The Insider's Guide to the Top 20 Careers in Business and Management

Also by Tom Fischgrund

Match Wits with the Harvard MBA's

Edited by Tom Fischgrund

Barron's Top 50: An Inside Look at America's Best Colleges

Fischgrund's Insider's Guide to the Top 25 Colleges

The Insider's Guide to the Top Ten Business Schools

The Insider's Guide to the Top 20 Careers in Business and Management

What It's <u>Really</u> Like
to Work in Advertising,
Computers, Banking,
Management, and More

Tom Fischgrund EDITOR

McGraw-Hill, Inc.

New York San Francisco Washington, D.C. Auckland Bogotá
Caracas Lisbon London Madrid Mexico City Milan
Montreal New Delhi San Juan Singapore
Sydney Tokyo Toronto

Library of Congress Cataloging-in-Publication Data

The Insider's guide to the top 20 careers in business and management :
    what it's really like to work in advertising, computers, banking,
    management and more / Tom Fischgrund, editor.
        p.   cm.
    Includes index.
    ISBN 0-07-021210-4 : —ISBN 0-07-021211-2(pbk.) :
    1. Vocational guidance.   2. Management—Vocational guidance.
    3. Consultants—Vocational guidance.   4. Job descriptions.
    I. Fischgrund, Tom.   II. Title: Insider's guide to the top 20
    careers in business and management.
    HF5381.I55   1993
    331.7'02—dc20   93-35982
                                                              CIP

2 3 4 5 6 7 8 9 0   DOC/DOC   9 9 8 7 6 5 **(HC)**

ISBN 0-07-021210-4 (hc)
ISBN 0-07-021211-2 (pbk)

3 4 5 6 7 8 9 0   DOC/DOC   9 9 8 7 6 5 **(PBK)**

*The sponsoring editor for this book was Betsy N. Brown, the editing supervisor
was Nancy Young, and the production supervisor was Suzanne W. Babeuf.
This book was set in Palatino. It was composed by McGraw-Hill's Professional
Book Group composition unit.*

Printed and bound by R. R. Donnelley & Sons Company.

This book is printed on recycled, acid-free paper containing
a minimum of 50% recycled de-inked fiber.

Contents

Part 2. Career Tips

Contributors

Tom Fischgrund, Editor

Tom received a B.A. from Tufts, a Ph.D. from MIT, and an M.B.A. from Harvard. He has taught public administration and done government research. He has written four books, *Barron's Top 50: An Inside Look at America's Best Colleges*, *The Insider's Guide to the Top Ten Business Schools*, *Match Wits with the Harvard MBA's*, and *Fischgrund's Insider's Guide to the Top 25 Colleges*. He currently is a marketing executive with Coca-Cola.

Monica Benning

Monica is a Vice President and Director of Corporate Planning of Bank South Corporation in Atlanta, Georgia. She began her career in banking in 1982 as a management associate with Bank South, rising to the rank of Vice President and Manager of Credit Administration in 1985. She has been in Corporate Planning since 1989. Monica is a 1981 graduate of the University of North Carolina at Chapel Hill where she earned a B.A. in French and Spanish. She is a 1989 graduate of the Harvard Business School. (CHAP. 3)

William Benning

Bill is a Vice President and Commercial Lending Officer with the Merchant Bank of Atlanta. Prior to working at the Merchant Bank, Bill worked for BayBanks Middlesex for 2 years and Bank South for 5 years as an asset-based lender. He began his career in banking in 1981 with Bank South as a financial analyst in the Credit Department. Bill holds a B.S. and an M.S. in Finance from Georgia State University; he earned his undergraduate degree in 1981 and his masters degree in 1990. (CHAP. 3)

K. Page Boyer

Formerly a Financial Consultant with Merrill Lynch in Chicago, Page is currently working on her first novel. Prior to joining Merrill Lynch, Page worked in advertising account management at Leo Burnett USA on the Kraft General Foods, Hallmark, and Dean Witter accounts. She was awarded her M.B.A. with Honors in finance and marketing from the University of Chicago Graduate School of Business in 1988. Page graduated as a Rufus Choate scholar from Dartmouth, where she earned her B.A. in economics in 1984. (CHAP. 7)

Deborah Cashin

Deborah is a Vice President with SouthTrust Bank of Georgia. She has been in the credit and lending side of banking for over 10 years. Deborah was raised in Cumberland, Rhode Island, and moved to Atlanta in 1981. She is a graduate of Davidson College, Davidson, North Carolina, and is presently working on a Masters of Business Administration degree from Georgia State University, Atlanta, Georgia. (CHAP. 18)

Jason Cashin

Jason is a Restaurant Manager for Ernie's Steakhouse, a restaurant chain based in Atlanta, Georgia. Jason has been in the restaurant business working in various capacities for over 15 years. The first 13 years of his career were spent at Cashin's, a family owned and operated chain of casual dining restaurants based in Atlanta. Jason is originally from Cleveland, Ohio, where he lived until he moved to Atlanta in 1973. He is a graduate of the University of Georgia, Athens, Georgia. (CHAP. 18)

Sally Cohen

Sally is currently a Chain Marketing Manager at Coca-Cola, USA in Atlanta. After receiving her M.B.A. at Stanford University, Sally began her brand management career at General Mills. After stints on Hamburger Helper, Suddenly Salad, New Products, and Raisin Nut Bran Cereal, she moved to Kraft to work on New Ventures. Following Kraft, she spent several years doing marketing for a wine importer in Chicago and then moved to Coca-Cola to work in the fountain business. (CHAP. 14)

Robert W. Collins

Bob has spent his entire career at a *Fortune* 100 firm, joining its U.S. Consumer Products division as an Assistant Product Manager in 1980. He has enjoyed a variety of experiences in the retail, new products, and professional groups, progressing steadily up the management ranks to his latest position—Vice President of Marketing for a major U.S. division. Bob graduated from Tufts University, with a B.S. in psychology in 1978, and from the Harvard Business School, with an M.B.A. in 1980. He is currently completing his doctorate in marketing and finance at the Lubin Graduate School of Business at Pace University. (CHAP 8)

Patricia S. Connolly

Patricia works for LaSalle Partners, Ltd., a corporate real estate services firm headquartered in Chicago. She is currently General Manager of a 596,000-square-foot shopping mall which will undergo an expansion over the next 2 years which will double the size of the project. Prior to joining LaSalle Partners in 1989, Patricia obtained her M.B.A. degree from Harvard University. Before business school, she worked as a technical supervisor managing ten chemical processing employees within two manufacturing departments. She holds a Bachelor of Science degree in Chemical Engineering from Tufts University. (CHAP. 16)

David Crane

David is currently Senior Vice President of Glass Financial/John Hancock in Atlanta. After spending 8 years with a major oil company and receiving his M.B.A. from the University of Dayton in the process, he began his career in financial services. While focusing on both investments and insurance, David earned his C.F.P. (Certified Financial Planner) designation in 1986, as well as a securities license in 1985. In addition to managing his own clientele, David is responsible for managing 11 associates in his firm. He has been active in the International Association for Financial Planning, serving on the Board of the Georgia Chapter for 4 years. (CHAP. 12)

Davy Davidson

Davy is the President of Engineered Plastics, Inc., a manufacturer of diversified plastic products headquartered in Gibsonville, North

Carolina. Prior to joining this company in 1992, he worked in the investment banking business from 1980 to 1992, most recently as a Managing Director in the corporate finance department of PaineWebber Incorporated in New York. Davy is a 1977 graduate of the University of North Carolina at Chapel Hill where he earned a B.A. degree in economics. He is a 1980 graduate of the Harvard Business School. (CHAP. 11)

Joane H. Goodroe

Joane is currently the director of The Heart Institute, Saint Joseph's Hospital of Atlanta. She completed her B.S. degree in nursing from the Medical College of Georgia and her M.B.A. from Mercer University. Her work experience has included both clinical and management positions in cardiac-related areas. She is involved in health care planning and reform. As part of her current role, she lectures throughout the country and is active in publishing. (CHAP. 9)

Harriet Hinson

Harriet is a Broker Associate with Re/max Achievers in Atlanta, Georgia. After graduating from college in 1984, she became a licensed real estate agent. She has earned her Certified Residential Specialist and Graduate Realtors Institute designations. Harriet is a third-generation real estate broker. Since joining the Re/max Organization in 1986, she has consistently been a top agent in Atlanta. Being in the top 1 percent of all real estate agents in the United States in Education and Sales, Harriet has taught courses on How to Invest in Real Estate and How to Buy Your First Home. Harriet is a Lifetime Member of the Atlanta Board of Realtors Million Dollar Club. Harriet is also a graduate of Emory University and Auburn University. (CHAP. 17)

Mark Howorth

Mark is a Consultant in Bain & Company's San Francisco office. He joined Bain in 1987 as an Associate Consultant, after graduating with a degree in Finance from U.C. Berkeley. He spent 3 years at Bain concentrating on Financial Services and High Technology clients. He left Bain in 1990 to get an M.B.A. at Harvard. Despite the wealth of opportunities offered to a Harvard M.B.A., he chose to return to Bain in 1992. He is currently focusing exclusively on healthcare clients and has a team of Associate Consultants working with him. (CHAP. 13)

Janice M. Johnson

Janice is the Director of Tax Policy of the New York State Society of CPAs, where she is responsible for monitoring and commenting on federal and New York tax legislative and regulatory developments.

She appears regularly on CNN, CNBC, CBS network radio, and other television and radio shows to talk about tax topics. She also serves as an editor for tax articles appearing in *The CPA Journal*. Prior to joining the New York State Society of CPAs in November 1990, Janice was a Tax Partner at BDO Seidman in New York City. There she handled a full client roster, with a specialty in the brokerage industry. She also represented the firm nationally in taxes. She holds a B.A. with Honors in accounting from Millsaps College in Jackson, Mississippi, and a law degree from George Washington University in Washington, D.C. (CHAP. 1)

Gil Kemp

Gil is President and cofounder of Home Decorators Collection, a mail-order catalog for homeowners. He has spent 20 years in the mail-order business at companies such as Bantam Books, New American Library, and Harcourt Brace. He is a 1976 graduate of Harvard Business School; he graduated with honors from Swarthmore College in 1972. (CHAP. 5)

Shirley C. Mewborn

Shirley is a Vice President and member of the Board of Directors of Southern Engineering Company, an Atlanta, Georgia, based consulting engineering firm. She received her degree in electrical engineering from Georgia Tech. After graduation, she worked for IBM in the Research and Development Laboratory in Poughkeepsie, New York. She later returned to Atlanta and joined Southern Engineering. In addition to her duties at Southern Engineering, she spends a great deal of time encouraging students to pursue careers in engineering and science, visiting local (and not so local) schools, lecturing on the requirements and opportunities in engineering, and recruiting top students. (CHAP. 4)

Sarah Salant

Sarah is currently Brand Manager on Miracle Whip at Kraft-General Foods. A Wharton M.B.A., Sarah began her career at General Mills and worked her way through Tuna Helper, Kix Cereal, and Pop Secret, among other assignments. She moved to Kraft to take over the leadership of DiGiorno Pasta and Sauces as it was going into national distribution. Since the launch of DiGiorno, she served as Brand Manager on Kraft Mayonnaise and then switched over to Miracle Whip. (CHAP. 14)

David Sanderson

David is a manager in Bain & Company's San Francisco office. He holds degrees from the University of Massachusetts/Amherst (B.S. mathematics), Syracuse University (M.S. computer science), and

Stanford University (M.B.A.). He joined Bain as a Summer Associate in 1989 and started full time in 1990. Prior to joining Bain, he spent 6 years at IBM as a National Account Manager, a Systems Engineer, and a Systems Programmer. While at Bain his efforts have been focused primarily on the high technology and telecommunications industries, and he has spent time working with automotive consumer products, entertainment, financial services, and aerospace clients as well. (CHAP. 13)

Robert L. Savage

Bob is Secretary and Co-owner (with his wife) of a successful and fast-growing small retail business based in Atlanta, Georgia. Bob also designed, and directed the highly respected Economics Costs region-wide organization for BellSouth until voluntarily leaving that firm in 1991. During his more than 28 years with BellSouth, he testified very successfully as a general pricing/costs/demand witness in over 30 major rate cases, directed the Marketing district at Florida's Space Coast, and worked at AT&T as nationwide pricing manager for telephone equipment. Prior to joining BellSouth, he served 4 years as an Engineering Officer assigned jointly to the U.S. Navy's Bureau of Ships and the Naval Reactors Branch of the U.S. Atomic Energy Commission. (CHAP. 19)

Michael Soble

Michael is currently a Vice President and Budget Manager at Bank South in Atlanta. After receiving his B.B.A. in finance at the University of Georgia, he began his career in the management training program at Rich's Department Store in Atlanta where he worked in various financial-related jobs for 4 years. After going back to school at night at Georgia State University to study accounting, Michael became a CPA and went to work for SunTrust Banks, Inc., in the Budget Department as senior analyst. After becoming the budget manager at SunTrust, he went to work at Bank South. (CHAP. 6)

Bob Speroff

Bob is the Western Region Senior Personnel Manager for the Domestic Ground Operations Division at Federal Express Corporation. Currently located in Sacramento, California, he began his career with Federal Express 12 years ago as a District Personnel Representative in Ohio and has held several Human Resource positions in the Domestic Ground Operations and Air Operations Divisions along the way. Prior to Federal Express, he worked as a Human Resources Director for 6 years at two retail chains in the Midwest. He received his B.A. degree from Cleveland State University in Ohio and his M.S. degree from Golden Gate University in San Francisco, California. (CHAP. 10)

Scott T. Springer

Scott is currently Director, Program Management at Nielsen Media Research, a division of A.C. Nielsen. Prior to that, he spent 4 years at Dixie Yarns in various operations positions, including time as an Operations and Financial Analyst, as an Assistant Plant Manager, as a Plant Manager, and as a division-level Business Planning Manager. Scott is a 1978 graduate of Louisiana State University. He graduated from Harvard Business School in 1989, earning first-year honors. Prior to business school, Scott spent 8½ years in the USAF, where he flew F-111 fighter-bombers and T-43 training aircraft as a Navigator and Instructor Navigator. (CHAP. 15)

Fred Studier

Fred is a Manager in Bain & Company's San Francisco office. He has degrees from Pomona College (B.A. in economics) and Harvard Business School (M.B.A.). He joined Bain as an Associate Consultant in 1985, working in Bain's San Francisco, Boston, and London offices. He opted to return to Bain after business school. While at Bain his clients have ranged from automobile, cement, and vacuum tube manufacturers to a financial services company, a cruise line, and electric and gas utility companies. (CHAP 13)

Meril Thornton

Meril is currently a Senior Vice President for NationsBank. She received her Masters in Management from Georgia Institute of Technology. Her first position was a staff consultant at Andersen Consulting, where she had a variety of programming and analysis assignments. She was a programmer analyst at Coca-Cola, USA, supporting marketing research systems. She began her banking career at Bank of Boston, where she had a variety of systems analysts and management positions within the systems area. At NationsBank, she manages the Institutional Systems Division. (CHAP. 20)

Matt Wilson

Matt is a Vice President, Account Director at J. Walter Thompson's Atlanta office. After graduating from the University of Florida with a journalism degree, Matt worked as a speech writer for two senators on Capitol Hill in Washington, D.C. and then worked as the Sales Promotion Manager for a few years with Marriott. Matt began his career with J. Walter Thompson working on domestic and international advertising campaigns for several categories including airlines, hotels, railroads, unions, radio stations, and banks. (CHAP. 2)

Introduction

What do bankers really do? Besides setting up bank accounts and lending money, how do they actually spend their time? Do you have to be good with numbers to be a banker? What do marketing managers really do? What do they do in "marketing" a product? Is it just making television commercials or is there more to it? What do general managers do? Do they do everything themselves, or do they manage other people? What do you do when you "manage" a business? What do systems analysts do? Do they only work with computers? How much time do systems analysts actually spend on a computer keyboard versus working with people?

While these seem like pretty straightforward questions, most high school, college, and even graduate school students don't have a clue what it is actually like to work in a specific career. Job switchers also lack knowledge about new areas. Most people, for example, know that bankers work with money and that general managers "manage," but that doesn't tell you anything about what someone actually does. Unless you have actually worked or interned in a career, good inside knowledge about what someone really does is limited.

While this is troubling, since most of our waking hours are spent working, and you should be doing something you enjoy, this lack of basic knowledge is understandable. It is difficult if not impossible to get good inside information about different careers. For one, you can only try out or intern in a couple of different areas, and this is very time consuming. Second, almost all career guides concentrate on how to get a job rather than describe or relate what someone actually does in a given career. Third, asking friends or relatives about their jobs usually results in a 2- to 3-minute reply.

The media is of no help either, since who knows what television or movie characters do for a living. For instance, what did Ozzie Nelson, in *Ozzie and Harriet*, or Jim Anderson in *Father Knows Best*, do to earn a living? Even when occupations are known, such as Darren Stevens in *Bewitched* (advertising executive) or Al Bundy in *Married with Children* (shoe salesman), the job portrayals are highly inaccurate. Most careers are never even mentioned at all. So the problem for anyone looking for a career is how to find out about what people actually do in different occupations.

This book fills the great need for "insider" information about the top 20 business and management careers. Each career is profiled in eight to ten pages by someone who actually works in that career. The profiles are divided into two parts. Part 1, entitled "One Month in the Career of...," describes an actual month of work in that career. Three questions are answered:

1. What are you supposed to do?
2. What do you actually do?
3. What is a typical month like?

Part 2, "Commonly Asked Questions about a Career in...," provides information about activities, tasks, skills, compensation, and so forth. Answers to 15 questions are given in this section:

1. What tasks do you do most often?
2. How much work do you do with people? Numbers? Computers?
3. How much time do you spend in meetings? Writing? Other?
4. What skills do you use most often?
5. What training, education, and/or experience is the best preparation for this career?
6. How do most people get their jobs in this career?
7. What do people in this career have in common?
8. How much are you paid?
9. What is the salary or compensation potential?
10. What are the short- and long-term career opportunities?
11. What is the range of jobs in this career?
12. What provides the greatest satisfaction? Frustration?
13. What is the biggest misconception about the job?

14. What is the one thing you would have wanted someone to tell you about this career?

15. What three pieces of advice or wisdom would you give someone thinking about this career?

This book profiles the top 20 business and management careers. They were chosen because they are mainstream careers which offer the greatest job opportunity and salary potential. Alltogether, employment in these careers is over 15 million, which is one out of every eight jobs in America today. Moreover, they represent the best jobs available. Smaller, more esoteric, "hot" jobs were excluded because they employ only a few thousand as opposed to hundreds of thousands of people, they are low paid such as some technicians, or they represent current fads whose value will probably diminish over time. The careers profiled in this book, such as accounting, marketing, general management, systems analysis, and so on, provide the best long-term opportunities.

In addition to these profiles, this guide also offers useful tips on choosing a career, preparing a résumé, interviewing successfully, getting a great job, and succeeding on the job. So once a career is selected, this book also will be helpful in getting a good job in that area.

This insider's guide to careers is invaluable to high school, college, and graduate students and to career switchers. It should be used by anyone who is trying to decide on a new career. When you consider that a career often determines what you do, how much money you make, and to some extent who you are, the importance of picking the right career cannot be underestimated. Since career choices are critical, the more informed you are, the better the chances that you will select the career that is best for you.

Good luck in making this career choice.

The Insider's Guide to the Top 20 Careers in Business and Management

PART 1
The Top 20 Careers

1

Accounting

Janice M. Johnson
*Director, Tax Policy of the New York State
Societies of CPAs*

One Month in the Career of
an Accountant

I never imagined when I was in school that the life of a certified public accountant (CPA) could be so full of crises. Most people envision a CPA to be a dull and fairly sedentary numbers cruncher, when, in reality, there is rarely a dull moment. Even though I serve as a member of the tax department of a national CPA firm, I really function more as a business adviser to my clients, working with others from both the audit and tax departments of my firm who are part of the client service team.

When I walk into my office on any given day, I have a "to-do" list containing more than a dozen items, all of which need to be addressed with some degree of urgency. On my to-do list in any given month are an array of tax returns—both individual and business—that need to be moved out the door. Returns are due on pretty much a year-round basis, given the availability of 6-month extensions for filing and the fact that many businesses operate on other than a calendar year-end. This means that there really isn't a "tax season" for most tax professionals in larger firms. While the flow of tax work is fairly constant year-round, right before April 15th, the pace becomes especially hectic. Probably 20 percent of our returns are received only days before they're due. Nobody plans ahead—especially for taxes, birthdays, and highway construction.

Some individual clients bring their tax information to their tax accountants in a big brown envelope, or even in the proverbial shopping bag, right in the middle of the spring "busy season" for individual returns. These individuals generally meet with a tax partner or a senior-level tax accountant in the firm to discuss the information which they are giving to the accountant. Sometimes a junior-level staff member is also present at these meetings to take notes and to assist the more senior tax accountant.

Other individuals with more complex tax pictures, and most businesses, have ongoing dialogues with their tax professionals in order to fully understand their tax position throughout the year. The more interaction there is between the tax accountant and his or her client, the more effective the tax planning can be.

Once the information for a tax return has been gathered, a staff accountant inputs that information into the computer for the actual processing of the return. However, it is important for the staff accountant to think about what the range of the tax liability computed by the computer program might be. It is very easy for input errors to occur or for a "glitch" in the computer program to surface. Since it is possible for the liability to be dramatically miscalculated through the use of the computer, the preparer must be ever vigilant to ensure that slip-ups do not occur.

During the presentation process, it may also be necessary to call the client for further information or for an explanation of the information which has been provided. The junior-level accountant generally discusses the issue first with his or her boss and, if it still needs resolution, one of them will speak with the client. Once the computer has generated a copy of the return, the junior person will give it to a more senior tax professional to review. In most firms, an accountant who has been in the tax department around 5 years or so will have reached the level of tax supervisor. Although the position is not called this in every firm, the use of the "supervisor" title is fairly widespread throughout accounting firms.

My job, as a tax supervisor, is to check the return that the tax staff has produced and to make sure that it contains all of the information provided to me and the firm by our client. If there are errors or omissions, I will give the tax return back to the staff, with an explanation of the changes that I am making so that they can understand how to avoid the mistake in the future and can actually make the changes. After the return is finished, it will be "top-reviewed" by a partner in our firm. Then, either that partner or I, depending on what kind of relationship each of us has with the particular client, will actually deliver the return to the client and discuss it with him or her. Once I delivered a return to one of my very wealthy clients and received a major shock. We had deducted as a charitable contribution a gift to his college of $4 million worth of stock. We had spent many hours with him planning the transaction and thought it was a "done deal." However, when we sat down with his return, he announced that he had changed his mind at the last minute, had not made the gift, and had forgotten to tell us.

The role of the senior tax accountant or tax supervisor in a large CPA firm is part client relations, part tax technician, and part teacher. After several years in the accounting world, CPAs begin to decide whether they want to specialize in either auditing or taxation. Assuming they choose tax, they may find that they need to go back to school to pursue tax specialty courses. This is generally done at night (after a fairly long and demanding day in the office). Once a CPA chooses to make his or her career in tax, after working through basic tax returns and tax research projects, the CPA will gain more and more client responsibility. After about 5 years or so, in most firms the CPA will reach a level equivalent to that of tax supervisor, which is probably a level that is a little less than halfway to reaching the status of partner.

A tax supervisor is not only responsible for keeping clients happy but must also be available to execute more involved tax research projects for both tax and audit partners of the firm. All through a tax professional's career there will be training in technical tax topics, in time and people management, and in selling skills. Continuing professional education is very important to the development of any CPA's career and is emphasized in all the firms. The tax professional is responsible for helping more junior staff to develop their skills and for responding to many of their concerns with respect to their careers. Thus, the tax supervisor serves as a teacher and a career counselor. In addition, all CPAs who have reached a supervisory level are responsible for developing as much business for their firms as possible. This means that it is necessary for them to become active in business, community, and alumni organizations.

Finally, there is a never-ending stack of tax literature to read. There are daily, weekly, and monthly tax publications of general interest to tax professionals, along with specialized publications in areas such as corporate taxation, employee benefits, international taxation, and state and local taxation. On top of this, it is necessary to keep up with general business periodicals such as the *Wall Street Journal*, *Business Week*, *Forbes*, and *Fortune*.

Every day that I come into the office is a new adventure. Clients and staff are always bombarding me with new issues. For instance, a client called and told me he wanted to purchase a business. It turned out to make more sense from both a business and a tax point of view to simply purchase a few of the business's assets. If the business is a corporation, there are tax consequences related to the purchase of the stock in the corporation that are different from purchasing only the actual manufacturing facility owned by the corporation. My client really only wanted the facility, while the corporation, in fact, owned a number of other assets for which my client had no use. Furthermore, by purchasing all of the corporate stock, my client could have found himself having to cope with legal liabilities incurred by the corporation which could, in some cases, take many years and much money to resolve. Not only did we save that client several hundred thousand dollars in taxes but, perhaps, millions in potential legal liabilities. Although this is not specifically a tax issue, it is the kind of issue a tax professional can often raise to his or her client's benefit. Only when you start talking to clients and asking the right questions are you really able to help clients plan their business transactions and to save money. Often, one simple question leads to a host of others and may result in the opportunity for a client of a firm to save an enormous amount of money. This is the fun part of my job—helping to structure the business deals.

Yes, there is the drudgery of pushing tax forms out the door, but it is in that tax information reported on those forms that you often glean the tidbits necessary to come up with a brilliant tax planning idea.

All through the year the tax professional should try to do continuous tax planning for his or her clients. Tax accountants try to "train" their clients so that they will call and discuss a proposed transaction before they do something that could have significant tax consequences, like selling a large block of securities. Toward the end of the year, the tax accountant will also sit down with his or her individual tax clients and put together a projection of the taxes that they will owe. There are often things that can be done, such as selling stock at a loss or making additional charitable contributions, within the last few months of the year to reduce the client's tax liability.

A stream of calls come into my office every day concerning issues such as these. There are many days I walk into the office with the futile hope that today the telephone won't ring and I will be able to do some catching up on that backlog listed on my to-do list. However, that is almost never the case. Usually, when I leave the office at night, all of the original items remain on my to-do list, and several new ones have been added. The only way the list gets whittled away is to delegate even more work to my staff than I had planned or to work into the night and on the weekend, when I am able to carve out more than 5 minutes of uninterrupted time to sit and carry out a project. And when clients aren't calling to ask one tax question or another, tax staff are in my office to ask me about something they are trying to research and don't quite understand or to tell me that the computer system has gone down yet again and that the return I wanted this morning won't be available until late this afternoon. Or they may want to discuss problems they are having in working with someone else in the office. In a firm of several hundred professionals, there is generally at least one personal crisis every few days. So, when the clients aren't demanding something, the staff are. Last week I had to deal with one troubled marriage, one incompatible accountant and secretary, three staffers out with the flu, and two client emergencies.

Even when both the clients and the staff are behaving fairly well, the partners are screaming for something. Since our business is based on selling our time, it is important to keep detailed records of what we spend our time doing. Once the partners start billing the clients, there are always questions as to exactly what work was performed and how could it ever take so long? When the clients receive the bills for our services, there is usually another round of similar questions. Nothing in accounting is ever easy.

For business clients, a tax accountant works with the auditors in reviewing the business's financial picture. For corporations with audited financial statements, this includes reviewing the tax provision in the financial statements. Many tax-planning opportunities and tax-saving ideas come to light during this process. State taxes are also becoming more and more important in planning for a business. Often the availability of much lower taxes in one state will dictate where the business establishes the majority of its operations.

Through my tax reading, I am always trying to remain alert to opportunities from which my clients could benefit. For instance, although I am not a registered investment adviser and would, therefore, never give a client advice about investing in specific stocks, from my general business reading I may decide that Series EE bonds are now a good investment for certain of my individual clients. I will then discuss with them the possibility of investing $15,000 during the year in these bonds in order to earn a fairly high rate of return in relation to certificates of deposit and other interest-bearing instruments, while deferring federal taxes and permanently avoiding state and local taxes on the interest earned on the EE bonds. An individual does not have to pay federal tax on the EE bonds until they are sold or mature and interest earned on them is totally exempt from state and local taxes. From looking at my client's tax return, I can tell whether or not the interest paid on the EE bonds makes sense in light of the client's overall tax picture or whether an investment that generates taxable income will, on an after-tax basis, provide an even greater return to the particular client.

Many times my clients will call me concerning something that they have read about taxes in either the newspaper or a business magazine or that they have seen on television. This is another reason why it is so important that I keep fairly current in my reading and that I remain aware of what is happening in the business world. Clients seem to expect that I will immediately have read everything that is published in the business world and that I will have seen every business show and that I will be ready to discuss them. Therefore, even though I cannot possibly read and see everything, I do have to learn to be something of a speed reader and to keep at least one jump ahead of my clients by reading the most widely circulated business publications and paying attention to business shows when I can.

Not only is it a good idea for a tax professional to read the business publications, but it is also a very good business-development tool if he or she can find the time to write a tax-planning article every once in awhile. There are many trade journals published in almost every professional area, and all of them are constantly looking for good articles that contain sound tax-planning advice. Getting your name known through publishing articles in specialty journals is a good way to start marketing your services in a particular specialty area. For instance, there are tax professionals who spend the majority of their time advising the securities industry, while others may specialize in employee benefits and compensation issues and others may deal almost exclusively in the real estate industry. The more these professionals write articles for journals in their area of specialty, the better known they become as specialists in that area and the more clients they are likely to attract.

The tax law has become so complicated that it is almost impossible to keep current in every area of it. Therefore, the name of the game for many tax specialists has become further specialization—not just in tax but in a subset of tax. Once upon a time it was enough simply to become a CPA and to advise clients in every area of business and taxes. Now, while the CPA tax specialist still serves as a business adviser to his or her clients, the CPA must know when a problem is outside of his or her expertise and when to bring in CPAs that specialize in the pertinent areas. It is most important that they know what questions to ask and that they are alert to problem areas so that specialists can be brought in where appropriate. Often, the specialists will not just be other CPAs, but attorneys, appraisers, bankers, investment advisers, etc. Specialists outside the CPA firm serve as a major referral source for clients to the CPA firm.

Many times, dealing with other professionals in the tax area can be more fun than dealing with your clients. There will be times when the client seems to hold you personally responsible for the overwhelmingly confusing state of the tax law. You may have clients yelling at you for the complexity of a tax law you are incapable of changing or for the size of their tax liability or the size of your fee for reducing their tax liability. Furthermore, many people seem to take issues related to their personal wealth more seriously than anything else in their lives. I have clients call me at home on Saturday night because they started worrying about a particular business deal that it might be possible for them to enter into. One client called me at home once too often with a relatively trivial tax issue that could have waited until Monday morning. I finally told him rather curtly one Saturday night when he called at 10:30 asking whether or not I thought that now was the time to recognize his capital gains for tax purposes that (1) his broker couldn't execute the trade until Monday morning, (2) this was not a matter of life and death, and I had not gone to medical school because I didn't want to have to deal with emergencies from home on a

Saturday night, and (3) I would be happy to talk with him about it on Monday morning before the markets opened, when I had his file in front of me, to see if the trade made sense. Dealing with other professionals, however, you can use the tax jargon and legalese which has become a part of your life by now, and it is usually possible to reach a consensus relatively quickly and painlessly.

The goal of every tax specialist, and of every CPA in a CPA firm, is often to become a partner in that firm. Every large CPA firm has at least annual reviews of professional staff members to let them know how they are progressing within the firm. That review should evaluate both the professional's strengths and weaknesses and help him or her determine actions that must be taken to advance to the next level within the firm. Someone who is at a tax supervisor level within a CPA firm is also asked to evaluate the staff members who work for them. The supervisor is either asked to directly evaluate his or her staff or to provide evaluations to someone more senior within the firm who will actually provide the evaluation to the staff. This process helps all of the professionals determine with some degree of accuracy their chances of succeeding within a CPA firm. If the future begins to not look especially rosy, there are many career opportunities available in the tax departments of smaller CPA firms and in American industry.

Commonly Asked Questions About a Career as a CPA

What Tasks Do You Do Most Often?

A CPA who has been with a firm 5 to 7 years has reached a supervisory level. That person spends a large part of the time doing just that—supervising. He or she is responsible for getting returns out the door, keeping clients happy, keeping staff happy and busy, keeping partners happy, and making sure that projects for the partners get done both correctly and in a timely fashion. The schizophrenia of being a supervisor is that the supervisor is responding to requests from more senior management and partners within the firm to do research projects and to produce other products while attending a large number of meetings—with clients, with potential clients, with community organizations for professional development purposes, and with members of the firm for purposes of planning and continuing professional education. Only a small part of the CPA supervisor's time is ever spent adding and subtracting—particularly in the tax area.

How Much Work Do You Do with People? Numbers? Computers?

In a large accounting firm, the amount of interaction with people is much more significant than one would expect. First, the number of the firm's staff involved in any given project can be quite large. Second, the client may have an equal number of people devoted to the issue. It is important to maintain good relations with all those involved in a job, so people skills are a very important attribute. Not only is it important to work well with people, but as you move up the management ladder in an accounting firm, you must start supervising staff, reviewing them, and helping them plan their careers.

Numbers and computers, of course, play a substantial role in any CPA firm. However, the amount of number crunching that actually goes on has been dramatically reduced with the widespread use of computers. It should go without saying, however, that it is still important for the CPA to have a good understanding of numbers and financial concepts in order to do his or her job well.

How Much Time Do You Spend in Meetings? Writing? Other?

Meetings are a fact of life in a CPA firm. There are meetings to plan proposals to get client business; there are the actual proposal meetings to pitch the client business; there are meetings with the client; there are meetings with staff to plan for the client; there are meetings for staff reviews; there are meetings to plan strategy for the firm; and there are meetings to receive continuing professional education. The number of meetings on a monthly basis can be staggering.

There is also a great deal of writing that must be done, so it is important to have a good command of the English language and to be comfortable communicating in writing. In the tax area, there are many research projects where both the problem that is being researched and the conclusions that are reached must be reduced to writing. And in all areas of the CPA firm, it is often important to record in memo form discussions with clients, and advice given to them, so that no confusion exists later.

Research is often a major part of the job—to determine the proper accounting or tax treatment of a particular item. As you move up in the firm, you have to become capable of reviewing the research done by others and developing a comfort level as to the accuracy of their findings.

What Skills Do You Use
Most Often?

People and analytical skills are almost equally important in a CPA firm. There is always the need to build both client and staff relations. Also, it is always necessary to develop new business. On the other hand, once the business is in the door, it is necessary to be alert to both problems and opportunities that must be addressed. This requires substantial analytical skills. Practice in a CPA firm really requires that a person be a good mix of extrovert and introvert.

What Training, Education, and/or
Experience Are the Best
Preparation for This Career?

It is very useful to obtain an undergraduate accounting degree in order to both pass the CPA exam and go to work in a CPA firm. However, it is also an enormous advantage to have very good written and oral communication skills, and these aren't always offered as part of the accounting curriculum. A business writing course is invaluable to the individual who wants to excel in a CPA firm. Additionally, those who want to specialize in tax should probably obtain an advanced degree in a tax program that is offered as part of a graduate business program or should go on to law school and take as many tax specialty courses there as they can manage or go on for an LLM degree in taxation after law school. To go full-time to law school and then for the LLM in tax will, however, require an additional 4 years of school and a substantial amount of additional tuition.

How Do Most People Get Their
Jobs in This Career?

Most people are hired into CPA firms directly out of school. Many of the larger firms recruit on college and graduate school campuses. Those individuals who have managed to gain some basic accounting work experience during college generally have an edge in the hiring process because they have a better sense of the actual mechanics of accounting, and they have demonstrated that they are willing to work and were able to do it while pursuing their academic degree.

What Do People in This Career
Have in Common?

People in accounting careers are generally comfortable with numbers and have an interest in, and a flair for, business. They are fairly practical in their approach to business and to solving business problems. Many accountants *are* pretty conservative, but they are not necessarily the individuals who fare best in the profession.

How Much Are You Paid?

Pay, of course, depends on the region of the country in which you are working and the size of the firm. Someone with 5 years of experience in a relatively large CPA firm will probably be earning between $45,000 and $65,000. Keep in mind, however, that benefits in many CPA firms are not particularly good. There may be only a minimal retirement plan, if any, and not very extensive life and health insurance coverage. CPA firms have not been noted in the past for the range and generosity of their benefits packages.

What Is the Salary or Compensation Potential?

In the largest of the national CPA firms, the partners can earn well into the six figures, whereas in the smaller CPA firms partners are likely to be at the low end of the six-figure range and below that in smaller metropolitan areas. Partners in CPA firms are treated as self-employed by the tax law, so they are responsible for paying their own self-employment tax and health insurance and life insurance. They are also responsible for making capital contributions to their firm in a variety of different ways and amounts depending on the firm. When all of these additional financial responsibilities are taken into consideration, they can make being a partner much less lucrative than it might at first appear.

What Are the Short- and Long-Term Career Opportunities?

In the short term, large CPA firms are an excellent place to gain a wide variety of experience and to receive excellent training. It is unlikely that you will be bored, although you may be worked to death. In the longer term, not too many people ever actually rise to the level of partner. Many are weeded out by the firms as not having the specific skill set or drive that it takes to become a partner. Others weed themselves out, realizing that they are disenchanted with the number of work hours that many of the large firms demand.

Those CPAs who do stay to become a partner generally have to spend around 10 to 12 years at staff levels before they become a partner.

Additionally, the traditional pyramid structure in accounting firms is becoming less broad at the base, requiring fewer junior staff as more work can be done by computers. Added to this, fewer partners are being made out of the remaining staff since the work load for accounting firms is not expanding at the rate it once did. Thus, many firms are now developing some form of permanent manager position where certain professionals are not made partner but are also not encouraged to leave as they would have been in the traditional "up or out" system of the large accounting firms. For some accounting-firm CPAs, this permanent manager-type position may be a very attractive position in that it does not come with the financial risk of being a partner and it may come with lessened work-load responsibilities.

What Is the Range of Jobs in This Career?

Those who become CPAs have the option of specializing in either the tax or audit disciplines and further specializing in a specific area within either of those disciplines. There are also other specialties developing within the CPA discipline, such as bankruptcy and business valuation.

For someone who wishes to leave one of the large national firms, there is a wide range of opportunities. There are many smaller CPA firms with either specialized or general practices that are always ready to welcome CPAs with large-firm training. Then there are private industry and government—both of whom offer a number of interesting, though generally not as lucrative, career choices to CPAs trained in the larger firms. The CPA who is lucky enough and skilled enough to become the chief financial officer of a business can continue to pursue both a very interesting and lucrative career. Some CPAs go off to found their own businesses—either CPA firms or other types of small businesses where they can hone the business skills they have learned in a large CPA firm. Finally, some CPAs decide to teach. Generally, however, this requires going back to school for more advanced degrees.

What Provides the Greatest Satisfaction? Frustration?

The greatest satisfaction is provided when you do your job well and a deal is closed with all parties agreeing that they all got what they wanted at the least tax cost and in the most efficient manner possible. Life gets frustrating when clients come to you at the very last minute with complex problems that should have, and could have, been addressed months earlier. Now you and your staff have to work around the clock and run up large amounts of professional time to do as much of the job as you can when there is too little time to do it right.

What Is the Biggest Misconception About the Job?

Most people simply do not realize how much more there is to the accounting profession than just numbers. Of course, the CPA has to understand numbers and be good with them, but that is only the starting point. Then he or she has to be able to communicate with the client—to obtain information from the client and to communicate it to the client. The CPA has to be a good solid practical businessperson and has to convince the client of that fact. It is also necessary to practice more than a bit of psychology because people have strange attachments and sentiments when it comes to their money.

What Is the One Thing You Would Have Wanted Someone to Tell You About This Career?

I wish that someone had told me—or that I had fully comprehended— about the enormous number of hours that the CPA starting out in a large accounting firm must dedicate to the profession.

What Three Pieces of Advice or Wisdom Would You Give Someone Thinking About This Career?

1. Learn to communicate, both orally and in writing, very well. This will make your professional life *much* easier.

2. Decide upon your area of specialty in the profession—either tax or audit—as soon as possible. It will allow you to develop your skills in the specialty you choose much more rapidly and will lead to less frustration that you are not advancing rapidly enough.

3. Try to intern in a small accounting firm during your college days. It will give you a much better understanding of the building blocks of the profession than will starting in a large CPA firm directly out of school.

2
Advertising

Matt Wilson
Vice President, Account Director,
J. Walter Thompson

One Month in the Career of an Advertising Executive

A new business pitch includes everything an ad agency normally does only at hyper speed. What normally takes a year is done in a month. New business. Every time I hear that rally cry at the office I know what's coming. Domino's Pizza is in the process of fishing around for a new advertising agency, and we've been selected to pitch the account. In less than a month, I've got to mobilize an office of 125 people to exhibit the vital signs and marketing instincts that typically win accounts. We'll do everything we would do for a paying client in hopes of getting new business.

I will have to direct new research to discover the secrets of why people buy doughy saucers of cheese and pepperoni. I will have to brief our creative department so they develop savory advertising to convert nonbelievers to the Domino's faith. I will have to deliver pizza to get closer to ravenous dinner customers. I will have to lead the final presentation with the ease of a toastmaster and the fever of an evangelist. All on top of servicing the needs of my existing client base. All without making either side wary that my attention is elsewhere other than focused laser-like on their business. I am an advertising executive, or account manager, and I love it.

Ask an agency writer or art director to define an account manager's role and you'll get a clear response: "Help sell great creative work." Media, the department in charge of placing advertising, will say: "Help sell the value of additional expenditures in television." And so on throughout each discipline of the agency. An account manager's primary responsibility is focused on bringing together each agency resource (media, creative, research, production) into a dedicated team that will ultimately create the advertising for a particular client. Although it may seem that account people are jacks of all trades and masters of none, the essence of the job revolves around selling—selling a client's strategy to the agency departments and selling the agency recommendations back to the client.

> *The first indication that we were about to go into new-business hell came from Domino's regional vice president of marketing, who invited us to participate in a regionwide review of agency credentials. We know that most clients seeking new agencies often downplay this first step since in their eyes they are seeking to narrow down the pack to a manageable handful of agencies that will eventually compete toe to toe for the account. We view this step completely different. We'll never get a second chance to make a first impression, so our first volley has to count. We've got 1 week to assemble and present a dossier on our agency's billings, current client list, media and creative capabilities, and our fee requirements for their business.*

The management of new business and existing business starts at the top, and most agencies are led by a general manager who has earned his or her stripes in account service. Being the final arbiter on resource allocation, the general manager selects an account director to take the lead on an assignment. Once the account director is selected, he or she must assemble a team from all divisions of the agency to work on various phases of the project. For the Domino's pitch, the team will take on two profiles: (1) the presenters, senior managers who must be well versed on the needs and applicable agency resources for the prospective client and (2) the resource team, typically junior-level account coordinators who in turn are responsible for managing their counterparts in the agency's media, creative, and production departments.

> *I'm in the process of writing the credentials' presentation and have gathered the account team in a conference room to review our progress. Team members have been working with their assigned agency group and will make individual presentations to me. From these miniprogress reports, it will be my job to make our experience as applicable to a fast food account as possible. It's not enough to say that we have a seasoned broadcast buying department. We have to translate our strengths into terms that the prospective client will think most useful to their business. Reviewing the work of the account coordinators, it's obvious that all of the right pieces are there but not with the right amount of spin that will get us to the next stage of the presentation.*

I ask the account coordinator assigned to media to develop an overlay map for the region served by Domino's in the Southeast. We need to show that we buy more radio and television space at a less expensive price than any other advertising agency participating in the pitch. We know this because whenever we buy radio or television space in a given market, our spending volume and the prices we pay for the advertising are reported on a syndicated media tracking service along with similar data for competing agencies. Instead of showing how much we spend, we need to show how we blow everybody out of the market anytime we spend money. Let's put a "Domino's" logo on all of our markets where we can give Domino's the most influence.

On the new-idea side, an account executive (AE) came up with the idea to sell our creative department as a special "Pizza-Vision" television and radio production group. It's solid thinking and will appeal to Domino's need to quickly turn ad campaigns around in response to the competition. I've assigned the AE the responsibility of working with the creative director to develop a rough draft of how we would present this idea. We've got only 1 more day to assemble the credentials requirement for the pitch. An all-nighter is coming our way, and we still haven't figured out how much we need to charge the client so we can make a reasonable profit.

The account people who work on a pitch have followed a nontraditional path to upper management. One can't be trained to be an account person as one is trained to be a lawyer or doctor or even an agency writer. Most of an account person's training happens on the job. Account coordinators find their first job at an agency by exhibiting competent marketing and advertising skills gained through a solid academic background (marketing, advertising, or journalism) and by coming to the agency with at least two internships under their belts. The vicious cycle of "can't get a job without experience/can't get experience without a job" applies to this career path. More and more initiates are compensating for their lack of experience with advance degrees in psychology, business, or marketing. However, without any practical experience, there's virtually no chance of a job offer. Once an account coordinator has been with the agency for 2 years, the promotion route is to the position of account executive with assignment responsibilities on one account under the supervision of an account supervisor and account director.

Through the 1980s, the rule of thumb was one account person per $1 million in media billing for each account. Now, as agencies have followed their clients in downsizing (or rightsizing), the rule has been changed to one account person for each $3 million in billing. Once, where account managers had the luxury of many junior account managers or coordinators to handle the detail work of tracking data, working with the art department, or analyzing media buys, we now see senior-level personnel handling everything from strategic development to scrutinizing billing procedures.

> *We just got word that we made it to the next stage of the pitch. The all-nighter was exhausting but well worth it. We had a team of art directors working on desktop publishing systems to develop innovative presentation materials for our work. As recently as a few years ago, all agencies would have submitted work in a simple portfolio case and a three-ring binder. Now, with the computer-aided design software, the price of admission is full-color, customized presentation tools. Our credentials were delivered to the regional headquarters by a Domino's delivery person; all materials were contained in customized "J. Walter Domino's" Pizza boxes. They warmed to our approach and were specifically interested in our Pizza-Vision broadcast production team and our media buying clout.*
>
> *Five agencies were selected for the final round of reviews. Each agency was given the same project to be brought forward to the presentation scheduled in 2 weeks' time: We had to develop promotion plans, television and radio advertising concepts for two selected markets, actually prepare a media plan with affidavits from radio and television stations verifying the prices we would pay to run the advertising, and answer one extra-credit question: "If your agency was a famous person who would that person be?" No matter the sophistication of the client, they can't resist throwing a zinger at you. One client from a new business pitch a few years ago asked: "If you were a fish, what kind of fish would you be?" Our answer was a shark. Either they liked us or liked the answer or both—we got the business.*

Once an agency is selected for the final round, the fun part begins: creative development. However, advertising or promotion ideas can't be created without some type of strategic insight. The simple marketing drill of compiling a client history will yield rich information, for example:

1. *The product.* How's it made? How could it be improved? What else do they make? Why is it bought? Is it unique in any functional or physical way?

2. *The competition.* What is the product's competition? Who makes it? Are there any substitutions? What is their share of market? How are they strategically superior or inferior?

3. *The market.* Which market? What makes it grow? How does it work?

4. *The corporate culture.* What kind of company? Who owns it? What are its values? What are its policies and procedures? What is its history with advertising agencies?

5. *The business objectives.*   What are the targets? Are they realistic?
Where can we conquest more business? How are the goals going to
be achieved? What are the implications for success or failure?

In the instance of Domino's, they had found themselves in a very
precarious position. Tom Monaghan, the entrepreneurial leader who
built the chain to a $4 billion fast food giant, said the secret of their
business was that they were a dynamite delivery service that just happened to deliver pizza. They built their business on an irresistible
premise for the harried and hungry: in 30 minutes or less, a hot and
delicious pizza will be delivered to your door or your money back. But
they made the mistake that most successful market leaders make in
many businesses—they didn't believe anybody could catch them.

> *Strategically, I took the cue from Domino's. They had become addicted to
> discounting as a method of stopping share erosion. What began as a test
> for Pizza Hut burgeoned into a tough delivery competitor for Domino's.
> Little Caesars began a successful pizza franchise that didn't even have
> delivery. Customers had to pick up their pizza, but they got two pizzas for
> the price of one. Subsequently, eroding market share forced Domino's to
> rethink their approach to quick serve restaurant (QSR) marketing: a new
> agency in the Southeast would be part of their solution.*
>
> *The national agency had developed the slogan: "Something for noth-
> ing"—an advertising strategy built on giving the customer a low margin
> item like garlic bread or a liter of Coke. This gave the customer an extra
> reason to call Domino's while giving Domino's a discount exposure 80
> percent less than the current cash discounts offered by many franchises.
> The job of the new agency for local marketing efforts would be to get the
> franchises, who typically reject headquarters marketing, to adopt this
> strategy.*
>
> *We pulled the creative team assigned to the pitch into a brainstorming
> session. Our rule is that any idea is a good idea. Each new thought usual-
> ly sparks another idea that may be the crowd favorite. Eventually we cen-
> tered on one idea called "The Wheel of Pizza." The concept would be to
> create a giant spinning wheel à la Pat Sajak's famous game show; each
> spoke of the wheel would contain something that Domino's would give
> away free with each pizza. For television advertising, we would feature a
> local franchise manager spinning the wheel and splice in wheel-spinning
> footage that we would already have in the can. In one ad, we would make
> the franchise community participants in the advertising, we would build a
> promotional platform that allowed us to escape dollar-off discounting, and
> we could put together fun advertising in one simple package.*

It's never enough to have an idea. Testing creative concepts on consumers gives one a glimpse at the scientific nature that drives advertising. Obviously, the desired result is to motivate customers to buy

more of your product. So, it makes sense to sculpt raw ideas with consumer behavior. One favored method is focus group testing. In research parlance, focus groups provide qualitative (read: anecdotal) comments relative to the project. To be absolutely accurate, one would take a statistically representative population sample from a market, ask identical questions to each respondent, and look for a quantitative indication that the concepts would affect consumer behavior. For our preliminary work with Domino's, a gut check would be sufficient to indicate if a concept is a winner or requires a return trip to the drawing board.

With a tight budget, most agencies are adept at quick field research to get a campaign off the ground. The agency research director hires a professional moderator to lead the focus group and assemble the anecdotes into a concise, easy-to-read report with observations and conclusions. But it is the account group that provides the strategic direction that the research director will build the project around. In Domino's case, would customers respond to our promotional ideas more favorably than the current price discounting currently in place? That became the million dollar question. Or in terms of potential billing for this client, the $4 million question.

It's 7 p.m., two agency writers, two art directors, our research director, and the account coordinator assigned to oversee the test sit with me behind a one-way mirror to watch six-to-eight "pizza lovers" discourse on Domino's. Each participant was screened according to past purchase behavior; we wanted people who ordered out at least three times per month. We've thrown them a red herring: When they were recruited for the group session, we told them we wanted their opinion on pizza quality for a variety of manufacturers and restaurants. Now, after they have purged themselves of their opinions, we get to the root of our project, which is testing the ideas and finding those that are most motivating. All of the promotional concepts had been translated to storyboards, a "comic-book" method of showing the progression of an idea through the end of the commercial. They are rough, but they work.

One group was totally useless. A focus group participant with an opinion on everything dominated the group and intimidated the other group members into silence. Group dynamics usually produce one of these people and is the reason multiple groups are assembled to guard against an attitude skew. The other two groups delivered far better results. Our research director got terrific responses to the Wheel of Pizza. One clear thought from a respondent was to limit the "free" or value-added items once per week so we wouldn't confuse the public.

So, they told us that the choice for delivered pizza was now not clearly enough defined. First of all, they were tired of pizza and will often consider going out to pick something up just as often as ordering lunch or din-

ner for home delivery. The array of home-delivered choices had grown to fried chicken, Chinese food, steaks and burgers, and even gourmet meals. The group concurred that the menu items from Domino's offered nothing new and that Pizza Hut and Little Caesars were just as good if not better because of a broader menu selection. Now that we had the information, we had to do something with it—make it work within our strategic direction.

We didn't have to wait for an official meeting between the creative and account services departments. As the focus groups progressed, the account and creative teams worked on promotional ideas spurred by the comments of the focus group participants. The account team brainstormed on strategy platforms while the creative team put the words to music. In just under 3 hours, we developed a monthly menu change promotion featuring regional toppings (i.e., Miami would get the Cuban Sub topping, New Orleans would get the Cajun topping, and Atlanta would get the B-B-Q topping). You never know where to draw the line with ideas because many of them will require operational dollars in addition to marketing funds. But we had our targets behind the glass, tested the new ideas, got great reactions, and decided to move them forward to the presentation.

There is no other profession in the world that demands an equal blend of show business with serious business recommendations. Architects don't do it. Law firms don't do it. Pharmaceutical companies don't do it. But when it comes to advertising agencies, everybody expects the proverbial "dog and pony" show. Agencies have been known to rent billboards outside the meeting site to advance their cause. We've carpeted our conference room with sod to pitch a lawnmower account, sold vacuums door-to-door for a vacuum account, test driven a Boeing 737-300 simulator for an airline account, tested Jetski's in the dead of winter, and covered a conference room floor with mattresses for a bedding company. Anything to be remembered. Anything to set us apart from the competition. It's expected, and it indicates to the prospective client an agency's creative capabilities, energy, and desire for the business. It's not unlike creating a play: Lines must be written, a set and prop inventory must be created—all for an opening night that determines your future success.

Two days before the final presentation, Atlanta was hit with the largest blizzard in 100 years. No one could work on the final touches of the presentation. But we had a strong idea. We used my four-wheel drive truck to pick up pizza from a Domino's franchise (surprisingly open) and delivered them to shut-ins across the county. We captured our efforts on videotape for use in the presentation. It was our hope that this would demonstrate our ability to think outside the box and work outside the normal expectations of a client.

What usually takes a full complement of agency employees, we managed to accomplish with skeletal staff due to the blizzard—we put our pre-

sentation together. We started with Domino's last question of "Who would we be...?" Our position was that we were the Babe Ruth of advertising. A long-ball hitter that bought media cheaper, created the most effective advertising, and consistently brought solid work back to home base on target, on budget, and on time. With baseball and teamwork as our chosen theme, we managed to weave it through every aspect of the presentation.

On the day of the presentation, each member of the presentation team was introduced on an oversized Topps baseball card, our faces superimposed over kneeling or swinging rookies with our resumés presented as stat sheets on the back of each card. For the creative portion, our usual presentation method is to show finished animatics—or video cartoons—to give the client an idea of progression and communication. In this instance, we decided to use outsized props accompanied with a play-by-play announcer who we had previously recorded in our in-house studio. The prop for the Wheel of Pizza was an actual working wheel, 5 feet in diameter, with a click-stop mechanism. After demonstrating the idea, we showed video-tape excerpts from the focus groups to validate our direction.

To present the topping promotion, we had our ideas delivered into the room by a Domino's franchisee who had done his best to create our recipes. We snacked on the pizza while showing additional footage from the focus groups that supported the topping concepts. For media, our media director and an account executive discovered that we could save Domino's $150,000 over the course of the year compared to what Domino's was currently paying in media costs. So, we had a Brinks guard enter the room with a briefcase manacled to his wrist. As he opened the case $150,000 in cash was revealed as we explained our performance on the Domino's media test.

At the end we summarized our credentials, told them we were the Babe Ruth of advertising, and passed out full-size Louisville Slugger bats with the slogan "Domino's and JWT—Swinging for the Fences" silk-screened on the sweetspot.

Going in to presentations, we know that theatrics and props alone will not win accounts. And for that matter, the fabled "dog and pony" show is never responsible for selling a new idea to an existing client. Without solid strategic thinking, ideas go nowhere. But most people find that illustrating one's ideas with dramatic demonstrations is an effective sales tool in any business. In advertising it has become expected.

We've learned that new business is no different from selling new ideas to existing clients. You never get a second chance to make a first impression. I just got a phone message from the Domino's regional vice president regarding our performance and standing after the presentation. I wonder what the news is? Gotta go....

Commonly Asked Questions About a Career as an Advertising Executive

What Tasks Do You Do and Skills Do You Use Most Often?

Tasks and skills obviously go hand in hand, and the skills of a diplomat are essential in successful account work. One minute you will be coaxing a writer to move up the deadline of a rough draft by 24 hours. The next, you will be assembling a group of senior executives to convince them to invest agency funds in a test commercial that the client may or may not buy. An advertising executive is a people manager, able to balance a mix of schedules, personal agendas, and egos.

As far as tasks are concerned, an account manager's job is defined by the sheer weight of managing work that other people in the agency produce to get the work completed for the client. It's a task known as "slopping the hogs." Farmers are only as good as their feed buckets, and an account manager is only as good as his or her relationships with the other agency departments. At no stage is the account manager's role passive. It is an active and highly complex process that covers five broad areas:

1. *Information management.* Anything that may affect the development of the advertising is critical. Like the military listening stations in the Cold War that gave us an early warning in case the Soviets launched their missiles, account managers must keep their ears to the ground and maintain a constant flow of information to all agency departments ranging from client attitude to competitive activity.

2. *Coordination.* Account managers hold the baton; they conduct the symphony. Not only must they supervise the completion of work critical to the assignment, but they must do so in a manner so that each department contributes at the exact moment that the work is required. In the manufacturing world this process is called just-in-time production. In the service world of advertising, we do the same thing, but we manufacture commercials. Working a critical path back from the first air date of a commercial, account managers must coordinate the research that provides insight of consumer attitudes *before* the strategy is written and approved, *before* the storyboards are created and presented, *before* the commercial is produced, *before* a media plan is created to showcase the client's product in all of its finery.

3. *Assignment of responsibilities.*   Not only must an account manager give the right people the right tasks, but he or she must tell them exactly what is expected of them. Clear and precise goals, rewards, and penalties are central to a well-run account.

4. *Priority management.*   When advertising absolutely, positively must be done overnight, account managers really earn their stripes. In today's world where everything is done instantaneously, clients want their advertising done right now. Account managers must rein in overanxious clients and/or push others in the agency to stick to their deadlines.

5. *Consensus building.*   Good accounts have lots of discussion, arguments, and debate about what's right and wrong for the client. But at some point, an agency point of view must be reached. An account manager must be able to find the common ground and ensure that all members of the agency are prepared to live with the decision.

How Much Do You Work with People? Numbers? Computers?

Account work is people work. Face-to-face contact with agency personnel and clients is a necessity. There are so many different personalities and cultures on both sides. Clients can be conservative and safe, creative people want to push the creative envelope, media people can be numbers driven and analytical, and production people can be harried. In advertising there is a saying: "Account managers can be separated into two camps, "friendly folks and folks that act friendly." Successful account managers have a love for working with people.

Dexterity with numbers is an essential account management skill. On a given day, managers usually track competitive advertising expenditures, calculate profit margins on their assigned account, provide year-to-date analysis on production and media expenditures, prepare expense reports, and even calculate the 15 percent tip rate on a client meal or two. Typically, junior account managers are assigned the responsibility of coordinating all relevant budgets and profit reports as a way of building necessary math skills and keeping them intimately involved with the bloodstream of the business.

Gone are the days of scratching out a rough draft on legal paper, having a secretary provide a second draft, proofing the work, and sending it back for final corrections. Tom Peters, author of *In Search of Excellence*, notes that with the elimination of middle management in America, junior- and senior-level employees alike need a multiplicity of skills to keep the organization moving smoothly and efficiently. That includes knowing spread sheet, word processing, and presentation software inside and out.

How Much Time Do You Spend in Meetings? Writing? Other?

First of all, the calendar is king. Lose the calendar and perish. When agency people need a firm answer on "when and where," all heads swivel to the account manager. One peek inside a Dayrunner will reveal a blistering schedule of meetings, lunches, and appointments. Astute account managers find themselves in the office at 7:30 a.m. in order to catch 2 hours of quiet time for paperwork, writing, and thinking prior to the first bell of the day. Meetings are held continually, covering most departments of the agency. Each account has at least 30 to 50 projects in swing at a given time. at 10:00 a.m., a strategy meeting with the creative department; next, an 11:45 a.m. meeting with research to review mall intercepts with consumers. A lunch meeting will follow to plan the launch of a promotion in the second quarter of the year. Afternoons are usually reserved for phones and meetings with subordinates on your team to report the results of *their* meetings throughout the day. At 6:00 p.m., things begin to slow down and there is time to review the day's work, plan for the next day, write a few call reports and/or internal memos, and scoot for a client dinner at 8:00 p.m. (even that's a thinly disguised meeting).

The best managers have unmeetings. By utilizing management by walking around (MBWA), internal temperatures can be monitored, a few words of encouragement or advice dispensed, and schedules checked for project completion or postponement. In this way, all of the information of traditional meetings is gathered without having to root employees away from the work of the agency.

Writing, as mentioned above, is the keystone of internal and external communications. Producing 1500 documents a year, from a major presentation to a minor memo, is an average production load.

What Training, Experience, and/or Education Are the Best Preparation for This Career?

We eat our young. No jobs without experience. No experience without a job. There are no board exams, competency tests, or licensing procedures for new recruits in the advertising business. On the collegiate side, backgrounds in marketing, literature, business, psychology, commercial art, and journalism are helpful. Advanced degrees such as M.B.A.s are typically not the door openers on the agency side that they are on the client marketing side for one simple reason: M.B.A.s typically look to spend a few resumé-building years at an agency before settling down as a product marketer. Agencies know this and shy away from short timers.

The first job is the hardest job to land in the agency business. Internships in college with advertising agencies, newspapers, radio stations, or consumer marketing companies are critical to demonstrate early skills development. In the early years, many head to New York or Chicago where over half of all money spent in advertising is managed for worldwide clients. The larger flagship agencies have formalized training programs for young recruits and appreciate candidates who have added to their academic background with internship programs.

Two indispensable skills that must be honed are:

1. *Writing skills.*   Too many graduates and newcomers to the profession have concentrated on the vocational side of getting a job rather than polishing the language arts. Many agencies require candidates to take a writing exam before being considered for a position. J. Walter Thompson asks potential new hires to rip an ad out of a magazine and write a fictitious marketing brief about the ad and then present it to a management review board. Clear, succinct, and pithy prose will put resumés and careers at the top of the pile.

2. *Presentation skills.*   It's the day of the big presentation, you've memorized your speech, your turn has come, and you blank out. This is more familiar to most people than they would like to admit. Advertising professionals make presentations every day of the working week. Speech and acting instruction pay big dividends. The best idea can't be communicated if the speaker is sweating, nauseous, and stiff in delivery.

How Do Most People Get Their Jobs in This Career?

Account managers now must sell themselves like writers and art directors sell themselves: with a portfolio of accomplishments. It's called "the book" and it should contain at least three demonstrable projects. This is becoming the price of admission for account management jobs. Interviewers wish to establish a benchmark for technical experience and get a feeling for the candidates' aesthetic judgment on creative issues. These projects should be in addition to academic accomplishment. Successful candidates usually build their books by completing *pro bono* work with local charities, radio and television stations, and, for the lucky, advertising agencies.

Finding a job on the creative side is particularly challenging. There are only a few postgraduate schools in the country that are successful at making creative careers: Two of the best are the Portfolio Center in Atlanta, Georgia, and the Los Angeles Arts Center. Over 90 percent of students who graduate from these schools get a job in their chosen field.

Although New York and Chicago are certainly the best locations to look for work among the agency giants, one can find world-class agencies in some of the most remote areas of the planet—Minneapolis (Fallon/McGelliot), Detroit (Carmichael/Lynch), Portland, Oregon (Weiden & Kennedy), and Columbus, Ohio (Shelly Bremen Communications).

What Do People in This Career Have in Common?

You've got to love the business. People don't get into advertising for the dental plan. All successful advertising professionals are passionate about the business of producing the most effective and distinctive advertising on the planet. The creative product always comes first. Agency folks are bright, intelligent, inquisitive, and outgoing perfectionists—some would call them type A people. Advertising people would not be happy manufacturing widgets; happiness only comes when the work they produce makes the sales curve fly off the charts and the awards shelf bulge.

In summary, advertising people

1. *Are perennially dissatisfied.* The constant quest for excellence is a claim few can live up to but deep down top managers know that an ad, brochure, or coupon could be improved or could be done better, even if the client is happy.

2. *Always say "Why not?"* Account managers get presented with a bunch of problems every day; the best will have a "why not?" attitude when faced with another "it's not possible."

How Much Are You Paid?

Written on the walls of many agencies is the saying: "Advertising is a great place to work if your parents can afford to send you there." Don't get into advertising if you want to make a lot of money because for the first few years your credit rating will be in jeopardy. The first position many take is the account coordinator's job with an average starting salary (*Ad Age*, "Survey of Salaries, '93") of $20,000. This is in New York; smaller markets experience lower salary levels. Over about 10 years, working upward to the position of account director on a substantial account (billing $10 million), one can expect to make in the neighborhood of $65,000 to $85,000.

What Is the Salary or Compensation Potential?

Know one thing: there are far more people at the bottom than there are at the top. Agency personnel rosters are a constant tidal pool of professionals coming in and going out. If one is patient enough, just by attrition alone, one will be promoted reasonably fast. On large accounts with nationally branded products, account directors can earn a base of $150,000, exclusive of bonus and benefits.

What Are the Short- and Long-Term Career Opportunities?

Coming out of the "economic unpleasantness" of the early nineties, advertisers lived through the biggest marketing depression in history. Companies dramatically scaled back advertising expenditures; agencies in turn scaled back to weather the drop in revenue. For every paid job in advertising, there are over 20 people who are qualified to replace the gainfully employed. A glut of professionals with 3 or more years of street experience makes it a challenge for entry-level hopefuls to compete. It doesn't appear that agencies are currently looking to increase employee rosters to postrecession levels; they are only adding employees as new business dictates.

For the long term, there have been many debates regarding the future of advertising. Michael Ovitz of the Creative Artists Agency befouled the agency network by grabbing one of the biggest accounts on the globe: Coke. Here was this advertising novice apparently rubbing ad agencies out with a single stroke of a deal pen. The truth is that most agency professionals welcome anybody who can put a creative product together—agency or not. It doesn't matter where they come from. *Fortune* magazine recently outlined their predictions on the careers of the future, and advertising was near the top of the list. The facts are easy to review: Whether America makes products or somebody else does, people are going to buy things and someone has to sell them. We'll be here until socialism takes over.

What Is the Range of Jobs in This Career?

As with most professions, there are three levels of responsibility in the account management team. One can expect to spend approximately 5 years working through the initial training ground jobs of account coordinator, moving to account executive, and finally a senior account executive. The mid-level jobs for those who are looking to make a career in account service start with graduation to account supervisor (usually on multiple accounts), eventually adding a VP title to the function in 3 years. After approximately 10 years in the business, one begins the drive to the account director level, and after about 5 more years one enters the ranks of executive management of the company as an executive vice president, group account director.

Besides having the best cost-per-title value of any industry, the career path starts with entry-level responsibilities, builds with the employee's capability to supervise others, then direct responsibility over one account, then a group of accounts, and eventually the chore of running a regional office. Luck and a good deal of hubris can launch you into national or global agency management.

What Provides the Greatest Satisfaction? Frustration?

The greatest satisfaction comes from watching the creative department take a black and white strategy document and build elegant solutions to a client's marketing problems. It's a manufacturing business, but the product is a collection of ideas to be preserved on celluloid or paper.

The greatest frustration comes from watching solid, breakthrough creative concepts get destroyed by a review committee either on the client or agency side. Search the world over and you will be hard pressed to find a statue or monument dedicated to the "brilliant" work of a committee.

What Is the Biggest Misconception About the Job?

Remember Darren Stevens from the TV hit show *Bewitched?* That's the biggest misperception—that the business is a schmooz-fest, laden with long lunches and creative brainstorming sessions out in the country. Yes, this business does come with its share of perks, but it is also grueling, fast-paced work.

What Is the One Thing You Would Have Wanted Someone to Tell You About This Career?

After the 10+ years that I have worked in advertising, I am just beginning to understand the critical relationship between analysis and strategic planning to the development of solid creative work. I guess I wish someone would have told me it would take this long to understand the business. But that in itself is one of the true attractions to the job. Salespeople only have to learn the product once. For advertising agency professionals, the job continually changes and presents new challenges every day.

What Advice or Wisdom Would You Give Someone Thinking About This Career?

Usually the first job you get in the business is a stepping stone for the next job. One thing I have learned in this business is that patience and persistence are the best paymasters. Ad people are only as good as their last ad. Overnight success stories are rare. What's the rush? Many are consumed with having a career on the fast track by the time they are 30. The first years in the business should be thought of as getting a graduate degree in advertising. Stay put until the right opportunity comes along. Get into the office early, stay late, volunteer for extra work, figure out how to work every piece of audio-visual equipment in the building, master computers, subscribe to industry publications, and read every available book on advertising and marketing. Basic? Yes. But are you doing it? Claude Hopkins, the father of modern advertising, attributed his success to the fact that he worked twice as many hours as his coworkers and thus made his way up the ladder twice as fast.

Good people are hard to find in advertising; the champions will be honored with continued employment. Finding a mentor means entering into a symbiotic relationship that may take years to develop. To be honest, mentors aren't found, they find you. A number of my contemporaries bypassed the mentor track and have become "Young Admirals." They discovered this method upon reading about two young cadets in the Soviet Naval Academy. Both cadets admired each other, equals in skill and ambition. But their concern was with the laborious rise to favored positions that waited upon them upon graduation. So they made the following pact upon separating to their respective duty stations: If one of them was absent when dealing with senior party officials and navy officers, the attending cadet would make great efforts to talk about the other cadet in glowing terms. This grass roots campaign delivered big results: They were the youngest officers ever promoted to the rank of admiral in the Soviet Navy. A trick? Self-promotion? Maybe. But, as lottery slogans around the country say, "You've got to play to win."

3
Banking

Bill Benning
*Vice President and Commercial Lending
Officer, The Merchant Bank of Atlanta*

Monica Benning
*Vice President and Director of Corporate
Planning, Bank South Corporation*

One Month in the Career of a Banker

Sometimes I find it hard to believe that as a 28-year-old, earning $45,000 a year, I'm responsible for loaning $15,000,000. That's more than I'll earn in 10 lifetimes. It's like I have the keys to Fort Knox and the power to give all that money away. The only catches are that a higher authority usually has to approve my choice of customer, and the customer has to pay the money back. Oh well, nothing's perfect. Besides, it sure is nice to act like Michael Anthony of The Millionaire, *even if the customers do have to pay it back.*

A career in banking typically takes one of four paths: lending, trust/investments, operations, or internal staff support. However, most bankers perform the role of a lender. Within lending, there are two distinct career paths for lenders: consumer and commercial.

Consumer lenders make loans to individuals, including installment loans to purchase autos, recreational vehicles, and the like and lines of credit either unsecured or secured by a home. Consumer lenders also approve credit card applications.

The consumer-lending function is becoming increasingly automated as banks move to credit scoring and centralized credit approval. Many banks are adopting a strategy where a customer service representative is responsible for generating applications while a consumer lender reviews, approves, and/or declines the application from a central location. The implications for those considering a career in consumer lending are that actual contact with a customer may be reduced to a telephone conversation, if that.

Commercial lenders (like myself) make loans to companies of all sizes for a wide variety of purposes including lines of credit for working capital and term loans to purchase equipment, finance real estate or facilities, and acquire other companies. They are also responsible for introducing other bank services—which generate deposits and fee income for the bank—to their customers, such as trust, investments, and cash management services.

> *I began my career in banking as a financial analyst in the bank's Credit Department. In this capacity I supported loan officers by doing all the boring grunt work: preparing financial analyses, cash budgets, and projections for potential and existing bank customers. After 1 year as an analyst and having learned the basics of the business, I was promoted to assistant manager of the Credit Department, supervising 20 employees. This department was responsible for the management functions of the bank's loan portfolio, including historical trend reporting, analysis, and central credit files.*
>
> *After 2 years in management, I decided I wanted to be on the lending side of the business, so I accepted a position as an assistant vice president and auditor for the bank's Commercial Finance Department. In this role, I traveled throughout the state, auditing the inventory and accounts receivable of our major lending customers. One year later, I was promoted to my current position, vice president and commercial loan officer. In a period of only 4 years, I gained both management and lending experience, which is fairly typical of the opportunities available in banking.*

While some commercial lenders choose one specialty and stick with it throughout their career, there is much opportunity to gain experience in different types of lending, particularly during the first 5 to 7 years of a lending career.

All lenders have specific goals that fall into a number of categories. Like salespeople, most lenders have goals for the number of calls they must make each month and the volume of business they must generate.

> *Each month I have a goal of calling on at least 20 prospects and referral sources. That averages about one a day. Last month I made 22 calls; 15 were prospects and 7 were referral sources. My efforts generated two very promising leads and three average leads.*
>
> *My goal for loans booked this year is $15,000,000. The year is half over and I'm at $6,300,000, 42 percent of my goal. I have two deals that I*

expect to close this month, which will bring me to 51 percent of my goal. My target market includes small business, middle market, and private banking customers in the metro area.

Normally I try to schedule four or five calls each week; then I fill in the schedule with last minute appointments. It's always easier to get appointments with people who know you. When I want to meet with those who don't, I try to call early in the morning or late in the evening to get around the "gatekeepers," secretaries and assistants who are well trained to filter unwanted calls from aggressive salespeople such as myself.

Another goal of a commercial lender is to maintain no past dues. This is particularly challenging because customers who are past due always have "breakthrough" situations on the horizon that will enable them to make their loans current...but not until next month. A lender must balance his or her belief in the customer's ability to perform with the obligation to protect the bank. As the following situation illustrates, this is never an easy responsibility.

I have an appointment at 10:00 this morning with Tank, Inc. I have decided to downgrade this company's loan to a problem status. The loan is more than 90 days past due, and the company has been losing money for the last six quarters. My objective in our meeting will be to convince the owner that his company has a problem and to agree on a solution so that his goals will be the same as the bank's goals.

The cash flow forecast I prepared last week shows that the bank must loan an additional $1,000,000 to cover payroll and keep the plant operating. This should enable the company to ship out an order that will create sales of $1,500,000. In the past, this company has not always been able to meet production deadlines. If they miss this one, their accounts receivable collection will be extended, and they will have to meet another payroll, causing the cash situation to deteriorate further.

I have checked our loan documentation and reviewed our collateral position. All documents are in order, but there is not enough collateral to support the additional $1,000,000 loan. We are secured by accounts receivable, inventory, machinery, and equipment. The loan is personally guaranteed by the owner. The business has been in his family for three generations. The owner has three kids in high school, and his wife has just been diagnosed with a terminal illness.

At the meeting I suggest to the owner that the bank will advance the $1,000,000 if the goods are manufactured on time and the purchaser of the goods pays the bank directly. I will verify this with the purchaser and will monitor the situation daily. Now here's the kicker: I also tell the owner that I will not advance the additional $1,000,000 unless he pledges his home as additional collateral. While I don't like doing it because the owner could lose his house if there is a problem, I have a responsibility to protect the bank. After protesting that the house is in his wife's name, the owner realizes he has no choice and agrees.

Another important role a lender plays is as troubleshooter for the customer's problems with the bank. Lenders must have a strong network of individuals who work inside the bank operations division that they can contact when operational problems arise. These types of problems arise almost daily, and lenders, the primary bank contacts for customers, must manage both the internal people who can solve the problem and the customer's expectations.

> *I am in the process of documenting the meeting with Tank, Inc., when the phone rings. On the other end of the line is the chief financial officer of Diversified Manufacturing. Apparently some of his lock box deposits were lost and Diversified's account was credited for the deposits of another company. He is hopping mad because the bank screwed up and, moreover, the other company's deposits were not as great as his.*
>
> *I spend the remainder of the day calling internal staff people in our cash management, lock box, and operations departments who must be notified of the problem to get it resolved. I had to make five phone calls and stress the importance of correcting the mistakes quickly in order to resolve the matter that day.*
>
> *By 5:45 p.m. I am in a position to call the CFO of Diversified Manufacturing to let him know that everything has been resolved in his favor. We have located his deposits and will credit them to his account that evening. Frequently, however, it takes more than an afternoon to resolve customer operational problems, and the solution is not always palatable to the customer. Had a check bounced, causing embarrassment to the customer, Diversified might be looking for a new bank (and I might be looking for a new employer).*

In an effort to identify those credit-worthy customers who will help lenders to meet their annual new business goals, they must make numerous "cold calls" to potential customers. During these meetings, lenders use interpersonal, sales, communication, and character judgment skills as they try to sell themselves and their banks while carefully scrutinizing the potential borrower. In a way, it's like being a financial investigator.

> *Growth, Inc., looked promising from the start. The owner was a salesman with a large local paper wholesaler. He built a large customer base and developed relationships with several major vendors. He started his own company out of his home by brokering paper. The suppliers gave him 45 days to pay what he collected from his customers in 30 days. The business is now doing $45,000,000 in sales annually. He has outgrown his present bank and needs a larger line of credit. He would also like to build a new building. He brings home over $500,000 per year in salary and makes the company show a loss in order to avoid paying taxes. I ask to review his personal and corporate financial statements and to meet his CFO.*

Next we tour the existing facility. I look for a number of things and ask numerous questions including:

- *Are there dusty boxes (indicating old inventory)?*
- *How well organized does the warehouse appear?*
- *Do the employees seem busy or idle?*
- *How often is inventory taken?*
- *How easy it would be to steal a pallet of paper?*
- *Is there a fire alarm and sprinkler system?*

All appears satisfactory, and the answers to my questions are adequate. I close the meeting by telling the owner that I will call him at the end of the week to discuss potential terms of a deal.

Once a good prospect has been identified, the lender moves from the role of salesperson to that of financial analyst. This requires skills with numbers and computers to develop a comprehensive picture of the company's potential to repay the loan under consideration.

As a first step in my analysis of Growth, Inc., I order a Dun and Bradstreet report on the company and Credit Bureau reports on the two top principals. I place calls to the company's references, including three suppliers and the company's current bank. I avoid calling the officer who handles the company at the present time but will contact him prior to closing any deal to make sure that I'm not taking a problem account.

I begin my financial analysis by pulling the files of two current bank customers who are also in this line of business and by gathering the national industry average data. I start by looking at the financial statements of Growth, Inc., for the past 3 years and compare the key ratios of my prospect to the national averages and to our customers that are competing in this market.

As the responses to my credit investigation come in, it becomes apparent that Growth, Inc., is a good prospect. I begin to prepare a formal credit analysis and loan request for presentation to my boss and ultimately to the loan committee.

When not out calling on customers, solving a customer's problem, or performing a financial analysis, a lender is likely to be "in a meeting." Such meetings may include internal staff meetings, business development or sales meetings, loan committee meetings, and problem loan meetings.

During a business development or sales meeting, lenders discuss how close the lending group is to meeting loan and deposit goals. Then, loan officers each review the deals they have "in the pipeline" and what they expect to book this month and next. Frequently, a member of a specialty sales group such as Trust or Cash Management will come in to talk about how lenders can more effectively cross-sell their products and services. Finally, top lenders who exceed their annual goal are recognized. A major success such as the closing of a big deal may receive a special recognition.

During problem loan meetings, all problem loans exceeding a specific dollar amount are reviewed. The loan officer must present the status of both the company's problem and the bank's work-out plan to the senior credit officer and designated others. This forum provides an opportunity for the bank to recognize new problems and to affirm or redirect the work-out plans of existing problems. The meetings are tedious and unpleasant. No one enjoys discussing or being held accountable for problem loans.

While the loan approval process varies from bank to bank, most banks use a loan committee approval system. Designated individuals who make up a committee meet at regularly scheduled times to review, discuss, and approve, restructure, or decline loans which fall in a certain dollar range.

Presenting loans to a credit committee is an art form, not a science. Experience has taught me to always leave room to negotiate. Inevitably, there is a wise old credit person in the room who likes to improve the deal a couple of notches. My strategy is to highlight the positive while explaining why the negatives aren't as bad as they might appear to be. I summarize the loan request from a company called Household Products, Inc., and then present a verbal financial analysis. I like to discuss the positive trends first, then identify possible risks and explain how these risks will be mitigated.

Today the loan committee does not like the fact that the owner is draining so much money out of the company when it needs additional capital to grow. They want to place a $250,000 salary cap on the owner (he is currently drawing $300,000), increase the interest rate by $\frac{1}{2}$ percent and collect a 1 percent fee at closing. I had anticipated the rate increase but had not expected the salary cap and the fee.

Once I have sold the bank on a deal, I must then sell the customer on the terms the bank requires. I spend the rest of the committee meeting considering how I will present the new requirements to my customer. I plan to call him from home that evening.

When I reach the president of Household Products Inc., I draw on my negotiation and sales skills to communicate the approval and the changes. I tell him that his loan was approved with a couple of minor stipulations. First I bring up the salary cap. I tell him that if the company continues to be profitable and pays the bank on time, the bank will probably agree to increase the cap. He seems comfortable with this. Then I drop the fee bomb. While 1 percent does not seem like a lot of money, it means the customer has to pay an additional $15,000. He does not like the idea and is extremely irritated that we did not discuss the fee earlier in the negotiations. I tell him that the bank charges fees on all new loans, but that I had tried to get *his loan approved without one. He responds that he would like to receive the proposal in writing.*

I am immediately suspicious that he will try to beat our deal by shopping other banks. I ask him for a $10,000 deposit that will be refunded when the deal closes. When he agrees to provide this, I am more confident that he will accept the deal with the new terms.

Frequently, however, a customer turns down a deal you've worked long and hard to sell the bank on. This can be one of the most frustrating parts of a lender's job. Managing rejection effectively is an important skill a lender must develop.

Late one morning I receive a call from the prospect I'm supposed to have lunch with. She is calling to cancel lunch. Immediately I begin to wonder why she canceled lunch and what's coming next. Has she decided to go with another bank? My mind runs through her list of potential excuses:

- *When her company first started in business, my bank refused to loan her money.*
- *I took too long to get the loan approved.*
- *My bank is too big (or too small).*
- *My bank's branch is inconvenient.*
- *Another bank cut our rate by $\frac{1}{4}$ percent.*
- *Our terms are too restrictive.*
- *Our fee is too high.*
- *Our cash management department is no good.*
- *The other bank has a better looking loan officer.*
- *Or some variation or combination of the above.*

She has indeed decided to go with another bank. Her reasoning included our restrictive terms and a lower rate. I try to sell her on the high-quality, personal service she will receive with me as her banker, knowing that our loan committee will not budge on the rate and terms. I lose the deal and my shot at achieving 48 percent of my annual quota.

Once a lender has sold both the bank and the customer on a deal, the next important task is to close the loan. Loan closings are generally held at the office of the bank's attorney. In addition to the loan officer and the customer, the room is filled with attorneys: the bank's attorney, the customer's attorney, real estate attorneys, the selling company's attorneys, if a purchase is involved.

All the attorneys argue. Those making a large fee seem to be very happy; the parties paying the fees always get frustrated by the amount of time it takes to close a loan. If there are five attorneys in the room with individual billing rates of $200 per hour, each minute costs $16.67.

Deal closings almost always have last minute problems, but these are almost always resolved. Occasionally deal-killers creep in and destroy the deal, usually because you had to close fast and were not able to check everything properly in advance. It is always best to wait and resolve problems prior to closing rather than forcing a closing through.

Frequently, the bank treats the customer to an expensive dinner after the closing to relieve the sting of the fees and closing costs with an impressive meal and some vintage wine.

At the end of each month, loan officers review their scorecards and develop plans for the following month.

> *This month I make 23 calls and close two deals. Growth, Inc.'s, loan is approved by the loan committee along with another deal I had been working on. I reach 46 percent of my quota, not the 51 percent I wanted to attain, but I expect to close three deals next month which will bring me to 60 percent of my annual quota. I have one customer that developed severe problems during the month, and another customer that is a borderline problem. I will have to monitor these closely in the months to come to avoid any losses. All in all, it wasn't a bad month. Sales were up, no loans went completely south, and next month I'll make my quota, the ever-optimistic banker that I am.*

Commonly Asked Questions About a Career as a Banker

What Tasks Do You Do and Skills Do You Use Most Often?

The seven most common tasks and skills are: organizational, interpersonal, character judgment, analytical, sales, negotiation, and communication. Organizational tasks and skills are critical to successfully juggling a banker's many and diverse responsibilities. Rarely does a banker have the luxury of completing one project or task without some kind of interruption. In order to meet aggressive new business goals, lenders must work on several pieces of new business at once while maintaining the accounts of existing customers to their (and the bank's) satisfaction. Consequently, bankers must be very organized to manage business at hand and to stay ahead of potential problems.

Lenders must have excellent interpersonal skills to build and maintain strong networks of contacts. These networks are their most valuable resource and include fellow bankers, customers, community leaders, CPAs, attorneys, and the like. Bankers' networks are resources they can take with them wherever they go, provided that they maintain and nurture each contact.

While customers consider a number of factors when choosing a bank, their relationships with their lenders often supersede the strength of the financial institution and the rate on the deal. When lenders decide they want to work for a different bank, their personal reputations and abilities to bring strong relationships with them to the new institution can gain them significant salary enhancements.

Character judgment and quantitative analytical skills are of equal importance to lenders. They must be able to determine, through the use of financial analysis and cash flow projections, whether or not a deal will work. But, even if the numbers look terrific, lenders must believe that potential customers will indeed use the bank's money for the agreed-upon purpose. They also must consider how customers might act under the pressure of problems if things don't work out as expected.

Once a lender has built a relationship with a potential customer and has decided that he or she wants to do a deal, the lender must be a strong salesperson, negotiator, and communicator, both with the customer and with fellow bankers. A lender must sell each party on the merit and strength of the other, while negotiating terms that are favorable to both and communicating (both verbally and in writing) those terms in a clear, unambiguous manner.

How Much Work Do You Do with People? Numbers? Computers?

Bankers spend approximately 50 percent of their time working with people, 30 percent with numbers, and 20 percent with computers. Work with people includes contact with many diverse personalities. A banker must be able to relate to all kinds of people from the attorney or CPA who refers potential business to the banker to the customer who manufactures brassieres, owns a restaurant, or freezes donor organs.

Work with numbers is a very important part of a banker's job. A banker must be able to understand financial statements, many prepared by the customer rather than by a trained professional such as a CPA. A banker must know how to read and interpret personal financial statements, personal and corporate income tax returns, and accounts receivable and inventory agings and must be able to read between the lines to ask questions about the numbers that aren't readily apparent.

Work with computers primarily consists of basic spread sheet and word processing skills. Over the next few years, the amount of time spent working with computers will probably increase to 25 percent while time spent with people will decrease to 45 percent since information technology will bring information directly to the banker from host mainframe systems rather than requiring a lender to request information from another individual.

How Much Time Do You Spend in Meetings? Writing? Other?

Approximately 20 percent of a banker's time is spent on the phone. Whether scheduling meetings with prospective or existing customers or resolving problems with other bank departments, the telephone can be a lifeline to a banker's success and, sometimes, a source of unwanted interruption.

If not on the phone, a banker is probably out of the office or in a meeting. Experienced lenders are usually required to make 20 to 30 calls per month on new prospects, existing customers, and referral sources. This activity requires 35 percent of a banker's time. Meetings frequently occur at breakfast, lunch, or dinner, particularly when relationships with new prospects are being formed. Meetings with existing customers or referral sources may be held at the office of the banker, the customer, a CPA, or an attorney.

Bankers who aren't out of the office calling on customers or prospects or on the phone are likely involved in internal bank meetings. Regularly scheduled meetings include loan committee meetings where decisions are made by consensus as to which new deals will be approved, new business meetings where lenders report on the deals they have in the pipeline, and problem loan or credit review meetings where bankers discuss the approach they will take to manage the loans that aren't performing up to the bank's required standards. Informal meetings with peers and superiors to discuss deal structure and to obtain loan approval for smaller loans also occur frequently. Internal meetings account for 10 percent of a banker's time.

Because bankers must leave a trail of documentation on almost every activity, they spend 35 percent of their time writing memos to superiors and credit files, letters to customers, credit reviews on the condition of customers, financial analyses, and recommendations for new credit approvals. The purpose of this is to establish a history on customer relationships for superiors and successors as well as to satisfy the requirements of regulatory authorities.

What Training, Education, and/or Experience Are the Best Preparation for This Career?

At a minimum, a banker must have a college education. While a degree in business, finance, economics, or accounting is preferred, an individual with a liberal arts degree who is well grounded in accounting and has an aptitude for finance can succeed as a banker. Many banks offer intensive in-house credit training programs for potential lenders. These programs can be supplemented or preceded by evening classes at a local college or university or by classes offered through the local chapter of the American Institute of Banking (AIB).

AIB classes are taught at an undergraduate college level by fellow bankers. Topics include three levels of basic accounting, analyzing financial statements, business English, business writing, and many specialized courses. AIB classes are an excellent way to meet fellow bankers at other institutions and to gain valuable skills at a low cost (most are subsidized by your employer).

An M.B.A. is not required but can be helpful, particularly for understanding a customer's business, which may range from manufacturing to wholesaling to service.

In banking, there is no substitute for on-the-job training and experience. Early in their careers, bankers have very limited individual decision-making authority; instead, they work with experienced lenders and gain important contacts in other areas of the bank, such as operations and cash management, which are essential to customer problem resolution. During this "apprenticeship," bankers learn how to fill their roles as liaisons between customers and all other areas of the bank.

Most banks operate with teams of lenders composed of (at least) one senior lender, two or three junior lenders, two or three entry-level analysts, and one or two administrative support people. This structure enables the senior lender to leverage his or her expertise at building and maintaining relationships while the rest of the team gets valuable on-the-job training and handles the more routine administrative and analytical requirements. By working with experienced bankers and listening to and learning from "war stories," young bankers can develop a valuable frame of reference to begin to apply their technical skills to real-world situations.

How Do Most People Get Their Jobs in This Career?

Most bankers enter the profession from undergraduate school, typically with degrees in finance or economics. Most banks recruit at college campuses and have training programs for "officer candidates" that last 12 to 18 months.

Many bankers have worked in teller or clerical positions while earning their degree and enter the training program "from within" the company.

What Do People in This Career Have in Common?

Bankers tend to dress conservatively, probably to project an image of trustworthiness and credibility. They participate heavily in civic, community, and charitable activities to maintain visibility and promote goodwill. Most bankers enjoy entertaining customers, referral sources, and fellow bankers; they almost always have good tickets to the theater, symphony, and sporting events.

Bankers tend to think analytically, and while they don't like to be called salespeople, most possess strong sales and negotiation skills. They are inquisitive, posing probing questions at every opportunity. Most are fairly risk-averse, as evidenced by their salary structure. Bankers are really salespeople, but they consider their jobs to be more prestigious and more secure than those of "commissioned salespeople"; consequently, they sacrifice higher commission dollars (or incentives) for higher base salary and lower upside potential for financial reward.

How Much Are You Paid and What Is the Salary or Compensation Potential?

A banker's salary tends to fall into ranges based on years of experience. Some banks offer bonus programs for new business production, but these programs typically are not activated unless the bank or the lending group has met a preestablished profitability goal.

Banks are quick to give title promotions that seem impressive and salary increases that seem less impressive. Rarely does a lender with no management responsibility achieve a title of senior vice president; however, some banks have differentiating vice president titles such as first vice president and second vice president.

Salary ranges based on years of experience, potential bonus ranges, and likely titles follow:

Years of experience	Salary range ($)	Bonus (% of base salary)	Title
1 to 3	25,000 to 30,000	5	First Level Officer
3 to 5	30,000 to 40,000	5 to 10	Asst. Vice President
5 to 7	40,000 to 50,000	10 to 15	Vice President
7 to 10	50,000 to 60,000	15 to 20	Vice President
10 to 15	60,000 to 75,000	20	Vice President

Bankers typically receive annual performance appraisals and merit salary increases based on the individual performance rating. Guidelines for merit increases usually fall in the 3 to 10 percent range. Consequently, salary compression is a phenomenon that banks are struggling to manage. Unfortunately, an unwritten law for lenders is that the only way to achieve significant salary increases is to change banks, and switching banks for more money is a common practice among lenders.

What Are the Short- and Long-Term Career Opportunities?

Historically, the only way to achieve significant salary increases without switching banks has been to move into management, and many banks promoted their best lenders into management, relieving them of their customer contact and new business responsibilities. However, banks have learned from experience that the best commercial lenders are not necessarily the best managers. Consequently, many banks are developing career paths for lenders who want to stay in lending. These tend to take one of two courses. A lender may either manage bigger deals in terms of the dollar amount of the loan or may choose to manage other lenders in a team leader role, continuing to maintain customer contact and being responsible for bringing in new business.

Long-term options for experienced lenders include moving into a senior management role in banking, entering consulting for the types of industries in which they have lending experience, or moving into the financial end of private industry. Many bankers become chief financial officers for customers with whom they have established strong relationships.

What Is the Range of Jobs in This Career?

While this chapter focuses on the career of a commercial lender, a banker can also sell or administer trust services, manage a retail branch, work with the increasingly sophisticated and important information technology that supports the bank's systems, or work in the operations area, or "factory," that keeps the bank going 24 hours a day.

The background required for each of these jobs is as diverse as the responsibilities and skills required for each. Most participants in a bank's officer-training program choose to enter (in this order) commercial lending, retail branch management, or trust services.

What Provides the Greatest Satisfaction? Frustration?

The most pleasurable activities a lender engages in are meeting with customers and prospects and closing new business. Lenders achieve a great deal of personal satisfaction when deals they have worked on for weeks are approved by their banks, accepted by their customers, and put on the books. Also satisfying is the case where a lender's judgment proves to be correct. An example follows:

A lender convinces the bank to do a deal with a customer he or she believes in, despite a large number of fellow bankers who displayed a great deal of skepticism and concern about the customer's ability to perform. The customer performs as well as (or better than) the lender expects. Fellow bankers praise the lender for his or her insight and judgment, and he or she earns a greater degree of creditability and "voice" when recommending future deals.

Equally frustrating and unpleasant is having to turn down potential customers with whom you've built a relationship, either because they didn't qualify for their request or because you couldn't sell the bank on the deal. Also frustrating, but slightly less so, is when a prospective customer chooses another bank over yours. Managing these types of rejection often takes a personal toll on lenders which they must learn to reconcile internally in order to continue to do their jobs.

What Is the Biggest Misconception About the Job?

The biggest misconceptions about banking are that bankers' hours are from 9:00 a.m. to 4:00 p.m., that the job isn't demanding, and that a bank is a secure place to work. Most bankers work 45 to 55 hours per week, typically from about 8:00 a.m. to 6:00 p.m. Earlier or later hours are usually due to breakfast or dinner meetings. While weekend work is not common and banks do have 10 scheduled holidays each year, bankers are not on the golf course by 3:00 p.m. every afternoon.

A banker's day is quite demanding, filled with new business appointments, internal bank meetings, and administrative responsibilities. All activities are frequently interrupted by calls from customers with crises which must be managed immediately. A banker is frequently torn between obligations to protect the bank and a commitment and desire to meet the needs of a customer. Balancing these obligations and commitments can be stressful and demanding.

The old belief, "once hired by a bank to retire with the bank," has fallen by the wayside. With the current wave of bank mega-mergers and restructurings, bankers are finding that job security is diminishing. At the same time, personal lender liability is becoming an increasingly important issue.

While lender liability suits are not common, some lenders are finding themselves sued personally by companies that choose to take advantage of the increasingly litigious nature of today's business world. The motive behind these suits is usually to erect a barrier between the bank/lender and the customer's assets; rarely (if ever) has the court ruled against a lender personally in a lender liability case.

What Is the One Thing You Would Have Wanted Someone to Tell You About This Career?

One thing women should know when entering a career in banking is that the good-old-boy network is alive and well and is difficult, but not impossible, to break into. This applies both to building relationships with customers and achieving promotions within the bank. There are very few women in top management positions in any bank in the country. Those who are tend to be in human resources, marketing, or comptroller/treasurer roles rather than being managers of revenue-producing units.

This does not mean that women cannot be successful in banking or in lending; many are very successful. Increasingly, women are launching careers in lending, cash management, and investments, all critical revenue-producing units for banks. At the same time, the banking industry has not openly embraced the presence of women in its senior and executive management ranks; women considering entering a career in banking need to be aware of and prepared to meet the challenges ahead.

What Three Pieces of Advice or Wisdom Would You Give Someone Thinking About This Career?

Be prepared for change. The banking industry is currently undergoing a restructuring and will likely look very different in the next 5 to 10 years than it does today. A large number of banks and thrifts are experiencing narrowing margins and deteriorating credit quality that are resulting in reduced earnings, dividend cuts, layoffs, lower stock prices, and failures. At the same time, regulators are requiring increased capital and are more closely scrutinizing credit quality levels and standards. The challenge for banks is to find the right combination of revenue streams, geographic and product markets, and cost structures to improve earnings. The institutions with strong earnings and capital positions will be able to take advantage of others' adversities and make acquisitions that deepen their current market positions and expand their reach into new markets.

Choose your employer carefully. Know what you are getting into. The current wave of mergers and acquisitions and the inevitable lay-offs that will result should steer more cautious potential bankers to the stronger institutions which will take over those less powerful. However, many banks with problems are looking for talent to help with changes. An experienced hire must evaluate and weigh the risk/reward potential for joining a troubled institution.

Look at the financial condition of the bank by reading the most recent annual and quarterly reports. Are problem loans, charge-offs, and nonperforming assets high? If so, are these problems being addressed through a comprehensive plan which is managed by top management? Is the bank well capitalized? Which units have been profitable? Which have not? Request 2 to 3 years of annual reports to determine if there have been numerous changes in strategy, top management, or director appointments.

Get many and varied perspectives on the culture of the banks you are considering. Ask bankers, attorneys, CPAs, and local business people about the reputation of each institution. This will help you decide which institution might be the best fit for you and will help you present yourself appropriately in the interview.

4

Engineering

Shirley Mewhorn
Vice President and Member of Board of Directors, Southern Engineering Company

One Month in the Career of an Engineer

Our charge was to design an electrical system to serve a new industrial development. Simple enough for a team of experienced electrical engineers. We had done it 100 times or so before. But what about the economics, the environmental issues, the structural analysis, the regulatory issues? This reminded me of a Rubik's Cube—it looked simple until you tried it. We organized a project team composed of qualified engineers in each area of responsibility and set about gathering the necessary data. For our project, we used computer modeling techniques to determine initial design load and future load for the system. There are many classic statistical modeling programs available, but our task was to find one that fit our needs and, perhaps more importantly, to interpret the results. Computers can turn out vast arrays of numbers to great precision. It requires judgment (usually based on training and experience) on the part of the engineer to assess the accuracy and the reasonableness of these results. For this project we input ten million pieces of data, which is why we used the computer.

We had many questions to address. For example, we had to assure that our design would meet capacity requirements now and for the projected future at a reasonable cost. We spent hours—days—running different scenarios and changing the parameters until we arrived at what we agreed to be the optimal design. A good analogy for this project would be designing a highway. If you had to move 100,000 vehicles, you could design one lane. One vehicle would arrive first and the last some 100,000 vehicles later. Cheap but pretty slow. Or you could design a road with 200 lanes and allow for 500 vehicles to move through. Fast but not very practical. In

*the real world, what you would do is find some optimum design to move
the traffic most efficiently for the least cost.*

Webster's Ninth New Collegiate Dictionary describes engineering as
"the application of science and mathematics by which the properties of
matter and the sources of energy in nature are made useful to people
in structures, machines, products, systems, and processes." Engineers
apply the theories of science and the fundamentals of mathematics to
devise solutions to practical problems. Their task is to take a problem,
define it, analyze the causes, study the effects, create or apply possible
alternatives, and finally come up with the optimum solution. The engineer is frequently responsible for converting scientific breakthroughs
to solutions of practical problems. Engineers in one way or another are
involved in everything that is built.

Engineers design and develop aircraft and spacecraft. They deal with
every aspect of research, design, testing, and manufacturing of not only
automobiles but every type of self-propelled vehicle. They apply chemical, physical, and manufacturing principles to manufacturing processes in which materials undergo chemical changes. They are concerned
with producing and applying to useful purposes metals and other
familiar materials. Engineers are also involved in relating to the needs
of the community: the building of roads, tunnels, and bridges as well as
the complex societal issues such as water and air quality, safety from
hazardous materials, and transportation systems. Engineers work to
make electrical energy available and create designs to utilize it properly and safely. They combine the scientific knowledge of nuclear reactions to produce heat, power, and special nuclear products.

The tasks engineers are involved in include but are not limited to
design and development, testing, production, operation and maintenance, quality assurance, materials handling, and packaging. Some
engineers are in sales, where their technical knowledge enables them
to understand the complete solution of the customer's problem and
assist in the implementation of the solution.

*Once we had agreed on the load parameters upon which our design was to
be based, we began designing an electrical distribution system that would
most economically serve the initial load and the improvements necessary
for 5, 10, 20 years in the future. This is the stage where we find the need
for and appreciation of our college calculus and electrical engineering
courses. I can recall in college the great wail and cry that emanated when
the professor marked the answer wrong when perhaps we only missed a
decimal point or made an arithmetic mistake. On a project, a "simple
arithmetic error" could create a major unnecessary expense, an unaccept-
able system performance, or a major safety hazard. For example, if we
were off one decimal on this design, we would have enough energy to light*

either one store or all of Poland. Engineering is a demanding and exact science. But we are educated and disciplined for that, and we moved through the planning and design stages on schedule.

Engineers spend most of their day working with numbers—mathematical equations which describe how a machine, a structure, or a system operates. Most of them work in an office, but some work in factories, on construction sites, in laboratories, outdoors, or even in submarines and spacecraft. Some work normal office hours, but many times a project schedule will demand extended hours. Working around the clock is not unusual at certain times in certain fields—for example, the shuttle lift off.

At times, there can be a lot of pressure in this environment. Imagine the thrill the project team felt when the shuttle successfully landed. It was a great reward for those long hours. Of course, our project was only slightly less exciting than launching a spacecraft, but to us it was essential to come up with the very best, the very safest, and the most efficient design. This is dictated not only by professional ethics but by the pride engineers share in their completed projects.

Our "paper" design had to be played against the real world. The most direct route for distribution lines had to be adjusted for the geographic environment. This step included the actual field data collection and surveying, which was done by the civil engineering team. Again computers came to the rescue. A fairly recently implemented technology called Global Positioning Systems was used to mark the exact location of electric distribution facilities on the land base. This technology involves the use of satellites to identify particular locations. This is the same technology used in the Gulf Crisis to locate specific targets.

Although a great deal of a design engineer's day is spent in thinking, reviewing analyses, devising new analyses, researching similar problems, creating new designs, and similar independent work tasks, a considerable amount of time is also spent in working with others. Meetings are a way of life with most engineers. These meetings frequently not only involve other engineers and technical people but also business, financial, and legal specialists as well. Sometimes this makes for interesting discussions since each profession uses its own vocabulary, its own acronyms and expressions.

While the mechanical engineers reviewed all of the structural design, assuring the most economical design to meet all of the safety factors and meet code requirements, the issue of environmental impact was being studied. An environmental report was prepared and included for consideration on the same level as cost, service, and reliability. The financial analysis projected the cost of the various alternative designs, rate schedules to match the cost of service, financing plans, and return on invest-

ment. The use of spread sheets and computers removes the tedium once associated with such analyses.

Clearly there are many steps associated with each engineering project from initial design through computer simulation, through environmental impact and cost analysis, through construction, and finally through inspection and certification. The tasks at each stage vary from heavy analytical thinking to computer analysis to numerous meetings. The skills required and the number of engineers involved vary depending on the size and complexity of the project. What's interesting about being an engineer is that on large projects no two jobs are ever alike. There always is a different wrinkle or a different constraint. There may be technical difficulties, public opposition to the project, operational hassles, or millions of other things that could and do go wrong. The engineer is ultimately responsible for ensuring that the design works as specified, meets all government regulations, is safe, and comes in on or under budget—easy to plan but difficult to do.

In a project for an industrial load, it is unlikely anyone would be raising a TV antenna, sailing a sailboat under the lines, or driving a crop harvester under the line, but those are events design engineers encounter in some projects. In fact, there is an entire discipline, forensic engineering, in which specialists determine the cause of the disaster. Particularly in the field of electrical engineering, there are frequent requests for assistance in accident investigations and service as an expert witness. The case rests on whether the provider of electricity was within all of the safety codes. To illustrate this, the expert witness frequently builds a model of the site. For engineers who like to work with their hands, this model building is more play than work.

When the design was completed, the engineers' work was still not finished. Specifications had to be written, bids had to be let, construction had to be supervised, and finally, finally, upon completion, the work had to be inspected and certified. Of course, in the meantime our team members had reassembled as groups of other teams on other projects, but we all shared a moment of pride when the load was activated and our efforts had led to a successful conclusion.

Commonly Asked Questions About a Career as an Engineer

What Tasks Do You Do Most Often?

Although tasks vary widely depending on the type of engineering career being examined, in the consulting environment most of an engineer's time is spent on project-related tasks. This means time spent analyzing the problems, devising solutions, evaluating and selecting the preferred solution, and developing a plan for the implementation of that solution. The analysis of the problem may involve travel to the site, meetings with the client, and perhaps meetings with regulatory bodies. In one recent case, the engineer in charge spent a considerable amount of time at public forums, meeting with property owners and school PTAs before he could begin design of a high-voltage transmission line. Not only did he have to deal with "not in my backyard," but in a public forum he had to answer many questions regarding electric and magnetic fields (EMF). This issue has been receiving increasing amounts of press coverage. Engineers have to do extensive reading and research to stay informed.

The preparation of the report on results of the study also requires a considerable amount of an engineer's time. This may be divided among several participants on a project, but, singly or collectively, they must prepare a report to the client. This involves writing the narrative as well as preparing drawings and charts and giving the results of analyses. This is why it is important for engineers to have good written and verbal communication skills as well as technical skills.

For some engineers, most if not all of their time is spent outdoors. This would include construction-related tasks, field testing, supervision, surveying, inspection, etc. In the case of the petroleum industry, this outdoor assignment may actually be off-shore. In the case of the space industry, this outdoor assignment might be the moon.

Many engineers spend a lot of time traveling, usually making required visits to the site of the project or to where the problem is, but this may also be representing the client in meetings and negotiations.

How Much Do You Work with People? Numbers? Computers?

Although engineers can set aside time to work alone, virtually all of their time is spent interacting with other people. They stay in constant touch with clients in meetings, on phone calls, and with visits. They usually work with a team of other specialists on the project and are frequently involved with other members of the team. Engineers frequently interact with commissions or other regulatory bodies. They are also responsible for supervising technical aides and drafters, giving them direction and guidance. Engineers are involved with many constituents—the client, fellow engineers, commission members, and support staff.

There is no doubt that engineering is definitely a quantitative business. The curriculum for engineering studies has heavy emphasis on mathematics. A thorough understanding of math and the ability to derive mathematical solutions for real-world problems is fundamental to success in the engineering profession. While computers are widely used to process tons of tedious, repetitive computations, this does not minimize the need for engineers to have a thorough understanding of mathematically based solutions. A phrase often heard around engineering offices is that the computerized result may be very precise, but the engineer must determine if it is accurate. Discerning the difference between precision and accuracy is essential.

Possibly one of the most profound changes in the engineering profession is the proliferation of personal computers. While there is still a demand for high-speed mainframe computers, the personal computer has become a day-to-day tool for each engineer. It has been said that in the future all engineers may or may not have a telephone on their desks, but for sure they will have a computer on their desks. These personal computers are frequently used for project scheduling, word processing, spread sheets, application programs, terminal-to-host systems, network access (and even for balancing the checkbook and keeping up with basketball scores).

How Much Time Do You Spend in Meetings? Writing? Other?

Too much. But this is necessary to get the job done. Frequently days start with a breakfast meeting at 7:00 a.m. and may even include a get-together after tennis on Saturday morning to discuss a proposal. These meetings are held in conference rooms, hotel rooms, job sites, airports, restaurants, or anywhere the parties can get together. However, teleconferencing and video conferencing are proving to be very effective communication media and reduce the need for face-to-face meetings.

Several hours per week are spent in writing. Basically this is divided between writing proposals to get new projects and writing reports, with some time spent in correspondence. Occasionally additional time is required for writing magazine articles, technical papers, and/or contributing to a handbook.

What Skills Do You Use Most Often?

No doubt—technical skills are used most often by engineers. Technical capability is a basic requirement in the engineering profession. Whether it is a mathematical formula, a chemical formula, an equation from the physics textbook, or other technical questions, engineers have an obligation to the profession and to society to be technically competent.

It should be stressed, however, that communication skills are also very important. Training in both written and verbal communications is gaining more importance in college engineering curriculum. The consensus among recruiters is that graduates need to be more than technical whiz kids to achieve success. Those who have both technical and communication skills are in demand and can command higher salaries.

What Training, Education, and/or Experience Are the Best Preparation for This Career?

A degree in engineering from one of the many outstanding engineering schools in the country is a first step in entering this profession. Most universities offer a co-op program in which students split their college time between work quarters and school quarters. In addition to providing financial relief for tuition-paying parents, the more important aspect of this arrangement is the experience gained by the student. Co-op program directors work to assure students get work assignments in the field of their study. This provides them with valuable experience and valuable contacts for future job opportunities.

How Do Most People Get Their Jobs in This Career?

As graduation approaches, students sign up for interviews with several of the many companies which recruit on college campuses. At some institutions this is a highly structured, formalized process, whereby the students and companies are "matched." These interviews are followed by plant trips and, it is hoped, job offers.

Of course, in times of a depressed economy these offers may not be as numerous or generous as in better times. But this is still an avenue that provides most first-time employment opportunities. Many universities provide a job placement service for alumni who are looking for employment. As in all other professions and industries, networking is still a good way to obtain a job.

What Do Most People in This Career Have in Common?

Common denominators in this profession are a high regard for ethics, a desire to make a contribution to society, and a keen analytical sense enhanced by continued learning. Many engineers are "putterers" or "tinkerers" who like to work with their hands. Also there is an interesting correlation of a high level of interest in music; this has been attributed to the mathematical relationships found in music.

How Much Are You Paid?

The latest average salary offers for bachelor's degree candidates ranged from $29,000 to $39,000, with chemical engineering being the highest. For master's degree candidates, this average ranged from $33,000 to $45,000.

**What is the Salary
or Compensation
Potential?**

Salaries for engineers with 10 to 15 years of experience range from $60,000 to $70,000. Many engineers form their own businesses and have high earnings' potential. CEOs of some major companies are engineers—Delta Air Lines, American Express, Milliken. Their compensation is public knowledge. It is frequently measured in millions.

**What Are the Short- and Long-
Term Career Opportunities?**

Opportunities for engineers in today's down economy are still greater than in many other professions. As illustrated earlier, engineering crosses many industry boundaries. This diversity offers a particular advantage in tough economic times. Another important factor is that there are no geographic limitations. Big cities, small cities, rural areas, off-shore areas, international locations—all need engineers.

Engineering plays a major role in the fun side of things, too. Think of the engineering required to make roller coasters exciting, yet safe. Disney contains a treasure of engineering feats; in fact, some of the mechanically simulated things are so realistic that you forget they are not real. For those who think engineers are tied to a dull drafting table, dealing with monotonous calculations, these engineering opportunities will be a surprise.

Another area of great excitement for engineers is the space program. Dr. Jan Davis made history with the launch of the *Endeavor* when she and her husband, astronaut Mark Lee, became the first married couple to fly in space together. Prior to this exciting opportunity, she worked as an engineer for NASA. Engineering is not only a stepping stone to space but also to the CEO's office. Top management—CEOs, presidents, vice presidents—of the major corporations reached that point through a successful career in engineering. These companies include diversified industries—Boeing, Chase Manhattan Bank, Dow Chemical, IBM, Kelly Moore Paint, Northern Telecom, Russell, Shearson/American Express,

Delta Airlines, Waffle House, Phillips Petroleum, Traveler's Insurance, Florida Power and Light, and Georgia Power.

What Is the Range of Jobs in This Career?

There are more than 25 major specialties in engineering which are recognized by professional societies, and within each of these are many subdivisions. Even within each of these, engineers may specialize in one industry or in one technology. It becomes immediately obvious that the range of jobs in engineering increases exponentially.

Engineers in each specialty may work in many fields. For example, electrical engineers work in power distribution, missile guidance, communications, medical, computer, aircraft controls, and broadcasting fields. Many engineers work in design and development. Some work in production, operations, maintenance, and testing. A background in engineering prepares one for a variety of choices both in traditional engineering jobs and other related fields.

What Provides the Greatest Satisfaction? Frustration?

Seeing a project through from the embryo of definition to the implementation of a solution is the greatest satisfaction in this career. Even on major projects with multiple teams, engineers usually are intimately involved with the implementation of the solution. Whether it is a bridge, a substation, a textile process, or a satellite launching—engineers can usually feel, see, touch, hear, and enjoy the results of their designs.

The greatest frustration has to be when the technical implementation of a solution is stymied by political processes. This does not mean local, county, state, or federal policies, but typically it means office politics. This may be circumvented or at least minimized by interpersonal skills, working to increase understanding and cooperation.

What Is the Biggest Misconception About the Job?

Strange but true, some folks still think that engineers are those guys in striped caps who drive trains. Most people do not realize that engineers have walked on the moon, been president of the United States, built cities, designed supersonic aircraft, and developed the technology that enabled the United States to direct bombs with such precision that the Gulf Crisis was quickly brought under control.

**What Is the One Thing You Would
Have Wanted Someone to Tell You
About the Career?**

The first thing I would have liked to hear is how rewarding a career in
this field can be so I would have not spent time considering alternatives.
Because of the very diverse nature of the opportunities in this profession, it is overwhelming at times for those considering this choice.

The other thing I would have liked is to have had a role model. Role
models are very important to young people at the time they must
make choices regarding education and careers. Again, the diversity of
opportunities in this field makes it difficult to always identify the most
appropriate role model.

**What Three Pieces of Advice or
Wisdom Would You Give Someone
Thinking About This Career?**

1. Success comes when you plunge into the job, even if you have to
   flap like mad just to stay afloat. Perseverance and endurance are
   two of the most underrated talents in the world. In the words of
   Calvin Coolidge, "Nothing in the world can take the place of persistence. Persistence and determination are omnipotent." This is
   true in all of life but is most certainly applicable to the exacting and
   demanding career as an engineer.

2. Build a relationship with people. Market integrity, service, and the
   ability to solve problems. A recent panel discussion, "Making It to
   the Top," in which 10 people with engineering degrees participated, the one characteristic mentioned consistently by each participant as being essential to success was integrity—some called it
   ethics, some called it honesty, some called it integrity—but all
   agreed it was most essential.

3. Enjoy the process. Whether you see an opportunity or an obstacle is
   based on your attitude and your perception. Every challenge, every
   obstacle holds within it an opportunity. To be successful in doing
   something you must feel good about it. Enthusiasm and energy are
   essential characteristics of achievement in this field of technology,
   people, and machines. In the meantime, it is important to remember that happiness is not in having achieved something but in the
   journey of achieving.

5

Entrepreneurship

Gil Kemp

President and Founder, Home Decorators
Collection

One Month in the Career of an Entrepreneur

I was 39 years old with a background in publishing and direct marketing. I was fairly successful in the business world and had actually started several businesses for the large corporations which employed me. Now I wanted to be out on my own. But I had to figure out three simple things:

1. What was I going to do? What was my big idea?

2. How would I make it happen?

3. How would I support myself while I wasn't working for someone?

   This shouldn't be difficult, should it?

All entrepreneurs have to create businesses from scratch. It's not like most jobs where the products or services are established and all you have to do is keep them going. Entrepreneurs take on all the risk with limited chance of success. But entrepreneurs do have an advantage. They are doing what they want to do. And the rewards can be great. Being an entrepreneur is as much a state of mind as anything else. It is deciding that you want to do something and then doing it. A friend who started his own business once told me that the difference between someone who is an entrepreneur and someone who isn't is that we all think about opening that little toy store downtown right before Christmas, but an entrepreneur will actually go out and do it. It's like the Nike commercials—"Just do it."

But being an entrepreneur is not easy. An entrepreneur has to have a great idea or special competence to sell. Then money or capital must be raised. Then all the things someone does in a big corporation such as human resources, operations, finance, and so forth must be handled by the entrepreneur. The entrepreneur is always selling because if the business doesn't succeed, entrepreneurs lose personally.

> *I'm beginning my third year in the mail-order catalog business. I'm happy, solvent, and the business is prospering. I believe my good fortune stems from some very simple facts. My business is in a growth area, I have an excellent partner, the business combines professional and avocation interests and skills, and I learned something about my strengths and weaknesses in the almost 20 years I spent in business before launching this catalog.*
>
> *Before I started the mail order business, I considered publishing, since I had been in that field for a number of years. However, the margins and the cash flow were not good. I also thought about opening a small retail establishment but did not want to tie up capital in a small operation with little chance for quick growth. Mail order intrigued me since I had done direct mail before, and I could pick the product I wanted to sell. Besides, it didn't seem that difficult for L.L. Bean and Land's End. Therefore, I founded Home Decorators Collection, a mail-order catalog selling lighting, bath accessories, furniture, and hardware to individual homeowners.*

Even great ideas require capital. All businesses need money to start, and most lose money before they ever start making any. Raising capital occupies a great deal of time for most fledgling operators. What makes it difficult is that most banks and other investors only like to give money to people who don't need it, or they want a guarantee (i.e., collateral) to ensure that they will get their money back. Banks and investors also like entrepreneurs to take some of the risk by investing some of their own money.

However, in one sense it is best for entrepreneurs to provide as much of the initial capital as possible since by doing so they will own or keep most of the company. Investors always want as much of the company as possible in return for providing the start-up funds. Two-thirds of new ventures raise money from private sources as opposed to venture capitalists or banks. That means friends, family, business contacts, and potential merchandise vendors.

> *Raising money is never easy, but I was not prepared for the financial side of launching a new business. "Please sit down," I said to the banker as we entered the conference room which doubled as a part-time office. We had just finished a tour of the distribution center which was humming with the activity of almost a thousand orders being picked and packed. Now we were going to discuss the key topic—the ability of Home Decorators Collection to borrow to fund additional growth.*

"The operation is very impressive, Gil," said the banker. "But we have a problem at the bank. We don't like to lend to start-up or very young companies. It's simply too risky."

"But can't you lend against our inventory?" I asked. "It would be very easy to liquidate if worse came to worse."

"No," he said. "We just don't like to do that."

So, I did what a lot of entrepreneurs do—mortgage the house and use credit cards. I was lucky, since years ago when I was still working for a corporation, I had taken a friend's advice to apply for credit whenever it was offered to me. Don't wait until you need it because then you'll have a devil of a time borrowing it he had said. He was right, but keeping up with all the payments was quite stressful. While intellectually I knew that even 15 and 18 percent interest was cheaper to me than giving up more equity, emotionally (and because of cash flow) writing the checks for credit-card payments each month was quite hard. The pain was a good incentive to look for other sources of cash.

Money is a primary concern of a lot of entrepreneurs. Even discussions with suppliers and vendors often have financial overtones. What is many times taken for granted in an established company—that there is money to fund ongoing operations—in a small or new venture, money or lack thereof, is a continual problem. As a result, entrepreneurs are forced to become resourceful or entrepreneurial in securing new capital. What better way than to seek concessions or better terms from the people you do business with.

The next day I generated a printout of our top 20 vendors and how much business Home Decorators had done with them the preceding year. My goal was to switch from net 30- to net 60-day terms. The first call was to the president and owner of a bath accessories company.

"Pat, our business is going very well, but I've called because I need your help. As you know, our business with you is increasing nicely and our prospects are terrific. You know we strive to ship all orders the next working day, which means that we have to keep a sizable inventory. With all the different finishes in your line, Pat, we have to invest a lot of money in that inventory. And we've prided ourselves on paying you promptly for that inventory.

"My difficulty is this. We have two places we can put money—inventory or into more mailings. And it's mailings that drive the business. Inventory is just a necessary evil. We're in the very fortunate position of having lots of excellent lists which we can mail to, but we have limited funds. I don't want Home Decorators to get into a position of being overextended and not being able to pay you and other vendors on time.

"So what I'm suggesting is this. If you can extend our terms to net 60 days, we'll free up money for more mailings which will increase business for both of us. What do you think?"

Pat ultimately agreed to a compromise of net 45 days, and over half our vendors agreed to improved terms. The process of negotiating reminded me how much selling I have to do as an entrepreneur. The selling isn't always to customers.

Entrepreneurs always have to be concerned with whether or not the business is going to make it. Even a few bad months can force a new business, which is usually short of cash, into a perilous situation. At the same time, the entrepreneur must give the impression the business is doing well for the sake of employees, suppliers, and him- or herself. Remember, the U.S. government has lost money for years and still continues to operate. If only entrepreneurs could print money, everything would be okay.

Twice a year we have an off-site meeting for key managers. We review in detail the past 6 months and look ahead to the next year and beyond. Home Decorators has a sister company of three apparel catalogs, and the experience of most of our managers is with the much more established sister. Consequently, it's a difficult job to sell them—as it would be to most rational people—on the concept that losing money is not a terrible thing for a new company.

"Do you think Home Decorators is really going to make it?" The question came from the manager of the distribution center. She was looking at financial results that showed a significant loss the first partial year and another loss, albeit smaller, the first 6 months of the second year. I did not think the question was at all unreasonable, but I thought a positive response was absolutely essential. While I honestly believed that the business was on a terrific track that was going to generate exceptional returns in the relatively near future, I had to get Chris and the other managers to share my belief.

"Well," I said. "It's always hard to lose money, even if the rate of loss is getting smaller. A key thing for all of us to remember is that catalog businesses almost always lose money the first 3 or 4 years they're in business. We should start to make money in the next 6 months, which is something we can all feel proud about. There are very few catalogs in the last 10 years that have done as well. If you look at the results of each mailing in sequence, we have had real improvement. And operationally we are getting better month by month. I think all this pain of getting started and losing money is going to be well worth it. We just have to wait a little longer."

As I spoke, I looked around the table. While I didn't sense overwhelming joy at my explanation of where we were and where we are going to be shortly, I did sense a higher comfort level. It occurred to me that the principle of deferred gratification is essential not just for entrepreneurs to embrace but must be conveyed to those who are part of an entrepreneurial organization. Inevitably, lots of negative things happen on the way to good results. And dealing with problems is more stressful when you don't have much money in the bank or certainty that you will in fact succeed. Dealing with those uncertainties in yourself and in your colleagues is an essential task in equipping the organization so that it is capable of moving forward. A positive attitude is essential in motivating yourself and others during the bumpy times as a company establishes itself.

Entrepreneurs are always selling. Whether it is to customers, employees, or vendors, selling is critical. To customers, you are selling a product. To employees, you are selling a shared vision. To vendors, you are selling the idea that they will get paid and make money if they do business with you. If any link in this business transaction chain breaks, the new business may fail. In order to succeed, entrepreneurs must persuade and convince everyone that success is right around the corner.

As I walked the aisles of the annual Hardware Show, I was looking for manufacturers that might fit in the pages of Home Decorators. I almost walked by Kirkwood's small booth because at first I just saw dozens of pillows. Then I noticed various small pieces of upholstered furniture. We were having some success with contemporary upholstery, and these more traditional pieces looked as if they might complement our assortment. So, I decided to stop.

"Hi, my name is Gil Kemp, and I have a mail-order catalog called Home Decorators Collection. I'd like to learn more about your line." I was shaking hands with Charles Kirk, who, I later learned ran Kirkwood with his son Brennan. Charles's face brightened when I said mail order, and he explained that he had done business with a number of catalogs.

I then spent the next 10 minutes explaining how our orientation differed from other catalogs and how we strove to develop close relationships with our vendors. My strategy is to convince a potential vendor that Home Decorators is an excellent company to do business with. We work hard to deliver on that promise, but critical to success is gaining a vendor's enthusiasm at the beginning. The more enthusiastic they are about our prospects, the better service and prices I'm likely to get. The better prices I get, the better values I can offer my customer, and the more merchandise I can sell. And the more merchandise I sell, the happier both the vendor and I will be. I sincerely believe that I can create a win-win situation for Home Decorators and the vendor. And the better job I do convincing the potential vendor of that, the more likely it's going to happen.

Persuading current and potential vendors, bankers, and employees, and myself as well that this venture is without question the best thing for me to be devoting my energies to is a critical and ongoing task. This is true for all entrepreneurs. Believing in oneself and the ability to make it on your own is the first step in any entrepreneurial venture. Besides, once you're out on your own, could you ever do a regular job again?

Commonly Asked Questions About Being an Entrepreneur

What Tasks Do You Do Most Often?

Perhaps the nicest fringe benefit of starting your own business is the opportunity to structure it to let you focus on those tasks that you enjoy the most. For me, a short attention span makes variety the key to keeping business interesting; so my week is full of many different tasks.

The primary task is selling both the concept and the person. Since so many new businesses fail, it takes a lot of perseverance to succeed. This means selling or convincing bankers, investors, friends, family, and even one's spouse. Another task is managing a series of varied activities. Initially, the entrepreneur is general manager, operations manager, financial manager, and so on. There is no task an entrepreneur doesn't do.

How Much Work Do You Do with People? Numbers? Computers?

The interesting thing about being an entrepreneur is that you do a lot of things yourself—at least when you start out. You are your own staff. As the business grows, entrepreneurs add staff, but at the outset they cannot afford to have employees when no money is coming in.

No man or woman goes it alone for long, so people are critical. Most of the time is spent convincing others that the numbers make sense. Therefore, an equal amount of time is spent with people *and* numbers. It is critical in the early stages to keep the project moving forward. As a result, working with people needs to accomplish something, or it can waste a lot of time.

I much prefer working with people to computers; so there are other people in my organization who handle our computer work. They're much better at it than I would be even if I spent more time at it. I do spend a lot of time with numbers and the quantitative output of others' work on the computer, but that time is an inevitable consequence of numbers being a critical part of the mail-order business.

How Much Time Do You Spend in Meetings? Writing? Other?

I used to prefer memos to meetings and one-on-one sessions. But now I firmly believe that taking the time to talk with people is the best way to communicate. And it's not just the employees the entrepreneur has to worry about motivating. There are different constituencies to focus on. Outside the company there are banks, investors, key suppliers, and landlords. I have never heard a single regret from a manager who invested the time in getting to know his or her employees and communicating with them. Company newsletters are useful but can never supplant face-to-face communication.

There are times that long hours are unavoidable, but doing everything oneself is no better recipe for an entrepreneur than for a manager. The practice of time management should begin long before starting a business. Developing a sense of priorities and delegation are habits that all business people should cultivate. The planning process should be thorough enough to anticipate staffing needs so that horrible hours need not be continuous.

For those times when long hours are required, building-in family time can be a way of reducing the tensions that can disrupt even healthy relationships. For instance, locating the business close to home makes it practical to go home for an hour or two at dinner time and then returning to the office. Fax machines, laptops, and cellular phones make it easier to get away from the office without losing touch. Instead of deciding a vacation is impractical, it might be possible to take a week off and spend mornings working and afternoons vacationing. Someone based on the East Coast can travel to California and work for 3 or 4 early-morning hours and still have most of the day left.

What Skills Do You Use Most Often?

The most important skills are those that my formal education spent the least time on. For example, interpersonal and leadership skills are needed both inside and outside the company. The technical knowledge I learned in my M.B.A. program is long forgotten.

Still an entrepreneur has to be good or at least passable at everything. Selling, persuading, and managing are all key skills. If an entrepreneur has all three, he or she has at least a chance of making it. Another critical skill is decision making. No one else can, will, or should make the tough decisions. These will either make or break the new enterprise.

What Training, Education, and/or Experience Are the Best Preparation for This Career?

Work for people and organizations that have a lot to teach is excellent experience. Entrepreneurs typically do lots of different tasks, especially when their companies are small. The opportunity to learn when the risks are borne by someone else can be the chance to stretch one's skills. Focusing on industries for which one has an innate affinity improves the chance that specific knowledge will be useful later on. It's useful to focus on creating new businesses even under a corporate umbrella, for many of the tasks are the same that face the entrepreneur, who does not need the protection of the umbrella.

How Do Most People Get Their Jobs in This Career?

By doing something they like. After all, they'll be selling it to customers, employees, and themselves. Improving the odds that they'll end up doing something professionally which satisfies them may be the greatest benefit of becoming an entrepreneur. An entrepreneur gravitates to those businesses that provide the greatest personal fit as well as opportunity. Creating a catalog of home furnishings combined my professional interest in publishing and the process of communicating through the printed page with a long-standing avocational interest in home decor.

More than creating a broad occupational fit, starting a business makes it easier to structure an organization around personal strengths and weaknesses as well as likes and dislikes. Intellectually, I recognize how critical the fulfillment operation is to a mail-order catalog. If merchandise does not reach customers quickly and at low cost, a catalog can quickly wither. But running a distribution center is not my interest. So Home Decorators now has fulfillment managers who can do that job far better than I could and who gain a great deal more satisfaction from it than I would.

As things work out, a disproportionate number of business people become entrepreneurs in their mid- to late thirties. By that age many people have learned their industry, made contacts, saved some money, sharpened management skills, and, perhaps most importantly, developed a frame of mind or attitude that leads to action.

But the fact that some psychologists look to the late thirties as a stage in life that is conducive to becoming an entrepreneur should never discourage someone from starting earlier or later. Bill Gates and Sam Walton, who started their organizations at opposite sides of their thirties, would never have achieved their extraordinary successes if they had paid attention to psychologists. They listened to themselves.

What Do People in This Career Have in Common?

Very little. Entrepreneurs may—as some psychologists claim—be trying to outdo their fathers, but I don't see that drive so much as I see tremendously varied backgrounds and interests. And if there are some psychological traits in common, they're seemingly subordinated by the different characteristics leading entrepreneurs to different types of businesses.

How Much Are You Paid?

Earning less than you're used to is a common problem for entrepreneurs starting out. In fact, most entrepreneurs put money into the business initially, rather than get paid. If you are used to a good corporate salary with benefits, and that is important to you, entrepreneurship may not be the right path. However, if you have just been laid off or if you are tired of always having someone else tell you what to do, a high salary to start with may be less important.

It is important to have some money to live on. Consequently, securing lines of credit while still employed in the corporate world is a useful technique. More valuable is being an aggressive saver. The habit of being an aggressive saver has two distinct payoffs. The obvious one is creating capital. The second benefit is living below your means. Consequently, a drop in income does not necessarily require a significant sacrifice in lifestyle.

Another means of support is a working spouse. Odds are good these days that both spouses will work. It's a lot easier for one half of a working team to take a vocational risk than for a single person to do so.

What Is Salary or Compensation Potential?

Unlimited. Year after year the new entrants to the *Forbes* 400 are disproportionately entrepreneurs. But they also tend to be individuals for whom the money is secondary. The satisfaction of creating a business usually is more satisfying than a high net worth.

Although it's fun to read about those entrepreneurs who have lifestyles of the rich and famous, most entrepreneurs who I know live relatively modest lives. Personal extravagance is not especially satisfying to many successful people, and they often recognize that it causes tension within the organization. Those without a significant equity in the business may resent someone who they feel is profiting unduly from their labor and showing off with a Ferrari, yacht, or other ostentatious possessions. But the satisfaction of creating something is a pleasure that lasts.

What Are the Short- and Long-Term Career Opportunities?

Having more control over your time and your life is a powerful motivation. I have arranged my work so I have an office at my home where

I spend on average a day and a half a week. At 3:20 p.m., my children come home from school, and it's a delight to take a 10-minute break to find out how school went or to play a quick game of catch.

The career opportunities for an entrepreneur are what you make them. Some entrepreneurs grow their businesses into multibillion dollar operations, others sell out early, and others never make it. Unlike existing corporations where there is an established career progression path, an entrepreneur almost by definition rolls the dice of life.

What Is the Range of Jobs in This Career?

Our economy is so wonderfully huge that the range of entrepreneurial opportunities is unlimited. And every month new opportunities present themselves to individuals who are energetic and nimble enough to tackle them. Yet a fear of plunging in and getting one's hands dirty stops many people from becoming entrepreneurs.

Entrepreneurs open high-tech companies, new restaurants, mail services, print shops, and every imaginable field in between. At some time the business reaches a point when it needs to consolidate its gains and at that point the usually free-wheeling entrepreneur must decide to grow with the business à la Sam Walton or move on like Steven Jobs.

What Provides the Greatest Satisfaction? Frustration?

The greatest satisfaction for any entrepreneur is clearly building something on your own. In fact, the process of creation is often more satisfying than the end result itself.

In business school I had a professor of small business who observed that for the entrepreneurs he studied, getting there was *all* the fun. He observed a plague of problems for those who cashed in their chips and suddenly discovered that life was empty without the challenges of building a business.

When I started Home Decorators, a friend told me that raising the money would take twice as long and be twice as hard as I anticipated. He was right. I never anticipated, for example, just how hard it would be to achieve the proper balance in inventory. I didn't count on raising money during a war in the Persian Gulf or that the business would be launched during a recession. And while I anticipated needing more cash than we raised, I didn't think it would be as much more.

Hokey as they may be, self-help books are useful to have around in the early days because they can help you to deal with the inevitable setbacks and challenges. Simply considering problems to be challenges can improve one's attitude and free up energy to solve problems rather than worry about them.

What Is the Biggest Misconception About the Job?

Most people underestimate how unpredictable events can be. It's tough psychologically—but necessary to create a plan that factors in allowances for all reasonable contingencies. I find it useful to have three plans or scenarios. Plan A is success. The sizable profits of plan A are what motivate me to deal with all the angst and hard work of launching and growing the business. I don't completely believe that plan A is going to happen as projected. So plan B is a more realistic vision. I make most of my investment and other financial decisions based on the realism of plan B. Plan C is a doomsday scenario. I sketch out plan C and then throw it away without completing it. To my mind, planning for failure is a sure way to fail. If I start to fall short of plan B, I'll revise it to fit and adapt to the new reality, but I hope I never resort to budgeting for failure.

What Is the One Thing You Would Have Wanted Someone to Tell You About This Career?

Just do it! It's no accident that a high percentage of entrepreneurs don't become them until they're fired. Consciously or subconsciously many of us require a catalyst before striking out on our own. The challenge is to voluntarily make the move before circumstances may require it.

Taking the time to chart out a personal game plan for the next 5 to 10 years is a very helpful technique for controlling when you strike out on your own. Being fired and landing a generous severance package can seem a comfortable way to become an entrepreneur, but is it worth it? Being at the mercy of someone else's schedule may just postpone success, but it can also prevent it.

What Three Pieces of Advice or Wisdom Would You Give Someone Thinking About This Career?

1. *Decide if you need a partner.* I'm extremely fortunate to have terrific partners. I've also in the past had a partner who was excruciatingly

disappointing. While it may be impossible to generalize, one rule of thumb may prove helpful. Each partner should bring a special skill or asset to the partnership that makes him or her indispensable to the other partner. Many times partners join forces simply because it seems comforting to go through the trying times of launching a business with a kindred spirit. The key question is whether all partners will be needed after the business is running successfully.

2. *Ask yourself what happens if you fail?*   The lack of an answer to this question may be the single largest reason more individuals don't become entrepreneurs. The prosaic truth is that life goes on. If one door closes, another opens. If you can view life as a process, a failure can strengthen you and improve your chances of success the next time.

    Before starting Home Decorators Collection, I had started another similar catalog called Kemp & George. From a marketing perspective, Kemp & George succeeded, but we had major organizational and operational problems. I ended up selling my shares in the company for a very modest amount but retained the rights to launch a similar catalog, albeit without my name on the cover. So, after 2½ years, I was back at the beginning. Or almost. The learning experience at Kemp & George has proved invaluable and has led to Home Decorators being more satisfying and rewarding than I think Kemp & George would ever have been.

    Although the separation from Kemp & George was painful, it wasn't especially distressing. I had complete faith that the new venture would work. I also saw that this experience was only a portion of my life. My wife and children remained enormously satisfying. My health was fine. I still enjoyed gardening and raising money for United Way. What was happening in business was happening just to part of my life but not my whole life.

3. *Learn to worry as an entrepreneur.*   Fear of failure stops more would-be entrepreneurs than lack of capital. Cultivating a positive attitude makes it easier to overcome the fear. Contrary to what many people believe, a positive attitude can be acquired. An excellent guide to the subject is *Learned Optimism* by Martin Seligman. To deal with the stress once you have embarked on a venture, Dale Carnegie's classic *How to Stop Worrying and Start Living* is full of practical suggestions for controlling excessive worry and tension. For example, Carnegie urges his readers to ask themselves what is the worst that can happen—and then how to improve on the worst.

6
Finance

Michael Soble
Vice President and Budget Manager,
Bank South

One Month in the Career of
a Financial Manager

I was sitting in a meeting in the board room with the top executives of the company discussing the budget for the upcoming year. They were all talking in circles and not making any progress or decisions. I was looking around at all the pictures on the wall of the past senior executives of the company wondering if the budget process was the same then as it is now. Our bottom-line numbers were not satisfactory—revenues were down and expenses were up. The CEO of the company quoted a net income figure that we should strive to achieve—a "goal." We were $15 million away from our goal of $50 million. Discussions around the table lasted for what seemed like hours with everyone talking in circles. Finally, my boss asked if we could come back in a week after we made some changes. We came back 1 week later and went through the same process once again—and again—and again. Management decided to close and consolidate some branches and eliminate some back office personnel through attrition. A few layoffs would occur in the upcoming year. Instead of meeting the $50 million goal only through expense reduction, management came up with ways to improve revenues through new marketing programs, increasing fees, and cross-selling the bank's products more effectively. Finally, with the upcoming year at hand, top management finally made some hard decisions and finalized the budget for the whole company. Some of the decisions that had to be made were very difficult to make since they affected many people. "Rightsizing," "restructuring," "downsizing"—these were all discussed during budget meetings and were the most difficult decisions to make. At last, after months of negotiating and discussions, the goal was achieved with the budget agreed to by the board of directors.

The job responsibilities of a financial, or budget, manager include managing the annual budget process for the company, tracking actual versus budget performance, and maintaining the integrity of the data presented in financial statements. These are the manager's main responsibilities. However, he or she also performs other tasks and assignments related to the analysis of the financial performance of the company. "Special projects" always seem to come to the financial manager at the most inopportune times, and it is his or her responsibility to juggle and balance numerous assignments in the most efficient way possible. In many cases it is either feast or famine. During the budget season, the budget department barely has enough time to eat lunch much less work on special projects. During the "off-season," the department spends a lot of time trying to improve the process and make it more streamlined. One approach taken is the postmortem off-site meeting at which all the important players in the budget process get together to discuss what went right and what went wrong the past year. The sharing of information at this meeting helps uncover improvements that can be made in the upcoming budget year. Every year the department makes positive strides, but there are always ways to improve. The department has much more time to be creative during the spring after the budget is finalized.It is also a great time to take a vacation. It is taboo to take a vacation during the fall, during the budget season.

> *It amazes me how much difficulty people have in preparing a financial budget. Whenever I call someone, I feel like Darth Vader because I don't usually tell people they are doing a good job. I have to let them know that they have to do extra work. People always seem to put off doing their budget planning until the last minute because they don't understand how the numbers fit together. Once a manager planned to spend $200,000 in renovating an office. He did not realize that this was a capital expenditure and should have been depreciated over 10 years. He planned the entire $200,000 expenditure in the upcoming year's budget. He spent the next year explaining why he was so far under budget.*

Part of a financial manager's responsibility is to help the people in the field develop their plans and to help them understand how they contribute to the company's profitability. In a lot of ways the manager is like a teacher. The more he or she explains subjects, the better the teacher gets at teaching it.

There are numerous ways to prepare financial plans. One way is called a zero-based budget, which is preferred by most financial managers. This method requires a lot of thought by the individual preparing the budget. This person must consider all the necessary items (staffing, supplies, etc.) required for the upcoming year as well as the income that will be generated. The income piece is the most difficult to predict because it is dependent on so many variables. The budget preparer then compares the results to current results to see if the budget is in line with expectations.

One year, I worked at a company which was running into financial difficulty. The expense base had to be reduced. We were asked to assist in developing a "hit" list to reduce expenses. The expenses were divided into fixed and programmed costs. Each of these expense items was then planned individually and combined together for the total budget. By using this zero-based method, it was easier to determine which costs could be reduced without as much pain and difficulty.

Another way to budget is to only look at current year results and plan growth rates. This is not the best way because it does not consider unusual items; however, it is the easiest way. Most people use this method to prepare budgets because it is not as technical for nonfinancial people.

In one case, a manager used this method to prepare an annual budget. He did not remember that he received a one-time fee of $100,000 in the prior year. He used a growth rate and determined his budget incorporating this one-time source of revenue. He then had to explain why he missed his budget by $100,000.

There are other methods of developing budgets; however, these are the most popular. Each company has its own unique way of preparing, challenging, and finalizing budgets. Some companies use a combination approach. They instruct everyone to use the zero-base method, but most of the line managers are not sophisticated enough to understand how to prepare a budget using this method. The budget department is just happy if they put the numbers in the right account. As a company uses more computer technology, it becomes easier to perform sensitivity analysis on budgets and makes revisions easier. One type of software automates the consolidation process of a budget. It can help save countless hours of number crunching. Prior to the development of this software application, budget departments had to work every weekend for months to produce financial documents. The software revolutionized the way budgets are developed and analyzed.

There are numerous types of budgets financial managers must work with on a daily basis. Revenue, expense, balance sheet, and capital expenditure budgets are examples of the different types of budgets which are prepared and analyzed at most companies. Each type of budget has is own characteristics and must be planned accordingly. Inflation, interest rates, the economy, etc., all play a part in the development and analysis of an operating budget. To be successful in the financial arena, a financial manager must develop expertise in reviewing, analyzing, and developing budgets.

The biggest difficulty in working on a budget is that it never seems to end. There are so many revisions. Even after the budget is so called "final," people still want to make changes. We do our best to make everyone in the field happy, but sometimes you just have to say, "No more changes." Once the budget is final, the budget department is responsible for tracking actual versus plan performance.

> On a monthly basis, our department analyzes what happened in the month just ended to determine if, how, why, and where we missed the plan. For 2 weeks every month, we analyze each division's performance and present the information to senior management. We synthesize large volumes of information into understandable parts by using various systems. We also spend a lot of time on the telephone asking people lots of questions. Many times we feel like detectives trying to uncover exactly what went on in the previous month. We share the information with all those affected and ask for comments on how to make the process better in the future. Sometimes it is very awkward discussing results of a division in front of top management when the person responsible is also there listening. You hope you don't say anything that is incorrect or that will offend anyone, especially if the division did not have a particularly good month. One month, we pointed out the obvious in a meeting—new business was well below plan. The manager who was directly responsible did not take the comment very well and became very defensive. We probably should have added all the new business which was "in the pipeline" to soften the comment. Still numbers can be hard.

A budget department often has the responsibility of maintaining a database of financial information which the entire treasurer's division can access to develop analysis worksheets, pro formas, financial statements, etc. Each month actual data is downloaded from the mainframe computer and the information is imported into a local area network (LAN). From the LAN, anyone who needs to access the information is able to do so through the budget system. It is the financial manager's responsibility to ensure that the data is accurate. Any problems related to the database are his or her responsibility. The addition of a system like this can help save numerous hours of data entry work and streamline report creation.

The budget department is responsible for preparing financial information each quarter for the "CEO review," in which the CEO has meetings with each of the major divisions within the company. The financial information is reviewed from the previous quarter and all the strategies in place for the upcoming quarters are discussed. These meetings are a great way to develop an understanding of how the entire company fits together and how decisions by one group affect how another group operates.

The budget department must develop good working relationships with all areas of the company. In order to perform its job effectively, the department must get information from numerous sources and people. Therefore, it is critical to develop trust and credibility within the company. It takes time to develop these characteristics, but if you do, it will make your job a lot easier.

Strategic planning is another area of the company into which the budget department has input. Financial managers assist with the gathering of data and submission of this information to senior-level managers to help them with strategic decisions. Financial analysts assist them in running sensitivity analyses to determine what would be the results if various strategic decisions were made. Some of these decisions include exiting businesses and creating new businesses; they also review potential results from marketing campaigns, etc.

> *Sometimes you become an expert on a particular subject, such as forecasting, and everyone calls you for help in developing projections. It is a good feeling to help others achieve their goals, but when too many people ask for help at once, it sometimes turns into a stressful experience trying to balance everyone's needs. Once we were trying to institute an ongoing financial projection process with the budget department coordinating the project. Many managers would wait until the projection was due before reviewing the information and then would expect an analyst to drop everything to help them. What should have been a reasonable two-week review turned into a "we need it tomorrow" crisis. It can be difficult to manage your priorities as well as those of others outside of your area when you are trying to operate on a crises mentality.*

The budget department also assists other departments within the division in providing information for financial reporting and cost accounting. The cost accounting area is responsible for allocating all the overhead expenses to the profit centers to determine the profitability of each center and division. It is one of the most disliked departments in the company since it gives all the profit centers additional expenses and causes them to be less profitable. Since the budget department works closely with cost accounting, many people in the field think the budget department does the allocations, so they call and question why their allocations are so high. The budget department does the best it can to answer their questions, but usually they are still upset because they can "never be profitable with all the allocations charged against them." Such is the life of a financial manager.

Commonly Asked Questions About a Career as a Financial Manager

What Tasks Do You Do Most Often?

Financial, or budget, managers prepare countless variations of financial reports. They analyze financial information and the performance of each division within the company. Each division has its own characteristics and the nuances of each must be understood. They also spend a lot of time communicating with all areas in the company, getting or sharing pertinent information related to the respective divisions. One example of a task performed ritually is a financial notebook prepared for senior management each month. The notebook summarizes the financial performance of the company and of each major division within the company. The preparation of this notebook involves other departments within the division (i.e., general accounting and financial reporting), so it requires much teamwork. Once this notebook is complete, it is sent out to all the senior-level managers. Top-performing financial managers always search for better ways of measuring and monitoring financial performance of each division and the profitability of the company as a whole.

How Much Do You Work with People? Numbers? Computers?

The financial manager's entire existence depends on how well he or she works with people, numbers, and computers. All aspects of the position relate to these three areas. In order to understand the company and what's going on throughout it, the financial manager must communicate with numerous people in every area of the company on a daily basis. This communication involves a lot of whys and whats to determine if the numbers justify the explanations. At the end of each month, he or she has to ask probing questions to get satisfactory answers to ascertain why things happened the way they did. For example, the budget manager may need to ask the operations division why the postage expense missed plan by 25 percent in January or why service charges increased by 10 percent from last month and then has to communicate these findings in a monthly report to top management.

Financial managers have to understand the financial results and how they fit together. It is like a puzzle, and they have to know all the pieces. When they don't fit together, the financial manager has to find out why. For example, if the company had an advertising campaign that emphasized a certain product, a positive result for that particular product would be expected. If the results were not what was expected, he or she would have to find out why. A financial manager's entire job is based on numbers and being able to analyze numbers and results. In order to be successful in the financial arena, it helps to have a strong financial and/or accounting background.

Financial managers perform their jobs primarily using personal computers (PCs). The PC is sometimes a financial manager's best friend at work. You don't realize how important your computer is until it doesn't work and you realize you can't do a whole lot without it. We use our LAN, which links work stations throughout the organization. Therefore, it is possible for multiple users to share the same files and information. Computers have made financial professionals much more efficient and effective in their everyday work. Before the budget department became more automated with computers and systems, the staff would spend hours entering data into spread sheets and then hours checking the data. With this new technology, they can now produce a report in hours which used to take days. With new technology, they can spend more time understanding the financial results on reports as opposed to creating the reports.

How Much Time Do You Spend in Meetings? Writing? Other?

The amount of time financial managers spend in meetings varies from position to position and from company to company. During the budget season (September to February), financial managers may spend about 10 hours a week in meetings with other divisions assisting them with information related to the budget. During the off-season, they may spend about 2 or 3 hours a week in staff meetings with the analysts in the department and with the other managers within the division. Sometimes it appears that little gets accomplished at these meetings, and in some cases this is true, but meetings are the best way to share information that is pertinent between multiple departments. Meetings help ensure that everyone understands what is expected of each individual to achieve a certain common goal.

As a budget manager, you do not spend a great deal of time writing memos. Most of the writing involves write-up work which summarizes financial results for various divisions. The writing is mostly analytical in nature and very technical. In many cases, you have to write in a manner that nonfinancial people can understand. This is a skill that develops over time with experience.

What Skills Do You Use Most Often?

Financial analysis is the most important skill necessary to perform a financial manager's job well. Being able to understand the numbers—get "inside the numbers"—is critical to the success of a financial manager. Without these skills, a person should probably consider another field. Computer skills also play an important role in financial management and will probably become even more important. Younger professionals need to know and understand how to use computers to get the job done in an efficient manner.

Another skill that is important is being able to communicate with all levels of management throughout the company. You have to deal with front-line managers as well as senior-level managers. You must be able to adapt quickly to changing audiences.

Problem solving and time management are two other skills that are required to be successful in this field. There is not one right way to solve a problem, nor is there a set amount of time to complete projects. You must be able to juggle multiple projects simultaneously as well as solve everyday problems and still deliver the information in a timely manner.

What Training, Education, and/or Experience Are the Best Preparation for This Career?

A college degree in accounting or finance is the best educational background to get started in this field. Becoming a CPA or earning an M.B.A. is a big help because it gives you credibility in the field. Usually a person starts off in an entry-level position and performs a lot of manual tasks ("grunt work") until he or she develops a good understanding of what is required in the position. It usually takes 1 or 2 years before the person is ready for a higher level. It is not necessary to be a CPA or have an M.B.A., but it helps get your foot in the door.

Taking courses in specific industries (banking, retailing, etc.) also helps prepare a person to be successful. This helps in understanding how the financial performance is measured.

How Do Most People Get Their Jobs in This Career?

Most people get started in finance and accounting directly out of undergraduate school. There are many entry-level jobs in financial management since it is such a broad field. Almost every company has a finance or accounting department, and each has entry-level positions. The entry-level positions involve a lot of detailed work at the beginning, but this is the way to learn about the company and the industry. It is surprising how much you can learn by doing such detailed work.

What Do People in This Career Have in Common?

The main attribute that people have in common in the financial management field is a very analytical mind. Being able to break down a problem into parts to solve it is key to the success of a financial executive. Being able to adapt quickly to change is another trait that people have in common. The rules of financial reporting and accounting always seem to change, so it is important for people in this career to be able to adapt an ever-changing environment. Being able to understand numbers and financial statements is a must for people to be successful in this field. A person in this field needs to understand the underlying factors that make up the numbers in financial statements. This ability develops over time, but a person needs an aptitude to develop this ability.

How Much Are You Paid?

The amount a person is paid in this field varies among responsibilities, industries, and educational background. Each industry's compensation levels are different. An entry-level person can expect to be paid anywhere from $18,000 to $30,000 a year depending on these factors. As you move up the management ladder, your compensation should also increase. The number of people you manage and their experience levels also contribute to your compensation level. The range in salary of a budget manager is from $40,000 to $60,000 depending on the aforementioned items.

What Is the Salary or Compensation Potential?

As you move up the corporate management ladder, there are fewer but higher-paying positions. The higher you move within an organization, the higher your compensation. Currently, stock options are a popular form of compensation for senior management positions as are incentive bonuses. As you move up, these options and incentives become part of your compensation package. At entry- and middle-level management positions, your salary is usually the only source of compensation. The potential for a high salary is there, but there is a lot of competition for a few jobs.

What Are the Short- and Long-Term Career Opportunities?

There are many opportunities in the short term since there is such a broad level of positions in the financial field. Most medium and large companies have accounting and/or finance departments with entry-level staff positions. Most of these positions, which include staff accountants, financial analysts, etc., can be filled with people with 0 to 3 years' experience. There is usually a range of levels for similar jobs within a particular area such as accountant I, accountant II, accountant III, etc. As you move up, the number of opportunities narrow, with the ultimate achievement of becoming the chief financial officer and in some cases the chief executive officer. The broader a person's experience level, the more marketable his or her skill set is. The first 10 years in someone's career should involve much upward as well as lateral movement. In many cases, to move ahead in your career, you must move to another company. This appears to be a common element in many career fields. Before moving to another company, remember "the grass isn't always greener on the other side."

What Is the Range of Jobs in This Career?

There is a very broad range of jobs in this career, but they usually fall under the chief financial officer of the company. There are many aspects of financial management that a person can get involved with such as financial reporting, financial analysis, forecasting, general accounting, tax, audit, and investments just to name a few. All of these areas are interrelated in some form or another. Therefore, there is much opportunity in the short term to broaden your experience level and develop your skills. As you move ahead, however, the number of higher-level positions are much fewer. Some of the best industries for financial executives to enter are banking, investments, public accounting, and financial services.

What Provides the Greatest Satisfaction? Frustration?

The greatest satisfaction of being a budget manager is completing a "final" budget to be presented to the board of directors. It is the culmination of months of preparation and analysis. Once complete, people are forever wanting to move budgeted amounts from one place to another because of reorganizations.

Another satisfying element of a budget manager's job is finding more efficient ways of delivering financial information to the people who need the information. For example, our department installed a software application which helped us to become much more efficient in producing financial information in a much more timely manner. We ended up reducing a staff position while producing higher quality analysis. In addition, other areas within the company also began using our database application. This is a very rewarding aspect of my job.

The most frustrating element of my job is when senior management will not make any major decisions affecting the budget until the eleventh hour, and we are expected to turn around the entire company's budget in a very short period of time over the Thanksgiving holiday. In order to complete the budget, we need information from all areas of the company. When we don't receive this information, we cannot complete the preliminary pass of the budget. We always seem like the "bad guys" because we force people to make hard decisions. We are just the messengers trying to facilitate the budget process, but some people don't understand the process, and we get stuck in the middle.

Another equally frustrating aspect of my job is that I have to answer questions for people in the field who should be the ones answering the questions. For example, "Why is supplies expense $10,000 over plan this month in Savannah?" The manager in Savannah should know the answer before I do.

What Is the Biggest Misconception About the Job?

The biggest misconception about financial managers is that we only know about numbers and we don't understand what causes the numbers to be the way they are. We have to be perceptive and understanding the underlying reasons of how the business operates and how to assist top management with strategic business decisions.

Financial managers should not be resistant to changes. They should be ready to try new ways of performing tasks and achieving desired results. PCs and LANs are the way of the present and of the future. Financial managers need to be aware of the ways that PCs can improve efficiency and that there is always a way to improve a process.

What Is the One Thing You Would Have Wanted Someone to Tell You About This Career?

In any career, including that of a financial manager, always ask a lot of questions and challenge why things are done as they are. Sometimes, people get used to doing things a certain way and are unaware of other ways or unwilling to change. When you start in a new position, you bring a fresh way of looking at things, which could result in a better way of achieving the desired results.

Before starting in this career, I wish that I had found out more about career paths within this field. Many times, people are short-sighted and do not consider the long-term career choices that are available within the field of financial management. As you move up the corporate ladder, the career path becomes narrower and the options available are fewer. In choosing a career, one must think long term and not just "I want this job."

What Are Three Pieces of Advice or Wisdom You Would Give Someone Thinking About This Career?

1. Consider getting an M.B.A. or becoming a CPA if you plan on entering the field of financial management. The competition is tough and to get an edge, you need to have more qualifications than the other candidates. This applies not only to a current position but to future positions as well.

2. Always keep an open mind when dealing with issues and try to see the other person's point of view. Always try and come up with a better way of doing things without losing sight of the "big picture."

3. Keep current on the economy and what's going on in the world because it will have an effect on your company's business. All businesses go through cycles, and you need to keep current to understand what's going on and why.

7

Financial Consulting and Financial Services Sales

K. Page Boyer
Former Financial Consultant, Merrill Lynch

One Month in the Career of a Financial Consultant, or Financial Services Sales Representative

"Good morning, is Mr. Schwartz in, please."

"No. Who is this?"

"My name is Page Boyer. I am with Merrill Lynch in Chicago. Is this Mrs. Schwartz?"

"Yes."

"Good morning, ma'am. Could you tell me when is the best time to try and reach Mr. Schwartz?"

"If you want to talk to Mr. Schwartz, you will have to go over to Mt. Zion cemetery and dig 6 feet down." Click.

So begins another day of cold-calling, the activity which comprises the lion's share of a financial consultant's (FC's) time. The brokerage industry is as close as one can get to being an entrepreneur, while still having a 401(k) plan and major medical coverage. Every established FC at a full-service brokerage house—also known as financial services sales reps or brokers—had to begin in the business by single-handedly building a clientele. These are individuals who have repeatedly "survived" the 80+ percent annual attrition rate in the industry.

The first 3 months of employment are used as a training period for registration; one must pass a series of exams in order to receive one's securities license(s). The first and most difficult of these is the Series 7 (New York Stock Exchange, or NYSE) exam. The exam is given in two parts: a 3-hour session in the morning and a 3-hour session in the afternoon. The Series 7 is a comprehensive exam covering such topics as equities (common and preferred stock), municipal (tax-free) bonds, all other forms of fixed-income securities (corporate and government debt), options, limited partnerships, futures, and federal securities law. The second required exam is the Series 63, or "Blue Sky," exam. The Series 63 is given for the state in which one plans to practice. If an FC wanted to take on a new client who resides in a state other than the FC's, the FC would be required to file registration with the state in which the prospective client lives in order to be licensed with the proper authorities to trade in that state. The Series 63 exam covers—in much less detail—the same type of information as is found in the Series 7, the exception being that the Series 63 covers the state, rather than federal, law governing securities transactions for the state in which the FC intends to trade. The final exams required by most full-service brokerage houses are for the life, health, and accident insurance licenses. Since the distinction between banks, brokerage houses, and insurance companies has become quite blurred, the major full-service investment houses, as opposed to the discounters (i.e., Charles Schwab), expect their FCs to be "full service" in every sense: doing insurance and annuity business, stock and bond business, and, now, even retail mortgage business.

At a typical brokerage house, a new hire is expected for the first 3 months of employment to concurrently study for the Series 7 exam during office hours, as well as to fill in answering phones, typing, and filing for other brokers when their sales assistants are out. The best way to describe these tasks is grunt work. Most houses have a very strict policy concerning passing the Series 7: Those who do not pass the exam on the first try are terminated. The Series 7 exam preparation consists of 12 workbooks by topic (equities, municipal bonds, and so on) and internal computer-based comprehension tests, which simulate the Series 7. During the initial 3 months on the job, trainees also go through a teleconference sales training program; this occurs after one has passed the Series 7. Each new training class of FCs has about 40 members, scattered across the country. The program has live instructors hooked up by phone in a massive conference call with the 40 or so members in each class. The purpose of this portion of the training is to work on selling skills, developing scripts, handling and overcoming objections, probing, learning profiling skills, and so forth. Once one passes the Series 7, teleconference program, Series 63, insurance exams, and receives his or her FC production number, one is eligible to begin production.

> In one of our conference calls, a member of the class asked the instructor, "So how do we go about developing lists for cold-calling? I mean, we obviously need to be targeting people who have money." Other members of the class pointed out obvious sources: doctors, attorneys, small business owners, and the like. I could only imagine the ear-to-ear, self-satisfied grin on our instructor's face when he offered, "How about looking in the obituaries?" Absolute stunned silence. He continued, "Sure, you could check your local obits daily. They give a fair account of the occupation of the deceased, where he or she lived, the charities and educational institutions with which he or she was associated, and so on. I've even heard of a case where a broker called up the widow and said that he had spoken with her husband prior to his death and that they had reviewed his portfolio and were planning on making some adjustments. The broker then went on to offer his condolences and see if he might stop by to speak with the widow. Whether or not the broker did in fact ever speak with the husband was unclear." Pure chutzpah.

Most of the full-service investment houses provide an on-going 24-month professional development program for FCs once they are registered. The program is broken down into six 4-month intervals. An FC is expected to complete respective assignments for each of the six modules (i.e., mastery of a various product or product area, cold-calling the sales manager with a stock script, and so on). With the explosion and increasing sophistication of financial products, the brokerage industry recognizes the need for continuing professional education, just as is common practice in law and medicine.

The annual rate of return necessary to achieve the client's long-term goals is the foundation for all portfolio allocation decisions. The numbers that are relevant for equities are stock price, earnings per share, P/E ratios, and dividend rates. For fixed-income instruments, a client is most concerned about price (discount, par, or premium), coupon, yield, face value or maturity price, and any call features which would affect the yield or price. Clients expect FCs to use numbers to show them exactly what they have done for them lately. The accountability in this profession is absolute; everything is black and white. One either had stock that went up or went down. The numbers do not lie. And, since the popular press covers the market so closely, the majority of clients consider themselves to be experts. They know just enough to be dangerous.

FCs have all critical market and client information programmed into their Quotrons—an industry-specific computer system. This is a business where 5 minutes can make a significant difference in whether money is made or lost for the client. An FC is able to retrieve company research, up-to-the-minute news headlines and stories that affect the stock prices of their clients' holdings, competitors' historical performance statistics (i.e., mutual fund families), and similar pertinent information directly from the Quotron. Technology developed in the past year or so allows FCs to fill client orders electronically via their Quotron machines. One can send buy or sell order to the floor of the exchange by entering data on the Quotron for immediate action, rather than having to manually fill out an order ticket, send it to the wire room via pneumatic tube, and have it wired to the exchange, as was the traditional procedure.

An FC is measured monthly in three ways: new accounts opened, production (commissions) generated, and assets under management. Full-service brokerage firms rank their FCs by quintiles in each of these three areas, based upon an individual's length of service (LOS). Actuarially, the industry has enough statistical data to forecast—based upon quintiles (1s and 2s in all three areas are a must for longevity) and LOS—which individuals are going to be able to maintain the profession's stringent standards. An FC is expected to put all of his or her licensing, teleconference selling skills, and professional development training to use in building a client base. In addition, there are quarterly meetings held for all FCs with under 2 years of service to coach them on locating, servicing, and building long-term relationships with qualified prospects and clients.

The Chicago District quarterly meeting is usually held at a big hotel out by O'Hare. It is held on a Saturday morning and begins at 7:30 a.m. All of the approximately 100 LOS 2 and unders are required to be present. One has to remember that the big investment houses are one of the last remaining male bastions. In a district that has over 200 FCs, there are probably fewer than 10 female FCs. The number of female VPs within the firm is even more embarrassing. As a woman in this industry, I faced an uphill battle both internally and externally. Within the firm, women have a difficult time being "one of the guys" because they are outnumbered 20:1. The disadvantage of being cut out of the loop is that success in the business is very dependent upon quickly assimilating a vast, continuous flow of information, much of which is accomplished by cross-talk among FCs. Externally, the demographics of the most highly qualified prospect has traditionally been a white male in his 50s. Recalling that investors

*like to do business with people like themselves, I spent an inordinate
amount of my time trying to overcome the age and gender hurdles. While
the makeup of the brokerage industry is unarguably changing, change
comes very slowly.*

The working environment for an FC is dramatically different from
almost any other career which one might pursue. Brokerage houses
have traditionally preferred to hire individuals who are hungry to succeed. Metaphorically, this follows the "throw them against the wall
and see who sticks" school of thought. The career of an FC is as much
a function of *chutzpah* as anything else. After all, what fully sane individual would choose to call 200 to 300 strangers a day, knowing full
well one is going to be slam-dunked by 99 percent of them? It is not
uncommon for a sales manager to favor hiring a 35 or 40 year old with
two kids, a wife who stays at home, and has a second mortgage on the
house instead of a graduate of a top 10 M.D.A. program. The sales
manager figures that the first guy has to work his tail off to make ends
meet, given the meager starting salary—or base—that investment
houses pay. As a rule, M.B.A.s are a rarity in the retail brokerage
industry. Firms want hungry street fighters, not dilettantes. While
there are M.B.A.s who have made it, most are not willing to tolerate
the low initial starting base, lack of respect, and continuous rejection
that are part and parcel of building long-term success.

An FC does not have a "boss" per se but is accountable to a sales
manager. As long as one makes his or her new account, asset, and production goals, management is satisfied. Additionally, one may choose
any way one wishes to achieve these goals. The most frequently
employed methods are cold-calling, direct mail campaigns, seminars,
personal appointments, and networking. There are no "required"
office hours; FCs do not punch a time clock. Generally, since FCs are
building their own businesses, they put in the same long hours that
any small business owner does. Typically, the day runs from 7:00 a.m.
until 9:00 or 10:00 at night. It is quite common to work on Saturdays,
as well. Unlike the typical white-collar job, FCs rarely have internal
meetings, write memos, or meet with their "bosses." The sales manager recognizes that these activities do not affect the bottom line and,
therefore, are generally a waste of time—time away from cold-calling.

*I, like most other new FCs, decided to try every possible method of gener-
ating business. I did Nuveen tax-free direct mail campaigns using reverse
directories to wealthy neighborhoods, I cold-called every kind of contractor
you can imagine in Chicago (construction, heating, plumbing, stucco,
marble, lighting, etc.), and I made personal appointments with every type*

of qualified prospect who would see me, ranging from a multimillionaire farmer in Dwight, Illinois, to the head of the legal department for a national consumer-packaged goods firm based in Chicago. But my favorite prospecting war story revolves around a seminar I did at the Hyde Park Jewish Community Center. Bear in mind that the average age of my audience was 85. Nonetheless, the retired senior citizen market is ripe for prospecting, given their need for monthly income and today's historically low bank rates. I had prepared a presentation to be given with transparencies on an overhead. Mistake number 1. Half of the audience could not see well. I had also intended to stand up and speak without the use of a microphone, since there were only 15 or so people in the room. Mistake number 2. The other half was hard of hearing. Given that I had incorrectly targeted my audience, I ended up generating zero business from this group. Live and learn.

Most FCs develop a niche in which they are comfortable working, with clients who share a need for that FC's specialty: some do municipal bond business for very conservative, high-tax-bracket, income-seeking investors (i.e., reinvesting maturing proceeds in AAA-rated, MBIA-insured GOs for blue bloods), some are stock jocks for those seeking capital appreciation (i.e., "Hey, you have just *got* to take 500 shares of BJICA at 35½; Ben & Jerry's, Inc. is wreaking havoc on Pillsbury's Häagen-Dazs in the freezer case. Besides, have you tried their new Cookie Dough ice cream?), and some prefer working with those seeking preservation of capital with a better-than-money market rate of return (i.e., investing in utilities and governments for widows, orphans, and nonprofits).

The benefits of a career as an FC are numerous. The upside income potential is unlimited; one can earn as much as one is able. Also, one can choose the people with whom one works. It is common knowledge that over time one's client base begins to look very much like one's self. One can work exclusively with the people one finds enjoyable. One also has the option to "fire" or reassign those clients for whom the costs of working with them (time, aggravation) outweigh the benefits (enjoyment, strategic agreement, commissions).

When I got to the office on my first official day in production, I found an empty desk and a telephone waiting for me. My desk was located in what is affectionately termed "the bull pen." This is a less-than-glamorous "boardroom" with usually six to eight rows of desks, four to five deep. There is absolutely no privacy or status. We are talking stripped down, somewhat like government issue. With my Wall Street Journal read, the 6:45 a.m. morning call on the squawk box from our analysts in New York digested, and my first cup of Starbuck's caffè latte steaming on my desk, I was now about to begin what would become my daily ritual of "dialing for dollars," or what is more commonly known as cold-calling. It is 7:30 a.m.

An FC's job description does not change substantially over time; one is expected to open new accounts, gather assets, and generate production, whether it is one's first day or twenty-fifth year with the firm. Most FCs recognize from the start that success in this business is a "numbers game." Cold-calling tends to be the most efficient use of an FC's time for accomplishing the above-stated objectives. The breakdown looks something like this: If one makes 200 dials—or cold-calls—a day, one can expect to make roughly 35 "contacts." A contact is defined as a living and breathing person (i.e., someone who has a pulse) to whom the FC makes a sales presentation. Again, the presentation will depend upon the FC, who may choose a product-specific pitch (i.e., "Mr. Brown, with taxable money market rates currently under 3.0 percent, I am simply calling to see if you would have an interest in a AAA-rated, insured Chicago O'Hare bond paying 6.0 percent tax-free?") or may choose a generic approach (i.e., "Mrs. Smith, I help people build investment strategies to achieve their long-term goals. Have you ever had the opportunity to lay out a financial game plan for funding your retirement and/or your children's education?"). Out of 35 contacts, one can expect three qualified leads. To be a qualified lead, an FC needs to get answers to three questions: (1) Does this prospect have a need (minimizing taxes, growth, monthly income), (2) how much money does this prospect have to invest, and (3) when does this prospect expect to have money available to invest? The firm expects a first-year FC to open three new accounts per week (these could be IRAs, cash management accounts, custodial accounts for children, trust accounts, and so forth), to bring in roughly $100,000 in new assets per week, and to generate approximately $2000 dollars in commissions per week. Given that one starts from ground zero, these are quite aggressive goals.

If you have ever received a cold-call from a broker, you may have thought to yourself, "Why is this person so nosey? It is none of his or her damn business how much money I have or in what I am invested." While this is certainly the response most people have when they are called by a broker, it really is misguided. Think of it this way. When you go to your doctor, you do not say, "Hey, Doc, I am going to give you three guesses what is wrong with me. No, I do not intend to tell you my medical history or what my symptoms are. I expect you to be able to figure it out." Similarly, making a sound investment recommendation is 90 percent knowing the prospective investor's history (portfolio allocation) and 10 percent determining his or her symptoms (long-term objectives). While it is always amazing to me that people will move the kinds of monies I have seen via a phone call with a stranger, this is historically and pragmatically the way the business is done. It is not likely to change any time soon.

The most exciting sale I ever made was an order for $500,000 face value of municipal bonds from a prospect I had been working on for months. I was 22 years old and straight out of college. I often thought to myself, "Thank goodness this is a phone business; nobody in his or her right mind would invest their money with someone so young." As an aside, the FCs just out of college tend to prefer cold-calling to other forms of prospecting since they can hide behind the receiver. This prospect owned a national car-rental agency and was very specific in his parameters: "I am looking for a very short-term, top-quality municipal paper. I expect 6.0 percent tax-free on 2-year paper." Needless to say, this prospect was asking for a yield on 2-year paper that was being paid on 10-year paper. This is how I learned about commission structures. Generally, an FC is paid a commission of a point or two ($10 or $20, respectively) for each $1000 face value (one bond) that he or she sells. Given that this order was for 500 bonds, my commission would have been anywhere from $5000 to $10,000. Of this, the firms takes 65 percent and I would get 35 percent. However, I was not dealing with a beginner. This prospect was a millionaire many times over. He understood that he could increase his yield by forcing me to lower my cut. Given that he dealt with every major house and could wait for the yield he wanted, I decided that a percentage of something was better than a bigger percentage of nothing.

Commonly Asked Questions About a Career as a Financial Consultant, or Financial Services Sales Representative

What Tasks Do You Do Most Often?

Being an FC is a contact sport. Contact, contact, contact. Successful FCs spend 99 percent of their time talking to people, either through cold-calling, doing seminars, or making appointments. Since FCs are paid on a commission basis, they must be opening accounts and gathering assets. Otherwise, there is nothing on which to generate production credits (PCs) or commission dollars. During the first 2 to 3 years in the business, the typical FC will spend 8 to 10 hours a day prospecting for new clients. Once a large enough client base (usually close to 300 accounts) has been built up, the FC will spend half to three-quarters of his or her day servicing the client base. The million-dollar-plus producers in the firm, as measured in production credits, always continue to prospect. They are constantly trying to upgrade their clientele, replacing unproductive and departing clients with more affluent and sophisticated investors.

How Much Do You Work with People? Numbers? Computers?

Ideally, 100 percent of an FC's time should be spent with people. FCs who are not talking to people are not going to open accounts, gather assets, or generate production credits. Self-interest is the motivating force here; if one does not generate production credits, one does not eat. Period. Consequently, an FC should be on the phone talking with people about their financial needs, discretionary investment assets, constraints, risk tolerances, and long-term goals in order to be able to add the value through offering the best investment advice and most innovative financial products available on Wall Street.

FCs obviously need to be well versed in terms of numbers. They are competing for the client's business against every bank, insurance company, and discount brokerage house. It truly is a jungle out there. The prospective client has to come to believe that you, the FC, have something to offer him or her that is more appropriate or better suited to his or her needs than any of the competitors' recommendations. Therefore, an FC needs to determine—through profiling the prospect (i.e., what is the prospect's net worth, income, retirement plan value, insurance cash and face value?)—the starting dollars available, the future value of dollars needed to achieve long-term objectives (i.e., "I wish to be able to retire with a $50,000 retirement income at 55 years old" or "I wish to be able to send my children—one is 2 and the other is 5—to the best colleges to which they can gain admittance"), and, finally, given the starting dollars today, the future value of dollars needed at some specific point down the road, and the prospective client's temperament for risk, what type of annual return will have to be earned to get the prospect from point A (today) to point B (tomorrow).

Since all FCs have Quotron machines at their desks, which are linked directly to the NYSE, computers play a critical role. All stock quotes (bid and ask), regardless of the exchange on which they are traded, are accessible via the Quotron. The same holds true for all issuer, price, yield, and call feature data on municipal, corporate, and government bond issues. Gold, silver, and all other commodities quotes are on the Quotron.

How Much Time Do You Spend in Meetings? Writing? Other?

The only corporate-sponsored meetings an FC attends are those arranged to introduce a new financial product. Usually once a week, for example, a mutual fund distributor's rep (i.e., Nuveen, Franklin,

Kemper) will come to the firm's offices in a given district to introduce a new fund, provide sales literature, and answer questions. All meetings are very brief—normally less than half-an-hour—and to the point. Again, time spent sitting at a meeting is time away from talking to people. Contact, contact, contact.

The type of meetings FCs like to schedule are prospect and client appointments. Anyone in sales will attest to the fact that the closing rate is dramatically improved by face-to-face contact. Consequently, a key objective of cold-calling—after profiling and qualifying—is to set an appointment. On average, a successful FC tries to go out on three appointments per week. These are usually scheduled for evenings and weekends at the prospect's or client's home, not during market hours.

The only type of writing an FC does is productive writing which furthers the prospecting or business-building effort. We do not write internal memos. There is no paper chase. The investment industry does not give credit for, nor is it impressed with, a voluminous paper trail. Unlike many occupations, FCs do not get bonuses based upon the weight of the paper they have generated during the year. FCs write brief, personalized, handwritten notes to be included with any direct mail campaign they may execute. Short, handwritten notes are standard practice for inclusion in follow-up mailings to qualified leads located during daily cold-calling. The most comprehensive form of writing that FCs do is client proposals—and these consist primarily of numbers. Like appointments with prospects or clients, all writing is usually done before 7:30 a.m. or in the evenings or on weekends. It is not done during market hours.

Meetings and memos are not part of the daily routine of an FC. Time spent on both of these activities is time away from the phone talking to people. Both appointments and written communication are necessary supplemental evils. They are not of primary importance.

What Skills Do You Use Most Often?

Listening is the most crucial skill for success as an FC. In order to be able to turn a qualified lead into a prospect and, ultimately, into a client, an FC must understand the client's needs. An FC must ask the appropriate questions to be able to form a complete profile of the prospect. Prospects will simply not do business with FCs who have not earned their trust. The best way to gain trust is to make a concerted effort to understand the prospect's past investment experiences, needs, goals, and dreams.

There are two schools of thought on the art of selling. One maintains that a "hard sell" (selling concept) is necessary to move unsought products; persistence, aggressiveness, and persuasion are needed to overcome prospects' inertia or resistance to buying what is in their best interest because they are too naive or ignorant to know what is in their best interest. The selling concept has been the traditional approach utilized by pushy, obnoxious brokers. These brokers start from the premise that they are going to sell the "product of the month," regardless of whether it is appropriate for the prospect in question. The second approach is a "soft sell" (marketing concept). The marketing concept is predicated on the notion of determining the needs of a prospect and then filling those needs better than the competition. The marketing concept focuses on needs first, products second.

While persuasion and the ability to close a sale are critical to an FC's livelihood, most of the major investment houses are refocusing their sales forces away from the selling concept and toward the marketing concept. Although monthly "product pushes" still and probably always will exist, many of the more visionary FCs are concentrating on profiling, financial planning, and overall asset allocation to provide more value than competitors.

What Training, Education, and/or Experience Are the Best Preparation for this Career?

FCs are—for all intents and purposes—self-employed. The first day in production is similar to being made a partner in a law firm or medical practice or the owner of a small business on one's first day. The best training for this field is not learned in a traditional classroom environment—it is learned in the trenches. Doing is the best experience. FCs come from all types of previous careers (teachers, real estate agents or developers, advertising executives, new college graduates, car salespersons). There is no preferred training, per se. More important than educational background is the psychographic makeup of an individual. One must be self-motivated, self-disciplined, able to handle constant rejection, extremely focused, goal-oriented, and driven to succeed. Advanced degrees are virtually unheard of and college degrees are not absolutely necessary. In fact, both are often viewed as frivolous. In a field where everyone's daily, weekly, and monthly numbers (new accounts, assets gathered, and commissions generated) are posted for the entire office to see, proof of being able to consistently "hit the bottom line" is what is required for long-term success.

How Do Most People Get Their Jobs in This Career?

The brokerage industry is relatively small and quite cliquish. It has tra-ditionally been—and continues to be—a boys' club. Those who are not insiders (i.e., with friends or family in the business), have to do an excellent job of selling themselves to the sales manager. Most houses require an applicant to take a math test (to prove that one can work with eighths), as well as a psychographic test. The psychographic test is similar to the type of test the military used to require. Questions include: When did you learn to play chess? At what age did you have your first sexual experience? At what age did you smoke your first cig-arette, if ever? When are you most alert—morning, afternoon, evening, or all the time? Brokerage firms have hired enough FCs over time to have a fairly good idea of the type of individual who has a shot at suc-ceeding. If one does not pass both tests during the application period, the process terminates. Those who pass both exams are scheduled first for an interview with the sales manager. If the sales manager feels that the applicant would be a good hire, a second interview is set up with the resident manager (the sales manager's boss). If the sales manager and the resident manager do not agree on the hiring decision, no job offer is made. If both the sales manager and the resident manager con-cur on hiring the applicant, it is a done deal and a job offer is extended.

What Do People in This Career Have in Common?

The majority of FCs share a number of strikingly similar characteris-tics, both positive and negative. As a group, successful FCs are some of the most efficient, productive, industrious professionals in business. The majority of FCs have a very high degree of integrity and provide an extremely important service for their clients. The average U.S. citi-zen, if left to his or her own devices, would be terribly ill prepared for sending his or her children to college, being able to retire comfortably, or financially managing a major medical catastrophe. The incentive structure by which FCs are compensated encourages workaholism. Most FCs come from middle-class backgrounds, where a Puritan work ethic is second nature. The more one works, the more money one can make, the more prizes or trips one can win, and the more prestige one can garner vis-à-vis peers. It is common for individuals with 20 or more years in this industry to work 12 hour days, evenings, and week-ends, just like the rookies. In fact, one could argue that those who have tasted the lavish benefits of success have even more incentive to produce. The behavior becomes almost compulsive. FCs are extreme optimists and opportunists. They cannot sit back and wait for things to happen. They have to make things happen. Whether the market and/or interest rates are up, down, or flat, FCs must still meet their monthly hurdles.

On the downside, FCs tend to lack balance in their lives. FCs' professional, personal, and social lives all tend to revolve around their careers. Since most successful FCs do not come from families with money (which explains why these individuals are highly motivated to achieve and to be richly rewarded), they tend to be exceedingly frugal. Consequently, they do not spend money freely. Investment houses finance a disproportionate amount of FCs' vacations and consumer purchases through prizes and gift vouchers. Most FCs read financial journals and periodicals extensively; whether they ever pick up a *New York Times* best seller or a classic work of literature is questionable, due to a lack of time, a lack of interest, or a combination of the two. Finally, the investment industry is almost exclusively male and is extremely macho in attitude. Arrogant and crude are appropriate adjectives. Given the way in which FCs go about building their businesses, these negative personality traits may actually be assets.

How Much Are You Paid?

New FCs are paid just enough of a base to cover their costs of living. The idea is to give new FCs every incentive to produce enough to cover their draws, or bases, so that they can begin earning commissions. Those who take jobs with major brokerage houses do not do so for the starting base. Those right out of college may have a base of $18,000, while an M.B.A. from a top-10 business school with 5 years of work experience may draw down a base of $22,000 (compared to the median M.B.A. starting salary of roughly $50,000 to $60,000 in investment banking and consulting). FCs bank on their ability to last long enough to reap the long-term rewards of a generous commission structure.

What Is the Salary or Compensation Potential?

Long-term potential is what makes the career of an FC economically attractive. In order to earn more than the monthly base, FCs must generate enough commissions to cover that base. An FC with a monthly base of $1000 would have to generate approximately $3000 in commissions to cover that base, given that corporate takes 65 percent of all commissions; the FC earns the remaining 35 percent. For all commissions above and beyond the $3000, the FC pockets 35 percent gross (before taxes). Commissions are earned as follows. When a client buys a mutual fund, for example, the client usually pays a "load" or sales charge. Even "no-load" funds pay a 1 percent commission to the FC. By law, mutual fund loads cannot exceed 8.5 percent; the majority average about 4 percent. Therefore, if a client buys $10,000 of a mutual fund having a 4 percent load, the gross commission is $400. Of this $400, the firm will take $260, leaving the FC with $140 before taxes.

The compensation potential for an FC is literally unlimited. There are FCs who produce $500,000 a year in commissions (take-home gross of $175,000), FCs who produce $1,000,000 a year in commissions (take-home gross of $350,000), and a few FCs who produce over $2,000,000 a year in commissions (take-home gross of over $700,000). The exciting issue to recognize is that one's take-home pay is less affected by political considerations than would be the case in most other careers. Success is production based; it makes no difference if one is male or female, black or white, young or old, straight or gay, a high school dropout or a Ph.D.

What Are the Short- and Long-Term Career Opportunities?

An FC's career opportunities do not change significantly over time. Building a business is a process. Like attorneys and physicians, FCs begin to develop a practice the first day in production. Likewise, the rewards of building one's practice are greater the longer one has been in the business. It takes a great deal of time and effort to develop a clientele. After about the fifth year, the business takes on a momentum of its own and referrals begin to be given to FCs by satisfied clients and they are able to spend more time on servicing their clients and less time having to do cold-calling.

Since the compensation potential of FCs is unlimited (in 1991, the *average* FC took home upwards of $100,000 in gross pay), there is very little desire on the part of FCs to make a career switch. The industry does award titles to FCs, based upon length of service and production levels, but these titles provide credibility more than anything else. A few FCs may decide to pursue a management track (i.e., as a sales manager, then a resident manager, and so forth), but their motivation is something other than dollars. Generally, FCs' day-to-day activities look remarkably similar in the first year as in the twentieth year in production.

What Is the Range of Jobs in This Career?

In the retail brokerage industry, the job of an FC does not change over time. Again, like lawyers and doctors, an FC's client base grows and he or she becomes more proficient and successful at the same tasks he or she did in the first year of production. In the financial industry, in general, there are a variety of occupations one may choose to pursue. Most M.B.A.s interested in finance seek jobs as investment bankers (the people who underwrite stock and bond offerings), mergers and acquisitions specialists, and institutional—as opposed to retail—brokerage positions (i.e., managing money for pension funds and corporations, rather than for individuals).

What Provides the Greatest Satisfaction? Frustration?

The most satisfying aspect of being an FC is helping people develop a plan for achieving their long-term goals and dreams. Most successful FCs find that their best clients become very close friends; they share a great deal in common. They are on the same team. It is highly rewarding to sit down with, say, a young couple in their early thirties, who have a brand new baby, and show them how—with an appropriate savings plan—they will be able to afford to send their daughter to an Ivy League college and still have money left over if she were to choose to go on to a top-10 graduate school, without having to take on an exorbitant amount of risk. Given that the average 55 year old in the United States has only $2300 in savings for his or her retirement, and the fact that most corporations are dramatically cutting back on pension benefits, an FC can advise receptive clients to start early and save consistently so that they will be able to retire at a reasonable age, without having to cut back on their standard of living.

The most frustrating aspect of being an FC is the general public's fixation on commissions and the concomitant distrust that goes along with that fixation. Movies like *Wall Street* and novels like *Den of Thieves* paint a terribly distorted, albeit commonly accepted, portrait of individuals within the investment community. As the old adage goes, "Fool me once, shame on you. Fool me twice, shame on me." Clients are not stupid. Given that FCs are building their practices for the long-haul—and would someday like to be able to run a referral business rather than having to forever do gut-wrenching cold-calling—it is simply not in an FC's best interest to take advantage of his or her clients. Consumers do not think twice about paying a waitperson a 15 percent gratuity, regardless of the service provided. Why most inexperienced investors—savers, to be more exact—view 2 to 4 percent as an unreasonably high price for sound financial guidance is unclear. While most savers (chronic certificate of deposit buyers and savings account holders), as opposed to investors, read publications like *Forbes*, *Money*, and the *Wall Street Journal*, their subscriptions alone do not register them with the SEC, license them with the NYSE, or make them credible investment counselors. Sadly, not even faithful and diligent viewing of *Wall Street Week* on a regular basis will accomplish this. Most individuals recognize that they are not qualified or licensed to practice law or medicine on themselves. Why they believe that financial management is distinctly different evades most investment advisors.

What Is the Biggest
Misconception About the Job?

The biggest misconception about the job of an FC is that it pays an exorbitant amount of money for very little work. Nothing could be further from the truth. While the compensation for FCs is unlimited, there are very few individuals in the general population who could perform the function of a successful FC. A million-dollar producer is an extremely valuable corporate asset. A million-dollar producer services more accounts and manages more assets than many corporation presidents and may be responsible for as much as $300 to $400 million dollars. Consequently, high producers pay a significantly larger portion of the corporate overhead than do the sales assistants or wire room or compliance personnel. A million-dollar producer is to an investment house what Michael Jordan was to the Chicago Bulls. Without star performers, the corporation would cease to be viable.

What Is the One Thing
You Would Have Wanted
Someone to Tell You About
This Career?

The most debilitating issue, of which most new FCs are genuinely unaware, is the awesome personal stamina required to handle constant rejection, general ignorance, and bald-faced hostility. One really cannot appreciate rejection until one has attempted cold-calling. Selling intangibles—like stocks and bonds—via telemarketing is as challenging a task as one can imagine.

What Three Pieces of Advise or Wisdom Would You Give Someone Thinking About This Career?

The first piece of wisdom one needs to recognize is that rejection is not personal. A prospect may be insecure about his or her investment knowledge, it may be a bad time for a phone call, or the prospect may not have any money but may be embarrassed to admit it.

The second piece of wisdom one needs to recognize is that building a business is an endurance contest. While it may seem like one is doing a lot of work and nothing is happening, one has to keep "filling the pipeline" with new prospects. This is a numbers game and if one keeps shoving the pipeline full, eventually something has to pop out of the other end.

The third piece of wisdom one needs to recognize is that the job of an FC is not 9:00 a.m. to 5:00 p.m. For the first 3 to 5 years, one will eat, sleep, and breathe prospecting. There is no way around it.

8

General Management

Bob Collins
General Manager, Fortune 100 company

A Month in the Life of a General Manager

The critical success factor for being a general manager is having a clear head and strong stomach. That's because the general manager is ultimately responsible for everything that happens in the organization, both good and bad. If the company has a great year, the general manager is rewarded accordingly with a bonus or stock options. Conversely, if the company loses money, the general manager's job may be in jeopardy. While a good general manager empowers his or her team and, ideally, pushes decision-making down into the organization, he or she is usually the final decision-maker in all major strategic areas from advertising to human resources.

The routine of a general manager is a good-news, bad-news deal. The good news is that no 2 days are ever alike. And that's the bad news; if you are a person who likes order and predictability in your job, forget about being a general manager. Most general managers thrive on variety, unpredictability, and yes, even chaos.

A general manager is always on the move. Very little time is, or should be, spent behind a desk. Instead, a general manager's time is filled with discussions, meetings, presentations, and coaching. Getting out into the field, talking to salespeople, the trade, and customers; seeing how the product looks on the shelf; and watching how the consumer makes a purchase decision are all part of the job. Then distilling this information, communicating it to the key members of the team, such as marketing, the advertising agency, and the R&D scientists, complete the management cycle. A general manager must oversee all aspects of the business.

For a general manager, time is the most precious asset. Waste time and the job will manage you. Managers can spend all their lives on details or make major decisions. And guess what—a general manager is paid the big bucks to make those major decisions.

Week 1

Monday
   8:00–10:00.   *Meet with controller. Review next year's budget preliminaries. Address 3-year decline in gross margin through aggressive cost-of-goods savings program. Request that extra savings be put into advertising.*
   10:00–11:00.   *Meet with ad agency/marketing group. Review and revise new ad campaign to initiate stronger point of difference versus competition.*
   11:00–12:00.   *Return phone calls. Meet with my administrative assistant to discuss meetings for week and travel plans.*
   12:00–2:00.   *Working lunch with vice president of research and development to discuss priorities and resources placed against new products. Make sure my division is getting its fair share of R&D's resources versus other divisions in corporation.*
   2:00–2:30.   *Give informal talk to group of visiting international business people. Large Japanese contingent, so I open with the 30 seconds of Japanese pleasantries that I can remember.*
   2:30–3:30.   *Impromptu meeting with my director of new products to discuss new opportunity. He's more excited than I am about it—I worry new product will cannibalize our profitable flagship brand.*
   3:30–4:00.   *Go to Product Evaluation Center. See new product demonstrated to consumer.*
   4:00.   *Hop in cab to airport. Fly to Chicago to have late dinner with regional sales manager.*

Tuesday
   8:00–12:00.   *Along with regional manager, call on our no. 3 customer. Formal presentation of upcoming programs by regional manager. Informal input by myself. Customer wants more "price-off" promotions. I explain that, strategically, we want to build demand through breakthrough advertising, not pricing.*
   12:00–2:00.   *Meeting goes well. Buy customer nice lunch.*
   2:00–5:00.   *While in field, visit stores. Talk to store personnel, observe consumers. Hop on 5:30 flight back to New York.*

Wednesday
   9:30–11:00.   *Go directly to ad agency on Madison Avenue (they never start before 9:30). See revised work. I like it, it's more hard-hitting. Informally share my field observations with creatives at agency.*

11:00–12:00. *Go back to office. Interview candidate for managerial opening.*

12:00–1:30. *Work out in company gym. (Hey, I'm entitled.) Have spontaneous status meeting with my boss, our worldwide president, who's on the Stairmaster next to me.*

1:30–2:30. *Catch up on mail, calls.*

2:30–6:00. *MBWTF (aka management by walking the floor). Casual discussions and updates with all levels of people.*

Thursday

9:00–10:00. *Give United Way keynote speech to 300 employees.*

10:00–12:00. *Reviews and merit raises presented to me by my managers and human resources. Approve some, revise others. Promote a key contributor.*

12:00–2:00. *Take promoted person out to lunch. Discuss plans we have for her in future. Very upbeat.*

2:00–4:00. *Research data is in on new product. Mixed reviews so we include R&D in meeting to try to determine how we can improve product. Some of my staff are willing to launch product as is. I tell them it would be disastrous to launch a less-than-perfect version of this product.*

4:00–4:30. *Fill my boss in on mixed research results. Better he hears it from me than someone else. Let him know what we are doing to remedy situation.*

4:30–5:30. *Meet with legal department to discuss contract for strategic alliance with another company. Set up conference call with legal counsel and president of other company to haggle out issues.*

5:30. *Get late workout.*

Friday

7:30–9:00. *Breakfast meeting with ex-coworker, turned consultant, who's pitching business.*

9:00–10:00. *Impromptu meeting with manager who's disgruntled with review and raise. Push back my 9:30 appointment. Resolving human resource issues and opportunities is the most important part of a general manager's job.*

10:00–11:00. *Go to product display room (simulated store) to see new packaging recommendation from graphics group. Approve it without any changes, expressing my heartfelt thanks to the team for a job well done.*

11:00–12:00. *B.S. session with vice presidents of sales and finance on likelihood of achieving our budgeted sales number. You never want any surprises among finance, sales, and marketing.*

12:00. *Split early to see my kid in a school play. And to pack for weekend trip. Return six calls from car phone.*

Saturday afternoon. *Leave for Washington D.C. for distributor convention. Have dinner with no. 1 customer that night.*

Sunday. *Meet with 7 of our top 10 distributors. My staff presents new product plans for upcoming year. Again, my involvement is mostly to address strategic or philosophical concerns of top consumers.*

Specialized functions such as marketing, R&D, finance, operations, etc., all report to a general manager who, as the title implies, must be a generalist—close enough to add value but distant enough to oversee everything.

Week 2

Monday
   Take 9:00 a.m. shuttle. Go directly to office to meet with my boss's boss, the vice chairman, to give monthly status of business. Fill him in, informally, on successful D.C. meetings.
   12:00–2:00. *My boss kicks my butt on tennis court. Smart move by moi.*
   2:00–7:00. *Lock myself in my office. Review final draft of marketing plans before my people present to my boss later this week. Give comments to my direct reports. I rarely close my office door; as a general manager, you find that "quiet time" is a rarity.*
   Tuesday and Wednesday. *Attend off-site executive seminar on "Global Marketing Strategies." Most of today's general managers are increasingly focused on worldwide opportunities. Focusing on just the domestic business is not enough.*

Thursday
   9:00–2:00. *Present marketing plans to management. With a few exceptions, everything goes smoothly. Make sure I give well-deserved kudos to my staff in front of our top management.*
   2:00–6:00. *Take my people out for pizza and beer to celebrate.*

Friday
   Had my secretary keep Friday clear of meetings. Catch up on paperwork, catch a workout, and leave early to have dinner with my family.

General management is people management. Good general managers can't do everything by themselves. They must rely on their teams. If the team is focused and motivated, it can make the general manager look great. On the other hand, if the team requires constant supervision, this will force the general manager to spend more time on day-to-day activities and less time on large strategic profit-making opportunities.

There are many facets of people management including directing, motivating, evaluating, rewarding, counseling, mentoring, and disciplining employees. The smart general manager makes people, not product, the top strategic priority of the organization. If a strong focus is put behind recruiting, training, and rewarding, a top-quality end product will always follow.

Obviously, life in an organization made up of all sorts of people is not always this simple. Things can, and do, go wrong. The most effective general manager acts quickly—rewarding good work and correcting poor work. General managers must be confident and forthright in their dealings with people; only then can they expect the same in return. General managers who create an atmosphere of trust, respect, and self-esteem can usually deal effectively and openly with both strong and weak performers.

Week 3

Monday
   Off-site meeting with my staff, ad agency, and R&D to brainstorm new product ideas. My boss pops in for lunch to give pep talk. Ends up staying for afternoon. I welcome his input—like a good boss he doesn't try to take over but instead coaches, motivates, and empowers his team.

Tuesday
   9:00–11:00.   Go to Columbia University. Give talk about our company to M.B.A. students. Stick around for reception. Commitment to continuously recruiting top talent is a big part of a general manager's responsibility. On cab ride back with some of my managers, listen to idea they have for new consumer promotion. Tell them to give it a try but set dollar limit for them to experiment with. Grab quick lunch with them.
   2:00.   Disgruntled employee quits. I decide not to try to change his mind (which surprises him). Since he's going to a competitor, I ask him to leave by close of business and not to take any large packages or files. For the balance of day I do more MBWT to counteract any negativism disgruntled employee might have been spreading.

Wednesday
   9:00–11:00.   Complete physical, required by company for all vice presidents. Cholesterol, blood pressure, everything looks good.
   11:00–2:00.   Rather than rush back to office, do some store checks. Then call old B-school buddy for quick lunch. It's nice to have some time away from the office to clear my head.
   2:00–3:00.   Call staff meeting to split up resigned employee's work. Ask if anyone has any replacement suggestions. Get a couple of good leads. Discuss possibilities with human resources.
   3:00–4:00.   Meet with finance to determine why cost of goods is unfavorable in latest version of P&L. Again, a dollar saved in cost of goods is an extra dollar I can use to invest in my business.
   4:00–4:30.   Hang out with some of our newer hires. Pick their brain and vice versa. Good, aggressive, talented bunch of people who appreciate the general manager taking the time to listen to them.
   4:30–6:00.   Write draft for sales meeting speech I'll have to give in a couple of weeks to 200 people. As always, focus of speech is motivational and strategy, versus tactical and pedantic.
   6:00–8:00.   Take one of the leads to replace employee who quit out to dinner. She's terrific. Make offer on the spot. She needs 48 hours.

Thursday
   All-day meeting of top 50 managers in company to work on global marketing strategy. Too many people to be productive. We decide to form breakout groups. Get "volunteered" to be on subcommittee to lead next meeting. Great....

Friday
   8:00–9:30.   Look at slides for sales meeting speech. Make a bundle of changes. I'm a perfectionist when it comes to public speaking.
   9:30–10:30.   Write first formal memo in about a month to my management to revise our bonus incentive system. As a general manager, you must be an advocate for your people. The best incentives for top people are job opportunity and financial compensation.
   10:30–Noon.   Drop in on some focus groups being held in-house. Sit behind the two-way mirror, listen for about $\frac{1}{2}$ hour and then pull my director aside for impromptu discussion on creative strategy.
   Afternoon.   Honestly, it's a blur. Put out a couple of fires, make a couple of calls, read a couple of memos, do a little thinking, a little coaching, a little motivating. By being accessible and roaming throughout my organization, I actually felt I had a very productive afternoon.

The variety of tasks and issues a general manager handles can be staggering. Often a general manager arrives at work before 8:00 a.m. and finishes the day with a client dinner, arriving home after 11:00 p.m. Within this context, it becomes a major challenge to balance work and family. If general managers aren't careful, family can take second place, although as someone once said, no general managers ever said on their deathbeds that they wished they had spent more time at work.

However, balancing activities and managing time are major skills a general manager must have in order to be successful. General Managers who can't control their schedules wouldn't last long anyway. In the end, the rewards are worth it. Since the general manager is usually the highest paid employee in the organization, the money and, even more important, the satisfaction from running your own show far outweigh the negatives.

Week 4

Monday
   7:30–10:30.   Breakfast meeting with my boss and his boss and a few others to discuss the upcoming Strategic Planning process. We evolve into a follow-up discussion on last week's global meeting. Someone else gets tabbed to head the Strategic Planning process. Great. Don't get me wrong—task forces are a great experience and great visibility but can drain time away from running the actual business.

10:30–11:30. *The vice chairman asks me to stop by. Asks me if I would be interested in an international assignment—nothing specific yet but running a major country, perhaps. I'm flattered and interested.*

11:30–1:00. *Beat the crowds at the gym.*

1:00–2:30. *Late lunch with a younger manager who I am mentoring. He's a little discouraged—his boss has not been showcasing his talents. I tell him to hang in there, making a mental note to discreetly talk to my mentee's boss, who's a peer of mine.*

2:30–3:30. *Take call from person I offered job to other night. She accepted but wants $10,000 more. I give her $5000. She's happy. Good people don't come cheap. That's okay. I would rather overpay a top talent than underpay a mediocre one.*

3:00–3:15. *Impromptu staff meeting to let my people know of new hire. Always important they hear it from within, as opposed to from outside contacts.*

3:30. *My boss calls. He's tied up with his boss. Asks me to hustle to conference room to cover meeting for him with outside people who have new product idea. He gives me about 30 seconds of background and off I go, telling my secretary to push back my 3:30 appointment. Meeting turns out to be a waste of time, but you never know when that big idea might walk through the door.*

4:30. *Belated meeting with director of consumer promotion to discuss promotional strategy for next year. Spend more against consumer, less against the trade, we agree. Tie into our print advertising. Combine a strong product sell with more image.*

5:15–8:00. *Catch up on a mountain of mail, mostly useless. A couple of my people pop in for informal feedback on projects. We decide to tack a day onto upcoming sales meeting in Orlando for group brainstorming and bonding.*

Tuesday–Friday. *Four vacation days. Take family skiing. Most general managers get at least 4 weeks of vacation. Use them or lose them. Besides, I spend about 1 hour per day on phone with office. But believe it or not, they get along without me.*

Commonly Asked Questions About a Career as a General Manager

What Tasks Do You Do Most Often?

The first rule of general management is that no 2 days are ever alike. As a result, a general manager is less task related and much more people oriented. Very little time is spent writing, computing, or analyzing. Speaking, listening, coaching, and motivating are the primary tasks. My rule of thumb is to *not* spend a lot of time behind my desk.

Accessibility and approachability are critical traits for a successful general manager.

How Much Do You Work With People? Numbers? Computers?

A simple answer to a direct question—a lot, a little, not at all. People are everything to a general manager, who should listen to their recommendations on how to grow the business and certainly pay attention to the numbers involved in their analysis. But mostly, he or she should react to the conviction and credibility his or her people bring to the party. As for computers, while general managers should certainly be computer literate, computers can eat large chunks of time, taking them away from people and the action.

How Much Time Do You Spend in Meetings? Writing? Other?

Too much. Like computers, meetings can be a big drain of time. The best meetings are those that happen spontaneously—in a hallway, during a workout, over a quick lunch. Informal, productive, candid discussion seems to diminish in the formality of meetings. I aggressively control my calendar. It's impossible to be in meetings 10 hours a day and still have time to lead an organization.

As for writing, I haven't written a memo in years. A general manager is primarily an oral communicator, whether it's a formal speech to 200 sales people or an informal coaching session to a dozen marketing managers. Other tasks include listening, more specifically, active listening which means comprehension, distillation, and useful feedback.

What Skills Do You Use Most Often?

Easy. Leadership, motivation, and decision making. Life in a big corporation isn't always rosy. As a general manager, I need to set a positive, professional example and keep people "pumped up" and productive. Decision making is what I'm paid the big bucks for—listening to the various recommendations people bring forward and "pulling the trigger." If my decision misfires, it can literally cost the company hundreds of thousands of dollars. But if I make the right call (and I usually do) it's "hero-time" as market share goes up and the sales start pouring in. The other area of decision making is about people. Hiring, firing, promoting, evaluating—I'm responsible for molding my organization. The key is, as general manager, I am ultimately held responsible, not the lower-level manager, who forwarded the initial recommendation. The general manager who pulled the trigger has to deal with the consequences. As I mentioned before, a clear head and strong stomach are required.

What Training, Education, and/or Experience Are the Best Preparation for This Career?

Well, educationally, you can't beat the classical M.B.A. from a top school. However, what has been most useful to me is my experience climbing up the ladder in my organization. There is virtually no problem or situation that I haven't previously come across. People respect experience when you have paid your dues. And they sense confidence based on experience.

Of course, the best preparation for a career in general management is a solid upbringing that stresses confidence, self-esteem, common sense, and a respect for others. Unfortunately, for most people, upbringing is out of their control.

How Do Most People Get Their Jobs in This Career?

One of two ways. You work your way up through the organization or you "jump ship," leveraging your current position and accomplishments at your existing company to even a higher position at a new company. Remember, the pyramid gets very narrow at the top, which is why many competent people need to leave their companies in search of the big job.

What Do People in This Career Have in Common?

Not all general managers are the best motivators, leaders, or decision makers. But what they *all* have in common is a desire to be *in charge*. There are essentially two types of people in business—those who enjoy taking charge and those who don't. General managers are the former.

How Much Are You Paid?

Most general managers of *Fortune* 1000 companies start at a minimum of $100,000 base salary for running a small division to well over seven digits for running the whole shooting match. And of course, there are perks galore—stock options, company car, financial planning, travel to glamorous places, etc. While it's not always as rewarding as what we read about in *Barbarians at the Gate,* one can certainly make a terrific living as a general manager.

A general manager of a smaller organization may not have the same level of perks, but often they get some that are even better, a "piece of action" (i.e., an equity position).

What Is the Salary or Compensation Potential?

Limitless. That's one of the nice things about being a general manager. While the competition gets tougher and the work gets more intense, the rewards are greater. At most top companies, if you produce, you get rewarded—big time. And on these big base salaries, even small percentage raises can seem like exponential increases.

What Are the Short- and Long-Term Career Opportunities?

Excellent. Even though the "fast track" has slowed at many companies, terrific opportunities exist for general managers to improve their learning curves through lateral, cross-fertilizing types of moves. For instance, the general manager of a health and beauty division of a major corporation may be laterally transferred to run an OTC pharmaceutical division of the same corporation. Same level of management but a great broadening of experiences. And of course, as big companies go global, the domestic general manager of today is considered for the international general manager spot of tomorrow. My former boss was recently promoted to run our company's United Kingdom business and, in 3 years or so, may either be promoted to run Europe or may be promoted back to the States to run a major piece of the business here.

And of course, general managers of big, blue-chip companies are highly sought after by other big, blue-chip companies. Also, smaller companies often try to woo experienced highly trained general managers to run their businesses. In fact, a divisional general manager of a big company can often leverage his or her experience into a president/CEO job at a smaller company.

What Is the Range of Jobs in This Career?

Smart general managers usually manage their careers as aggressively as they manage their businesses. And, as they approach their businesses, most general managers approach their careers with a focused strategy...a game plan. Many general managers want to climb to the ultimate rung of the corporate ladder—chairman of the board of a major corporation. Other general managers want to leverage the wealth, networks, and experience they have accumulated into an entrepreneurial venture. Still others go into consulting, some teach, some retire early.

With proper planning, smart general managers can usually write their own ticket into any range of potential jobs and careers.

What Provides the Greatest Satisfaction? Frustration?

Easy. The greatest satisfaction is developing an organization, hiring the right people—training, coaching, and mentoring—and developing rising stars who can eventually take your place so you can move on to bigger and better things as well.

As a general manager, you can directly affect dozens, if not hundreds, of careers and lives. Rewarding? Of course. A scary responsibility? No doubt.

Biggest frustration? Probably all the corporate bureaucracy which can sometimes get in the way of running the business. However, deft general managers don't allow the bureaucracy to overwhelm them—they rise above it.

What Is the Biggest Misconception About the Job?

I think a lot of people have the misconception that the higher up one gets on the corporate ladder the easier and cushier one's job becomes. Wrong. I'm working much, much harder now than I did earlier in my career. I've internalized my responsibilities and feel a personal commitment to making my business succeed. There are longer hours and more stress. Of course, the work is more challenging and you can't beat the pay.

What Is the One Thing You Would Have Wanted Someone to Tell You About This Career?

Well, fortunately my father-in-law shared this with me early in my career and I'll pass it along since it has served me in good stead: "Be nice to the people you meet on the way up because you will meet the same people on the way down." Now, I'm not on my way down yet, but I have seen a number of my colleagues take advantage of people, only to have it bite them in the rear down the road. Machiavellian reasons aside, I firmly believe you should not set your sights on being a general manager unless you truly care and respect the people you work with.

What Three Pieces of Advice or Wisdom Would You Give Someone Thinking About This Career?

1. *Prepare yourself.*   Get an M.B.A. from a top school. Start with a blue-chip company that will train you. Learn your profession and work your way up. Concentrate on honing key skills such as leadership, communicating, coaching, and decision making.

2. *Enjoy yourself.*   The rise up should be as much fun as getting there. Stop and smell the roses. Not everyone makes it to a general manager position, so you might as well enjoy the ride.

3. *Trust yourself.*   A career is a long-term proposition (one hopes) so go with your gut, your instinct. Have the confidence to be yourself. You are a member of a team but never feel obliged to give in to total conformity. Remember, you are paid for *your* opinions, *your* individual talents, and *your* commitment.

9

Health Care Administration

Joane H. Goodroe
Director, The Heart Institute,
Saint Joseph's Hospital

One Month in the Career of a Health Care Administrator

It is Monday and I was supposed to be off this past weekend. Unlike many other professions, I am faced with the 24-hour, 7-days-a-week service that hospitals demand. When I left on Friday, everything seemed settled. By Sunday morning, the number of emergencies was 3 times what we could accommodate. An extra team had to be called into the operating room for open heart surgery, and then extra staff were needed for the cardiac intensive care unit. Everyone had to be paid at time and a half and then of course there was the shift differential. When everything was staffed, I stepped back and realized that in the long term I just exceeded budget because of this one weekend.

Nothing is more important than the day-to-day care that patients receive in a hospital. With the shortages of specialized health care professionals, administrators are faced with difficulties in providing care for patients, especially on evening, night, weekend, and holiday shifts. Unlike many other businesses, hospitals must be able to always provide the same level of service, especially during emergency situations. For example, in the above situation, I not only needed a nurse to work, I needed a nurse who was certified to take care of critically ill cardiac patients. Patient care cannot wait until someone has the opportunity to answer a request. It is not like a report that can be written later if there is another priority. All patient care demands immediate attention and must be delivered at a specific time or the patient will be compromised.

> *It is 4:00 p.m. on Wednesday. A 42-year-old man had a massive heart attack and irreversible heart damage. There is only one hope—a temporary heart device to "bridge" him until a heart becomes available for transplantation. The surgeon and an incredible team of people are ready to coordinate this event. I find myself in multiple roles. I check on the operating room, the intensive care, and the family of the patient. The operation is tough, but the patient makes it to intensive care. This is just the start of many difficult times that this patient and family will face in the hours and days ahead.*

No two patient care situations are the same. Some administrator roles require closer involvement with direct patient care than others do. The administrator assures that the system will operate effectively so that every opportunity will be given to each patient. A "hands-on" approach encourages collaboration among hospital personnel. There is nothing as powerful to enhance relationships with physicians than to be on the front line involved with patient care. Patient care is a physician's business and an administrator who stays in an office cannot be an integral part of the system.

> *I received a telephone call this morning from a very anxious man. His father lived out of state and was very sick. He had had a heart attack about a week ago and was in a very small hospital. This hospital did not have open heart surgery, and his son wanted him transferred to our institution. His father was 5 hours away and was too unstable to make the trip. I got the name of the physician treating him in his home town. I had one of our physicians call him, and he agreed that the patient would benefit from open heart surgery. I began calling medical plane and helicopter services to see what would work out the best. The son was very relieved that we were helping.*

Everyday the health care administrator is faced with situations that require difficult choices because they involve the life of a patient. Family, friends, and patients put their trust in hospitals. No duties of an administrator are more important than making sure that trust is earned every time. The administrator could have told the son of the critically ill patient to have his father's doctor contact one of the physicians on staff at the hospital. Instead, an administrator can make the decision to do extra work for the patient and family. At the same time, an administrator must continually weigh issues which affect the financial viability of the institution.

> *There are no empty beds in the hospital this morning, and we have 30 scheduled admissions. Of course, there will be the usual emergencies that*

will also have to be accommodated. Admissions would like to notify some of the physicians that we need to cancel patients. I know that if we do that, they will admit the patients to a competitor hospital. I also know that once the physicians make patient care rounds today, we may have enough beds. Sure it will be tight and we may need to hold some patients in the emergency room, but in the long term, it is better than losing the business.

It is always difficult in a hospital to balance between the patient care and business issues. In the past, most hospitals did not look at their work as a business. Therefore, if beds seemed tight on a particular day, they may have suggested that another hospital be used. Can you imagine a car dealership that is extremely busy one day sending their customers to the dealership down the street. In the past, health care institutions were not run as competitive businesses. It is only in the last 10 years that hospitals have begun to develop strategies for growth of strong services.

The administrator has to be aware of the daily census and how patients are being channeled through the system. A person with very good intentions may think that he or she is appropriately solving the bed "crunch," but that person may not understand the market sensitivities and competitive approach that should always be considered.

One of our principal physicians has just stopped me in the hall and requested that the hospital purchase an experimental laser. The cost of the laser is over half a million dollars. Since it is not a federally approved device, there would be no reimbursement for the procedure. The effectiveness of this type of treatment is not known. This physician is very cost effective and certainly is responsible for a large portion of the net income to the hospital. He also practices at a competing center. When I told him that I was not sure we would be able to purchase the laser, he told me that he could take most of his cases to the other hospital because they said that they would be happy to work with him to purchase this equipment.

Nothing describes this type of situation better than "being between a rock and a hard place." The physicians are important customers to the hospital. Many of them practice at competing hospitals, so you are always aware of the threat of losing them. With the advances in technology, an administrator is faced with very tough decisions. How do you use resources wisely without losing your competitive edge? It is like throwing a dart in the dark. No one can predict what technology will be effective, and there is always the element of using this new technology as a marketing tool to separate you from your competition. Many times telling the public about new technology will increase overall business to the hospital. There are no clear answers—just many questions and issues that have to be sorted out.

A vendor with whom we do over three million dollars worth of business in a year came to meet with me today. He sees us as a valued customer and wants to know what things we like and do not like about their product. This product is chosen by the physicians; therefore, I feel more like an intermediary. I want to negotiate a better deal, but I need to remember that the physician is an important part of this equation. If the physician perceives that I am jeopardizing his or her relationship with the vendor, it could cause me more problems.

Many of the products that are used by a hospital are specifically chosen by the physicians. Vendors usually have relationships with both the hospital and the physicians. Since the physicians are using the product and the hospital is the one buying the product, price is a secondary consideration. The only time that price becomes an issue to the physician is if the benefits from using the product are the same.

Administrators talking with a vendor need to understand which decisions are physician oriented and which decisions are left to the administrator. Some institutions have begun mandating these types of decisions to physicians. This is very risky in a competitive environment where a physician can choose to practice at another institution.

Negotiating with vendors and persuading physicians is an important role for an administrator. There are hundreds of vendors, so time must be allocated to spend it with the most appropriate ones. There also can be from 1 to over 100 physicians who need to be consulted with regarding decisions that need to be made. Each administrator chooses a different path to handle these issues based on the uniqueness of the service and which physicians generate the most revenue for the hospital.

The routine standing meetings on my calendar seem to occupy a significant portion of my time. There is the biweekly administrative staff meeting, the weekly department meetings, the monthly management staff meetings, and the monthly physician meetings to name a few. It is amazing how much is communicated through each of these meetings, the amount of dependence each of us has on other departments in order to be successful.

Hospitals have accreditation standards to meet from organizations such as the Joint Commission of Accreditation of Hospitals Organization. They evaluate a hospital's performance versus the standards. It takes coordination and tremendous documentation to assure that standards are met. Documentation in a health care setting is a part of everyone's function. Direct patient care givers must meet certain standards of documentation in the patients' charts. Quality assurance programs have to be developed that monitor all aspects of how care is given throughout the institution. Overseeing the development and continuation of these types of programs provide important roles for the health care administrator.

The day-to-day operations of a hospital are challenging, but positioning a hospital for long-term survival in today's market has become the most difficult. In the past, physicians were seen as customers. The more patients that a physician admitted to your hospital, the better the profitability for the hospital was. However, with the relentless escalation of health care cost, more and more payers have begun paying a fixed fee. Physicians play the largest role in controlling the amount of services given to any patient. With the stroke of a pen, thousands of dollars of tests and services can be ordered on any patient. Under a fixed reimbursement, the hospital is at substantial risk, and there are no incentives to encourage a physician to practice effectively. Therefore, there are no clear answers to the escalation of health care cost.

The administrator has to be able to energize the climate in order to control costs and facilitate change. Educating the hospital staff is also key to making changes. Teaching everyone the economics of health care becomes the responsibility of the administrator. Each day, administrators find that health care reform is an integral part of their jobs.

Each month, I carefully analyze and review the revenue and expense report for the previous month for each of the departments that I oversee. In my areas alone, I am managing an operating budget in excess of fifteen million dollars. There are over 100 employees who report to my area of responsibility; if each employee worked 1 hour of overtime a day, it would add an additional $850,000 of expense to the budget.

Health care administrators often have the amount of responsibility that equals that of the chief executive officer of a midsize company. Assuring that revenues and expense budgets are appropriately forecast requires due diligence. Constant analysis of the monthly expenses and revenues becomes important for the outcome of the institution in general. With the unpredictable labor and procedure issues that occur in a hospital, the administrator has to be able to evaluate the long-term impact of variances.

Two months ago, we began doing a new cardiac procedure with lasers. It is cutting-edge technology and not everything is known about the long-term outcome for the patient. Very few institutions in the country have the ability to do this procedure, so there is a good marketing opportunity. I have set up a meeting with the marketing staff, key physicians, and myself to brainstorm on how to use this to our advantage. Is advertising the way to go or should we encourage media interest to focus on scientific applications? We decided to go with the scientific applications since the media would be interested in doing news stories, and it would not cost us anything.

The multifocus role of the health care administrator includes marketing. Defining what audience to target is often difficult and confusing. Potential customers can be the public, physicians, payers, and employers. There are times when advertising campaigns to the general public are appropriate and other times when this would be a waste of money. The staff in the marketing department, using expertise from the administrator, can develop strong marketing plans that enhance the bottom line of the institution.

> *Since health care reform is an issue touching every American, I have become very proactive with state and national legislative representatives. I had breakfast today with one of the state legislators, who discussed pending legislation with me; there were some alarming issues. One bill would limit the role of the nurse significantly. After discussing the issue, it was obvious that his subcommittee was missing some important information. If nurses' roles were limited, all health care providers would face alarming increases in costs in order to make up for services nurses provide. As I left the meeting, I realized that I would need to become more involved with all reform.*

Five years ago the major issue facing an administrator was related to staffing the clinical areas. Today administrators must focus on how to compete in the changing health care environment. This means reviewing costs for open heart surgery with some competitor profiles. For example, our hospital needs to reduce cost by 8 percent this year just to maintain our market advantage.

The health care administrator of today has a multifocused role with both external and internal focus. Ensuring quality patient care, competitively priced care, and value-added services are all critical areas for the administrator.

Commonly Asked Questions About a Career as a Health Care Administrator

What Tasks Do You Do Most Often?

The role of the health care administrator is diverse. Time is spent evaluating and planning day-to-day operations. This includes meeting management staff in order to make appropriate plans. An effective administrator also spends time speaking with patients and their families. From these meetings, an evaluation of how the hospital is perceived can be made.

Physicians also demand an administrator's time. Administrators serve on different committees with physicians and meet with individual doctors to see how they feel about hospital services. Since physicians tend to be scheduled tightly throughout the day, these meetings usually occur at 7 in the morning or after 6 at night.

In the future, health care administrators will spend more time meeting with payers and negotiating contracts for future business. Hospitals will be competing for business; in the past physicians and patients made the choice of which hospitals to use.

How Much Do You Work with People? Numbers? Computers?

At one time, health care administrators worked mostly with people. This included staff, physicians, and patients. Although a significant amount of time is still spent working with people, there is an important integration of finance and planning into the equation. An administrator must be able to evaluate the "numbers" and then determine priorities.

Computers have increased productivity for all businesses, including health care. The administrator who wants to be on the leading edge must be proficient with computer skills. In order to increase efficiency, most large health care institutions now communicate through electronic mail and have moved many manual functions to computerized systems.

How Much Time Do You Spend in Meetings? Writing? Other?

Meetings are a part of the daily schedule. Assuring that daily operations of the hospital flow smoothly requires meetings to discuss policies, to look at opportunities, and to understand threats. Many meetings have routine times and meet either weekly, biweekly, or monthly. When new issues arise, a task force may be formed.

Communication with others both in the institution and outside requires time spent writing. Letters and memos are dictated on a daily basis to all customers of the hospital and also to the staff. Some of the most important communication occurs informally. An unscheduled hall conversation with a physician may enhance relationships, reveal a competitor's strategies, or alert the administrator to a possible problem.

What Skills Do You Use Most Often?

Obtaining and sharing information are the most important skills that an administrator uses, and these skills are used in the majority of work each day. The effective administrator has mastered communication skills and knows how to empower staff, negotiate with vendors, identify opportunities in the marketplace, and make the customers feel cared about and valued.

Strategic planning is also a skill that an administrator uses daily. The day-to-day decisions affect the viability of the institution in the future. Therefore, the administrator must be able to evaluate a situation very quickly and make some decisions without a written analysis.

What Training, Education, and/or Experience Are the Best Preparation for This Career?

Health care administrators come from varied backgrounds. In the past few years, a graduate degree has become the standard for the administrator and now is even seen at the management level of the organization.

Administrators may have clinical backgrounds with even clinical graduate degrees. They have usually proved their abilities through years of experience in different management positions. These administrators often have excellent communication skills because they have worked closely with physicians and with patients in other positions. Others may choose to augment their clinical education with a graduate degree in business or health care administration.

Many administrators have undergraduate degrees in business or related fields and complement those degrees with a graduate degree in health or business administration. The people with purely business backgrounds usually have worked in the health care setting at other levels before entering the administrative level.

There are very few administrative positions open to people who have only met the educational requirements. To be competitive in the marketplace, it is best to have experience in a health care setting.

How Do Most People Get Their Jobs in This Career?

As in many other careers, many health care administrators have landed in their positions without a grand plan. Since the technology associated with health care is constantly changing, many people are able to secure positions by demonstrating knowledge and ability in a new and emerging field. For example, many cardiac administrators worked somewhere in a cardiac clinical setting and established a reputation of being able to get things done. Usually these people also have excellent communication skills that they have used throughout the institution.

For people who are completing their education but have no formal experience in the health care setting, an administrative internship or residency enhances their credibility. This is also an excellent way to evaluate the many different types of positions that are available in health care administration. Management positions are usually open to people who have good references from an internship or residency program.

What Do People in This Career Have in Common?

People who choose a career in health care administration usually enjoy the dynamic, challenging environment. They like being around people and providing service to others. The most effective health care administrators are energized by challenges and accept them readily. They are constantly searching for opportunities to enhance the present experience. Administrators today welcome change and are often part of the process to create change.

How Much Are You Paid?

There is no set answer to this question. Since there are many different types of administrative positions in the health care industry, there is as much variation in the salary. For example, a rural hospital with 50 beds may pay their top administrator as much as a tertiary center pays an administrator who is overseeing only one aspect of the hospital.

One thing is for sure. Just like any other position, the market often dictates the salary. A position that requires a specialty expertise or that is strategic to the survival of the hospital demands the greatest salary. Administrators who have previous experience in health care and competitive educational backgrounds command salaries of at least $50,000 and greater. For the most part, the chief executive officer of a health care institution does not command a salary equivalent to that of a major corporation. However, in the past few years health care administration has seen an enhancement of salaries and benefits that has made these positions very attractive and competitive with other businesses.

What Is the Salary or Compensation Potential?

With the diversity of health care settings, there is very good potential for growth in salary and compensation. The position of a health care administrator can mean many different things. Working your way up the administrative ladder is compensated with an increase in pay and other benefits.

Most well-established settings have salaries plus bonus programs that reward those who are achievers. There are usually very good retirement programs and other types of incentives that are equal to others in the marketplace.

What Are the Short- and Long-Term Career Opportunities?

The dynamics of the health care market are changing both the short- and long-term opportunities. In today's market, administrators with skills to deal with the emerging health care issues are in high demand. Restructuring the health care system to deliver care in a high-quality, cost-effective manner is the greatest challenge. People who are able to demonstrate an ability to be a change agent, understand the market, and create new business opportunities will be able to find excellent positions.

As health care reform becomes a reality, the long-term prospective is hard to predict. One thing is certain. Some people who have held administrative positions in health care for many years will not be interested in or even able to accept the new challenges. This will create openings for new people. Currently, there is about a 30 percent turnover in administrative positions in this country. This number will probably increase. There are also opportunities to publish, lecture, and consult.

What Is the Range of Jobs in This Career?

There are as many different types of administrative positions in the health care field as there are institutions. Positions can be very focused or very broad. There are also the traditional and new product line approaches. In larger institutions, it is necessary to have a specialized focus. In these positions, one person may be the administrator of specialized services such as radiology and laboratory diagnostics. Finance is another area that requires a special focus. Another position could only deal with nursing areas. In smaller institutions, these positions are combined so that one administrator deals with many of these areas. This model is the traditional approach.

As health care has faced increasing competitiveness, a product line approach has developed. This has been modeled after the manufacturing approach where one person oversees the development and production of the product from beginning to end. Specialized services such as oncology, cardiac, and orthopedics are examples that have been channeled through this new approach. The administrator of these areas oversees these specialties including their clinical and financial aspects. The product line approach is in the development stages at most health care institutions. There is no doubt that this concept will open up new opportunities for the health care administrator.

What Provides the Greatest Satisfaction? Frustration?

The health care administrator is in a demanding field. The one thing that brings the greatest satisfaction is knowing that you are part of something that is helping others. As a service industry, health care is at the top of the line for the gratification that a person receives from working in the field.

The other satisfaction in the field of health care administration is job security. There are a large range of positions that are available in every area in the country. If you are willing to relocate, entry-level positions are available. Through continued relocation, a person can "climb" the corporate ladder rapidly. If you are not able to relocate, opportunities of advancement are still available, although they are not as frequent.

The greatest frustration for a health care administrator is the crisis in health care cost, which is affecting everyone in the United States; the administrator is facing issues that have developed over 100 years. A large amount of criticism results. *Wanting* to fix the problem is not enough. Major national policy changes are needed in order to begin the change process.

What Is the Biggest Misconception About the Job?

The biggest misconception about the job is that all health care administrators perform the same functions. In reality, the field is so diverse that there is specialization in finance, clinical, and service areas. Therefore, when someone makes a decision to enter health care administration, the options are enormous and the skill background can be diverse.

What Is the One Thing You Would Have Wanted Someone to Tell You About This Career?

One of the key elements that most people do not understand about health care is the interdependence on physicians, who are not a part of the hospital structure. This element is very difficult to even explain. Physicians control a majority of the cost in any institution, but there is no incentive for them to be cost efficient. Therefore, a health care administrator who is trying to ensure profitability and to conserve resources has little authority to actually control them.

No person can solve this issue. It is the basis for a large part of the health care crisis, but it is not ever clearly identified as an issue. It is the one element of health care that no one talks about, and yet it affects the ability of an administrator to do the job.

What Three Pieces of Advice or Wisdom Would You Give Someone Thinking About This Career?

1. *Be willing to accept the challenges as opportunities.*   In the years to come, health care administrators will be faced with more challenges than any other profession. Health care as we know it may cease to exist, and, therefore, tough decisions will need to be made. A person who wants to work with the predictable will not enjoy the health care environment of today.

2. *Be creative in your thinking.*   As new solutions are needed in health care, it is an excellent opportunity for people to use creativity. Planning health care in a different manner from the past will begin to solve some of the health care issues.

3. *Determine the type of administrative role you want.*   First, it is important to build a plan to achieve it. Once a determination is made of which clinical areas are preferable, clinical training can be obtained to complement other backgrounds. With such a wide range of positions, it is best to narrow the focus. The more knowledgeable one is about the options, the easier it is to make the right decisions.

10

Human Resources

Robert Speroff
Western Region Senior Personnel Manager,
Federal Express Corporation

One Month in the Career of a Human Resources Manager

A few years back, I recall doing some Christmas shopping for my human resource managers and staff. I found an interesting craft bazaar with loads of booths. It had top notch artists creating some unusual pieces. I had a feeling I'd find the elusive perfect gift that day. While walking through the endless maze of booths, I spotted a display of the most inventive caricatures of occupations. The artist was there working on a picture of a dentist. He had a completed supply, alphabetically arranged, to the side and several framed around the booth that were proudly displayed. I went to the bin and looked through to the Ps. Here I found painter, pianist, plumber, psychologist, but no personnel. I checked the Hs for human resources, thinking this artist must be an enlightened and informed individual; no human resource occupations there either.

I needed some assistance, so I asked the artist for some help in finding a caricature of a human resource professional. He looked up at the ceiling, shaking his head and said, "Sir, I don't even know what a human resource is." At that moment I no longer saw an artist. I saw a Christmas scrooge dashing my hopes of the perfect Christmas gifts for my staff. I was saddened that personnel or human resources (HR) wasn't as easily recognized as the doctor, lawyer, or the bug exterminator.

This got me thinking about how hard it is to pin down the exact nature of HR managers, because they assume so many roles—counselor, teacher, recruiter, and detective. At any given time, the circumstances might require the HR manager to wear a variety of hats and be able to change them without much notice when dealing with employees and members of

upper management. So many roles to play and hats to wear. Yes, that's it,
I'll get them hats for Christmas.

HR managers are responsible for the recruitment and selection of
employees. They not only screen applicants but also promote the
proper corporate image to prospective applicants who are hoping to
advance their careers. The challenge is to find the right person and
match that person with the open job. Searching for the right person
usually takes two paths, either outside or inside the company.

External recruiting can involve anywhere from one to thousands of
positions, depending on the need. It can be a long and arduous
process. Internal recruitment is not as involved as external mass hiring
for special operational purposes, but it can be just as complicated and
equally time consuming, particularly when recruiting and developing
management candidates. At Federal Express, we have established an
internal selection procedure from which management candidates are
identified. The process is called LEAP (Leadership Evaluation and
Awareness Process).

Here I am as a member of a panel interview committee, listening to a can-
didate defend his answers to a series of questions that he has already
responded to in writing. We ask the candidate to expand his response and
to provide us with greater detail. Our objective is to decide whether or not
the candidate has demonstrated "individual consideration," one of nine
skill dimensions that we feel are important to the success of a manager in
the company. The candidate is successful. At the conclusion of the inter-
view, he asks the panel if he can take our picture for his career scrapbook.
He claims that he has photographs of what he considered critical turning
points in his career. We go along with his request—good thing he was
eventually hired because he knew exactly who we were and what we
looked like.

HR managers also play detective roles because they spend much of
their time investigating employee relations' issues, verifying facts,
interviewing complainants, taking statements, and compiling information in an effort to determine the facts in a given situation.

I remember the employee who had a minor accident with his delivery van
and then attempted to repair the damages by himself on his lunch break to
avoid reporting the accident to the company. The situation was discovered
by his manager when he returned to the facility and was talking to a fel-
low employee. When the manager leaned against the side of the truck, he
soon discovered that the paint was still wet. In an effort to assist the
employee in presenting his position to the accident review committee, I
found myself borrowing my son's toy cars so the employee could demon-
strate the particulars involved in the accident. The Accident Review Board

*could then determine the preventability of the accident. From that time
on, I carried those toy cars with me to future accident review boards.*

There are also those times when you play the good guy and the bad
guy roles because one of the HR manager's chief functions is to balance the needs of the company with the needs of the employee.
Effectively facilitating a dispute between management and nonmanagement employees is at the core of the employee relations role of the
HR manager.

*I remember the time that I was in a grievance meeting reviewing a termi-
nation with the manager and the employee. The employee claimed that she
was unfairly terminated because she was not aware that she could not
ship personal items through the network without being charged. The manager felt certain that the rules were communicated clearly and that it was
reasonable to assume that the employee should have known the proper procedures. In this situation, it was decided that the communication of the
discount shipping policy was not adequately communicated and, therefore, the employee was returned to work with a less severe penalty.*

Although time-consuming, ensuring that employee issues are addressed
thoroughly and as expeditiously as possible is critical. The objective in
reviewing these cases is to do "the right thing" in terms of fairness to
the individual, while taking into account past practices, personnel policy interpretation, and any other circumstances that might mitigate the
situation.

HR managers need to keep up with what is current in the HR field if
they expect to remain on the leading edges in their industries. At Federal
Express, one such development course is called Exploring Leadership and
is modeled after the Outward Bound experience. In this setting, managers
are put through a series of "events" that they wouldn't ordinarily perform. The objectives are to be aware of your leadership skills and to realize the process that you use in order to address work problems. Although
there were a number of events, one sticks out in my mind.

*The event involved a 35-foot telephone pole, at the top of which was a
round platform no more than 12 inches in diameter that swiveled. The
object was to climb the pole, stand on the platform, and jump to a trapeze
suspended a mere 6 feet away. It was performed with the assistance of
guide ropes secured at the other end by my teammates, or belayers. While
climbing the pole, I thought how crazy I must be to put myself through
this. What in the world does this have to do with human resources? They
never said that I would be required to do this in my job interview. It was
afterward that it hit me. Regardless of how difficult the situation might
be, if you focus on the task at hand, you can accomplish just about anything you put your mind to.*

HR managers need to remain in touch with employees in order to better understand the nature of the business and how employees react to changes in the company. They do this by visiting employees at their work stations. At Federal Express we have multiple facilities in states across the country, which makes the logistics a challenge. We refer to these trips as "fly arounds." So it's time to go on a "fly around" to visit the troops. With all the "hats" packed in the suitcase, the HR manager heads for the field.

A typical field trip takes you away from home for 3 to 4 days, sometimes 2 weeks per month, depending upon other priorities. HR managers usually use time and resources best by conducting a number of tasks that can be completed simultaneously while on the trip. These trips make for some very long days.

> *I arrive at a station or ramp facility between 6:30 and 7:00 a.m. I meet informally with the employees as a group while they load their trucks with the day's deliveries. The couriers leave the building by 8:00 a.m. in order to meet the service commitment time of 10:30 a.m. I ride along with one of the couriers for a "dose of reality." I find that employees really enjoy their jobs and are quite proud of showing off their skills. This allows me the opportunity to "see how things are going" and to listen to concerns and answer questions.*
>
> *On one such trip, Ralph, the courier, had asked me for a favor. A customer on his route had told him that he collected model airplanes as a hobby. Ralph, wanting to get on the customer's good side in order to get additional business, promised that he could get the customer a FedEx airplane for his collection. The next time I visited Ralph's station, I brought the model airplane with me and we both hit the road. When we pulled up into the Latrobe Country Club in Latrobe, Pennsylvania, I knew the recipient—Arnold Palmer.*

After a full day of pick-ups and deliveries, we arrive back at the facility by 5:30 p.m. All the day's freight needs to be sorted and loaded into larger vehicles and transported to the airport to be loaded onto the airplane. This is another great opportunity to work with the people.

> *The freight needs to be loaded into "the cans," which are large containers shaped in such a manner that allows them to fit onto the airplane as tightly as a hand in a glove. Each container is marked for certain destinations. As the freight moves down the belt, handlers take the packages off the belt and pack them in containers in a systematic fashion. The handler has to "build" the container so that there is no "dead" space. After the sort, a well-built container resembles a Rubic's cube; each piece of freight is packed away in its own space. This is usually where I find myself, helping load the containers. The folks are very helpful and tolerant of my many questions. "Where does this one go again?"*

By the time it's 6:15 p.m., the *containerized transport vehicle* (CTV) departs for the airport with the end results of a great many people's hard work. This is the best time to meet with folks informally. At times, soft drinks and pizza are provided by the station manager as we talk about the business at hand.

> *Here I am in a courier uniform, having pizza and soda with the employees, when someone asks why they didn't get a market-level salary increase this year. I explain the procedures that compensation uses to determine whether or not a market increase is warranted and where the data is collected from to determine prevailing wages and cost-of-living considerations. Other questions come up, such as, "What is the competition doing?" and "How is our company performing financially?" and "Why was this new change made to the Retirement Savings Program?" Good thing the HR manager brought all those hats along. You never can tell what kind of questions will be asked.*

The meeting typically breaks up about 7:30 p.m. I depart for the next location and arrive at the hotel at 9:00 p.m., grab a quick bite to eat, and start this cycle again at 6:30 a.m. the next morning at another facility. Approximately 30 percent or more of the HR manager's time is spent on the road visiting with employees when multiple locations are involved.

There are also various administrative duties, in addition to the HR responsibilities, which are managerial in nature. Although not as exciting as the field visits, performance reviews, budget responsibilities, personnel requisitions, and capital equipment requests are all part of the job duties of an HR manager.

Reflecting on my Christmas shopping experience, I can now see why some people are confused with what HR managers do. Actually, HR managers perform a variety of functions. They remain focused on the human element while making business decisions and helping employees solve work issues.

Commonly Asked Questions About a Career as a Human Resources Manager

What Tasks Do You Do Most Often?

Unquestionably the one thing that HR managers do most often is to communicate with people, formally and informally. Regardless of the culture and size of the company, they accomplish this through a variety of media, such as video broadcasts (live and taped), electronic mail (e-mail), oral communications and presentations, and written communication. Many hours are spent daily on the phone and attending meetings with management and nonmanagement employees, discussing issues that each person considers important. There seems to be a never-ending number of topics that require your consultation. Typical subjects include policy interpretation and administration, staffing, complaint resolutions, career counseling, hiring, disciplinary action, compensation and benefits, organizational effectiveness, and training and development issues.

The amount of time spent consulting depends on how generally or specifically the duties of the HR position are defined by the company. It is not uncommon to find the responsibilities of HR positions to be very general and more encompassing in smaller organizations and more specialized in larger organizations where there are compensation specialists, benefits specialists, pension specialists, safety specialists, security specialists, etc., on staff.

How Much Work Do You Do with People? Numbers? Computers?

HR managers solve business problems that involve the human element. Problems that involve labor disputes, grievance proceedings, terminations, and employment selections are often dealt with on a regular basis. A great deal of time is spent interacting with people at various levels of the company. HR managers interact with front-line employees, and other times they meet with upper management to discuss changes in operating plans.

In addition to dealing with people, a general knowledge of accounting and statistics is required because businesses are driven by numbers. In order for an HR department to speak the language of business, the HR manager has to deal with numbers. Employees, customers, and stockholders want information about the company and how it is performing. Line management wants to know information about turnover, absenteeism, cost per hire, relocation costs, exempt and nonexempt headcount, wage rates, salary compression rates, etc. Much of this information is computer based. Knowledge of *management information systems* (MIS) is necessary to develop an analysis of trends in the HR area within the company.

Depending on the size of the company and the allocated HR budget, computerized employee records and a variety of management activity reports are also used by the HR manager. Activities such as wage increases, performance evaluations, and required training are tracked and monitored. Various regulatory agencies require documents to be kept on file. A human resources' MIS allows the records to be kept, tracked for completeness and accuracy, and retrieved when necessary.

Don't think for 1 minute that a career in human resources is for noncomputer, non-finance-oriented types. Although much time is spent interacting with people, you cannot lose sight of the fact that an effective HR professional is a business person who focuses on developing people programs that provide a return on the company's investment. It is not a career for those who cannot make it elsewhere in the "real business" world. Count on spending a good portion of your time working with numbers and using the computer as your means to get them.

How Much Time Is Spent in Meetings? Writing? Other?

An HR manager spends a good deal of time attending meetings on a variety of subjects that could involve anything from new hire orientation to employee grievance hearings to involuntary terminations. When these meetings are not scheduled, there are usually policy drafts to approve and comment on, individual counseling sessions, or formal presentations to prepare for— sometimes for upper management and sometimes for other companies.

There is a fair amount of routine paperwork that needs to be reviewed, and the status of assignments that have been delegated to staff members for completion need to be monitored. Don't forget the time spent on quality action teams or other "special" assignments that require the human resource manager's input.

An HR manager has budgetary responsibilities as well. Planning in this area is vital and necessary in order to accomplish departmental tasks, which are in part driven by the HR manager's ability to prioritize projects and prepare justifications to obtain funding in support of those projects.

Some HR managers are responsible for multiple facilities in various locations, which may require a fair amount of overnight travel. Business travel may seem glamorous to some but not to others. Don't expect to have time to see the sights when traveling on business. Consider this aspect carefully when looking for a job. After all, face-to-face communication with employees is far more effective than any other means.

What Skills Do You Use Most Often?

The ability to convince others to take action that they otherwise might not take is the power of persuasion. In most companies, HR managers don't have the authority to dictate; they must persuade line management to follow their advice. The skill of gathering information (i.e., facts, numbers, statistics, statements, policies, laws, etc.) and using it to present your position in a logical manner is most often needed.

At times, employees must be convinced that the company's actions or policies are appropriate. Employees may believe that their pay doesn't reflect the current prevailing wage rates in a market area. A group discussion might be necessary in order to explain the company's position on compensation. With the ever-increasing high costs associated with health care, it may become necessary to explain to employees why certain changes are made to a group health plan and what the changes mean to them personally.

Not only is the ability to persuade others important, but I consider the "approachability index" equally important. This is my personal unscientific measurement of how comfortable people are in interacting with you. This does not mean that you always need to give people warm fuzzies, but you should have a natural ability to make people feel reasonably comfortable with your presence. Your candid feedback and respect of the individual's privacy will promote a high comfort level in those you counsel.

What Training, Education, and/or Experience Are the Best Preparation for This Career?

A Bachelor's degree in Business Administration or some other general business degree is a good start. It's tough to return to school later in life to take economics, accounting, and marketing classes because they just weren't required in a liberal arts degree. Some colleges now offer HR options in their business departments. Students might be required to take courses in human resources management, employment law, policy administration, and compensation. This is a great way to get the best of both worlds—a degree in business with an emphasis in HR.

A Master's degree might not be necessary to initially begin your career, but if you want to advance to higher levels in the HR field, an advanced degree gives you a competitive advantage. If you have a Liberal Arts degree, an M.B.A. with an emphasis in human resources will round out your education. If your undergraduate degree is in business, a graduate degree in human resources will work too. There are 120 universities and colleges that offer undergraduate specialization in human resources and an additional eight that specialize in labor and industrial relations.

In terms of experience, you are just not going to be offered the chief personnel officer position of a *Fortune* 500 company fresh out of school. Just like any other career, you need to "pay your dues" and work your way up from the bottom. However, there are some strategies that you can use. You need to focus on broadening your base of practical experience. You can accomplish this by working in various HR positions in compensation, benefits, employee relations, and employment, for example. If you develop a particular interest in any of these areas, you can specialize and follow a different career path. If not, you can mold your career in a more general fashion by being a jack of all trades and master of some.

Finally, I would recommend that you also build a peer network with other HR professionals by joining national or local HR chapters. The Society of Human Resource Management (SHRM) is the largest national professional HR organization. Joining it will give you an opportunity to meet people who can advance your career. These professional organizations also offer training that you can benefit from. Their monthly publications give you a great update on current HR issues in the field.

How Do Most People Get Their Jobs in This Career?

Some get into HR careers by accident and others by design. But, either way, timing is everything. Sometimes simply being at the right place at the right time is the key. It is hard to break into the HR field in many respects because companies and firms are looking for people with experience. How does a person get a job in the HR field without having experience? It's not easy; people who are discouraged easily will fall by the wayside—quickly. Others who really want to have a career in HR will find one, if they are persistent.

One way of gaining experience in the HR field is through the military. Recruiters, job analysts, trainers, and other HR positions in the military can provide some very good, comprehensive experience which can be immediately applied to HR positions in the civilian world either in the private or public sectors.

Another way to gain experience is by working as a trainee or a personnel assistant for a consulting firm. Working for a consultant is a great way to increase the exposure to various industries and can provide experience in a number of HR disciplines such as compensation, benefits, employee relations, pension administration, etc. Many employment agencies, private and state funded, offer positions as job interviewers or placement trainees. This area is also a good place to start to sharpen your interviewing and selection skills.

Although these are but a few examples, there are many more possibilities. There are entry-level positions in the private and public sectors. Some companies have intern programs for college students, particularly those pursuing graduate degrees. Each situation can offer you a wealth of experience upon which to build your career. In summary, don't quit, work hard, increase your responsibility as you grow professionally, and be willing to forget that you are a recent college graduate; take the entry-level job no matter where you may find it.

What Do People in This Career Have in Common?

HR professionals like the challenge of helping people solve their problems in the workplace. They possess good listening and communication skills and are good organizers of information. They are not afraid to make hard decisions, like deciding the fate of a person's livelihood, yet at the same time, they make those gut-wrenching decisions not only with their intellects, but with their hearts.

HR professionals practice what they preach and set an example for others in dealing with human relations. They believe in the value of the individual and the synergism of people working together. Successful HR professionals feel at home with people and are as comfortable with one person as they are with 100 people. They have a high regard and respect for others and their ideas.

How Much Are You Paid and What Is the Salary or Compensation Potential?

Not enough! It never is, is it? Pay ranges vary from position to position and from company to company. Geographic differences as well as the prevailing market for recruitment and retention purposes also account for pay variations. In general, the salary for an HR director position in a small company ranges from $50,000 to $72,000 annually. However, in larger companies the salary range increases to between $80,000 and $132,000. The wages are even higher for HR directors with experience in labor relations. In these positions, the salary range is between $94,000 and $149,000. The size of the company is determined by factors such as the number of employees and the amount of revenue generated, the service or product produced, and the number of locations a company has.

In many situations, compensation packages are made up of a base salary and bonus or some sort of incentive compensation program.

Incentive programs are normally tied to profit objectives; others are tied to personal objectives such as a *Management by Objective* (MBO) program. Many incentive compensation programs are a function of both. Usually, the higher the level of the HR position, the greater the incentive compensation package. When evaluating job offers, look closely at the total compensation package. Don't forget that a strong benefits program may actually be worth more than the difference in base wages.

What Are the Short- and Long- Term Career Opportunities?

A career in HR looks more promising now than ever before for several reasons. First, the role of the HR professional has grown and matured since the 1950s. In the early postwar era, HR as a profession had come from the reputation of being a department staffed by those who could have never made it in the real business world. Today, true HR technicians are schooled in the art of dealing with people and know how to create a balance between the goals of the corporation and the needs of the individual. Companies are realizing that people are the key to their success and they look to the HR professional to assist in recruiting the best possible candidate and to develop programs that motivate the work force to perform at a level necessary to compete in a worldwide economy. Companies also look to the HR professional for ways to empower the work force with the knowledge and required confidence to manage themselves and to solve their daily work problems through Total Quality Management Systems. After all, who knows the job better than those who perform it?

Second, the work force is changing and becoming more diverse. As we approach the upcoming century, minorities and females will become more prominent. The work force will grow older and more disadvantaged. New jobs will require a higher level of skill than the jobs of today. Federal regulations and the enforcing regulatory agencies have placed additional requirements on companies through such acts as the Americans with Disabilities Act, the Family Leave Act, and the Civil Rights Act of 1991. It is expected that new federal regulations and changes to existing labor law will be proposed as the social and political conditions change. Demographic changes and new federal regulations will require companies to make adjustments in corporate personnel policies and procedures. The HR professional will be a primary player in orchestrating these changes.

Third, global competition will be greater than ever before as U.S. manufacturing decreases. As competition increases, companies will depend more on compensation and benefit programs that are closely connected with productivity. The HR professional will be responsible for creating compensation and reward systems that more closely match the profit goals of the corporation, such as incentive bonus plans, gain sharing plans, and creative profit sharing plans.

Finally, the education, health and welfare, and the needs of the family will be a primary focus. Training and development of new workers, retirement plans for the aging work force, health care provisions and cost controls for rising health care, child care for working parents, education for workers who are forced to change jobs due to modernization, and other similar challenges will give the HR professional many opportunities to contribute to an organization in the wake of these changes.

Career opportunities for the HR professional will not decline in the future for those who are trained and ready for the challenges that lie ahead.

What Is the Range of Jobs in This Career?

The range of jobs in the HR career field primarily falls into two categories: specialists and generalists. Specialist jobs focus on one area of HR, such as affirmative action, compensation, benefit administration, safety, employee relations, labor relations, training and development, organizational development, recruitment, or HR information systems. In each of these specialized areas, there are a variety of jobs. For example, in the area of compensation, there may be positions such as compensation analysts, who write job descriptions, evaluate the worth of the job as it compares to other jobs in the corporation, and determine the minimum requirements which are used for recruitment and placement. Other analysts may focus on determining the number of positions that are required in order to meet the projected work load based on the company's marketing forecasts. In the benefits administration area there might be positions that focus specifically on health, life and disability, or retirement plans.

Generally, a person moves within a specialized area while adding to his or her knowledge. In larger companies, there may be associate-level positions. These entry-level jobs are ideal for a person who has the education but no practical experience. As experience is gained, the person advances to senior-level positions in each specialized area and then into a management position or on to another specialized field within HR.

On the other hand, management positions in the HR field tend to be more general in nature because the focus is broader and encompasses a variety of responsibilities. Higher-level HR management positions, such as vice presidents, are even more general in nature and involve the development of broad-based strategies that are in concert with the company's business strategy. The HR generalist uses the expertise of the specialists in the development of HR strategies and tactics. The generalist uses this input to orchestrate changes.

What Provides the Greatest Satisfaction? Frustration?

The moment that provides the greatest level of satisfaction is the knowledge that your level of contribution made a difference, either to an individual or to the corporation. An effective HR strategy places the HR manager at the front end of corporate issues. Feedback is plentiful, which helps the HR manager make adjustments as conditions in the company change.

The inability at times to correctly determine the outcome of a situation because of unforeseen circumstances causes frustration. The necessity of working through the bureaucracy of a myriad of departments is frequently present in a large organization and is extremely time consuming. There is usually more than one way to solve HR problems. It's a matter of identifying risks and then making recommendations. Sometimes even though you believe your data indicate one course of action, another will be taken. A wise and thoughtful executive once told me that all people are entitled to their own opinions but not to their own set of facts. And so it goes. You learn to take it in stride and to come back the next time— better prepared. We all know what happened to dinosaurs when they were unable to adapt to the changing environment.

What Is the Biggest Misconception About the Job?

The biggest misconception about an HR manager's job is the stereotype that some non-HR professionals have of the position, that is, that an HR manager is an employee advocate regardless of the situation and that the HR function does not quantifiably add value to the corporation's operating profits. While I can understand the genesis of this stereotype, neither of these assumptions is correct. An effective HR manager is a business person first who brings a wealth of knowledge of the HR function to the company.

Most companies cannot operate without people performing some activity which produces some desired result. Operations management focuses on the business at hand. They are driven by corporate goals which are derived from production numbers and shareholders' expectations. Although line management does adequately balance the needs of the employee and the needs of the corporation, they are not HR technicians.

The HR manager specifically focuses on balancing the needs of the employee with the needs of the company. Sometimes this means not taking the side of the employee or management but rather the side of the company by interpreting policy and determining past practices as well as identifying risks. Other times, it may mean acting as a facilitator between management and nonmanagement employees in order to bring an equitable solution to an issue.

What Is the One Thing You Would Have Wanted Someone to Tell You About This Career?

I would have wanted someone to tell me how critical HR knowledge is to the overall foundation of the HR profession and how quickly the field changes. It is very easy to get caught up in the daily maintenance of routine activities and lose sight of the bigger picture. The HR manager must prioritize what needs to be done in the present and visualize the needs of the future. Future activities and strategies will be determined by current events as well as unpredictable factors, but without a vision, appropriate change will not occur. A strong educational foundation in HR and business will enhance the practical experience you will gain and will help you make sense of it. Awareness of political and social changes will tip you off to the future direction you need to pursue.

What Three Pieces of Advice or Wisdom Would You Give to Someone Thinking About This Career?

1. Human resources is as much an art as it is a science. Rarely will you deal in black and white issues but more often than not in shades of gray. Be tolerant of ambiguity.

2. Be sensitive to social pressures and knowledgeable of political changes that result from a dynamic and diverse culture. As political and social changes occur, so does the manner in which companies

are required to operate. Court decisions constantly challenge the "way it has always been done" and act as a catalyst for change. HR managers need to be on the cutting edge of these changes in order to better balance the needs of the employee and the company.

3. Don't suffer from paralysis by analysis. In other words, don't analyze things to death and be slow in taking action. Like all other positions, the HR manager is judged on the result of the services and not on how much effort is expended.

11

Investment Banking

Davy Davidson
Former Managing Director, Paine Webber

One Month in the Career of an Investment Banker

November 1

The champagne had been on ice for several hours, and the private dining room of the finest club in town looked stunning. Pretty soon, all of the invited guests would be arriving: officers and directors of America's newest public company, lawyers, investment bankers, accountants, and various other people. The initial public offering had been a "blowout" and the stock had traded well after the offering was completed. Consequently, the mood at the closing dinner was festive and jovial toasts and roasts would probably go on for hours. Everyone would leave with a bagful of gifts and mementos. Many would leave a lot richer. A few entrepreneurs had become multimillionaires almost overnight, and some investment bankers and lawyers took a big step toward paying for their children's education. This explains, of course, why a few hearty souls would assuredly carry the party on into the wee hours of the morning—and there would be a lot of laughs throughout. No question about it, on occasions like this, investment banking is a fun and glamorous job. Unfortunately, it is the other day-to-day aspects of the work that make this a tough way to earn a living.

The most misleading aspect of investment banking is that most deals and transactions like this one get tidied up with a nice party and a "tombstone" (the advertisement/announcement of a public securities offering which appears in the major financial publications immediately after the deal is completed). This belies the fact that most deals go through endless twists and turns, frustrations, and general chaos.

Most deals die a time or two. It is the investment banker who breathes life into them at critical points along the way.

An investment banker's job is basically to help companies raise money and to give them financial advice. It is a valuable service to many companies because there are different sources of money to consider, different types of securities which a company can issue, and complex financial issues that most companies must address.

The process through which a company raises money in the public securities market typically has four stages. The first stage is one in which a company recognizes its need to raise money and retains the services of an investment banker. This stage is often a very emotional and drawn-out process, and there is usually an intense level of competition among investment banking firms all seeking to be hired by the company. The second stage is primarily one of "due diligence" during which the investment banker spearheads a thorough investigation and analysis of the company so that all meaningful considerations—both good and bad—can be properly disclosed to prospective investors. The third stage is an exhausting marketing process during which the investment banker and the company "sell" the company's story to prospective investors. This stage is made all the more difficult because at any one point in time there will be a number of other companies aggressively competing to attract the same money from these investors. The fourth, and final, part of any securities offering can best be described as simply "getting the deal closed." In this final stage of a public securities offering, there are many disruptive factors that can work to prevent it from being completed, and overcoming these potential problems, or "deal-breakers," is when investment bankers really earn their fees.

Let's go back to the first stage of a deal—where an investment banker is called upon by a company seeking to go public because it has outgrown its ability to finance itself internally. I was the investment banker involved in the initial public offering of Global Brands Inc., and it is a deal which clearly stands out in my mind today.

September 15
It had been nearly 8 months since I first met the management of Global Brands, a rapidly-growing consumer products company which sold a broad range of diet and health foods. The company had recently launched a new line of diet foods that was doing extremely well in the marketplace. Both sales and profits were growing steadily. However, to keep pace with this growth, the company needed to raise money and both the management and shareholders of the company had made the important decision to "go public." Consequently, they had engaged my investment banking firm to manage the offering. In the intervening months, the team which I

headed within my organization had been carefully scrutinizing the company, its management team, financial statements, business practices, customers, vendors, competitors, and everything else which seemed relevant to our underwriting process. Naturally, we taste-tested the company's diet products and competing brands in the marketplace—and probably packed on a few pounds along the way, even though they were "diet" foods. The purpose of all of this detective work was not simply to become more knowledgeable about the company but to ultimately protect new investors and determine a true and "fair" offering value for the company's common stock. Because fair value in a public securities offering is often, at best, a subjective definition, one must be careful in interpreting what it really means.

The second stage in a securities offering—due diligence—includes a presentation by the investment banker to what is known within his or her organization as the Commitment Committee. The purpose of the Commitment Committee within any investment banking firm is to formally approve or disapprove that firm's involvement in an offering. Senior representatives of all major areas of an investment banking firm are represented in the Commitment Committee process: investment banking, sales, trading, and research. This committee is one of the most important hurdles to clear in the due diligence process. Indeed, no reputable investment banking firm will commit to underwrite a public securities offering without first completing this process. It is often a harrowing experience for the bankers involved in a transaction because any time you expose your firm and colleagues to millions of dollars of potential liability, the risks take on a very personal nature.

It may seem curious that 1 hour with this committee can put an end to a transaction that has been in the works for many months. However, such are the underwriting standards and rigors of a major, reputable investment banking firm. This type of scrutiny is one of the most important protections offered to a brokerage firm and its clients who buy the securities that they are selling.

September 20
Going into this particular Commitment Committee meeting, my team was well armed with the necessary facts, figures, and data accumulated over 7 months of thorough due diligence. We had carefully reviewed the history of our diet foods company and had developed a solid feel for where we thought the company was headed over the next few years. All we had to do now was sell the senior management of our organization on the company and its prospects. In short, we had to make them believe—as we did—that it would be a good investment for our firm's brokerage clients.

Once we had presented a brief overview of the company and its investment merits, the questions started flying. Tough questions. Irrelevant questions. Stupid questions (someone even asked if the company had a lean management team. Naturally, we resisted the urge to say that all senior managers of this diet foods company were skinny). Over the course of an hour or two, we subjected ourselves to a merciless grilling from the Commitment Committee but were able to think quickly on our feet and answer most of their questions. The committee members unanimously approved our participation in the Global Brands deal.

Once an investment banking firm "commits" to proceed with the offering, the next major step is the Organizational Meeting. This session, though a necessary one, is often little more than pomp and ceremony. It is a necessary forum in which all parties involved in a deal must meet as a large group in order to agree on a basic timetable for the offering and decide who will take responsibility for what particular assignment.

One thing always becomes apparent at this stage of an offering: Most of the documentation work will fall on the shoulders of the company's lawyers and accountants. The investment bankers, in many respects, will be responsible for keeping the whole process moving *forward.* I'm not sure which is a more accurate analogy for the banker's role in the process—a conductor leading a symphony orchestra or a cheerleader on the sidelines of a football game. Perhaps investment banking is a combination of both.

September 24
Today was the day of the Organizational Meeting for the Global Brands deal. All parties were represented, and this Organizational Meeting was like most others. Everyone voiced opinions as to how and when things should get done. A few opined as to which direction the stock market would go in the coming weeks and months—and some of these opinions were sheer BS. Nevertheless, at this session everyone's particular role in the process began to take shape, and we knew that from this day forward, the real hard work would begin in a final, frenzied push to get the deal completed. Many of us were meeting for the first time, and our roles would vary greatly over the following weeks. Some of us would assuredly hate each other by the time the process was over. All of us would inevitably carve out our own unique—if not peculiar—role in the transaction.

After the Organizational Meeting is over and the entire working group is squarely on board for the deal, the truly tedious work of drafting a registration statement begins. Much of this work and the related documentation is done to comply with disclosure requirements of the Securities and Exchange Commission (SEC) and other regulatory authorities. Most of it is technical or boring in nature, and for this reason, it is usually foisted on the shoulders of the lawyers. The investment banker's challenge, in large measure, is to translate many of these long and sterile disclosure documents into an effective sales pitch for the company and for the deal. This requires both marketing savvy and a working knowledge of—and respect for—the securities laws.

September 28
Today's drafting session was the first opportunity for all participants in the Global Brands deal to pore over a draft of the registration statement. The company's attorneys had put together a good first draft of a working document, but there would assuredly be plenty of changes. Perhaps it was particularly appropriate for the Global Brands offering that our first draft of the registration statement had a lot of fat that needed to be cut out of the document. During the course of an all-day, all-evening session around a large table in a windowless conference room, there were plenty of arguments and debates over seemingly meaningless words and phrases in the document. The most aggressive members of the working group wanted to use expressions like "excellent opportunities for growth"; the more conservative members insisted on "growth potential." For those in the group with thin skins and pride-of-authorship feelings, these were always tough exchanges.

Having spent 13 years in the investment business, I knew that drafting sessions like this were a painful but necessary part of the process to be endured. In addition, when the drafting work in a session like this became too tedious, the seasoned investment banker could always escape to make "an important phone call" or huddle separately with the client to plan a tentative "road show" schedule, during which time the company makes a presentation to major institutional investors in selected cities in both the United States and Europe. Planning a road show is much more fun than drafting a prospectus. A road show presentation—unlike the dry and legalistic prospectus—is filled with elaborate slides and graphics which are intended to aggressively market the offering. Road show presentations are technically not in compliance with the strict requirements of the SEC, but they are a common practice on Wall Street for new issues of securities. If done in a responsible manner, regulators and attorneys typically look the other way. In this particular deal, our schedule called for 18 U.S. and 6 European cities in 15 days—which meant that literally every meal which the traveling party would eat during this time would be on the run. We hoped the road show would generate enough interest in the stock along the way to justify all of the time and money which would be poured into it.

The due diligence phase of a securities offering is extremely important work since it generally identifies particularly delicate or problem issues that a company faces so that these risk factors can be adequately disclosed to prospective investors during the marketing process. Unfortunately, due diligence sessions are *always* long, tedious, and boring—occasionally they are confrontational—and it is the job of the investment banker to keep the sessions properly focused and moving forward. The investment banker knows all too well that, down the road, his or her greatest level of protection from disgruntled shareholders will reside in the thoroughness of this due diligence investigation.

October 2
Today's and tomorrow's schedules called for the roll-up-your-sleeves type
of due diligence. The entire working group would sit down with the
Global Brands management and fire an endless barrage of questions. It
was to be the major due diligence session for the offering, and everyone
involved—bankers, lawyers, accountants, etc.—would have the chance to
have questions answered. Financial projections would be scrutinized in
great detail, thorough plant tours would be conducted, and every type of
question would be fair game. No stones would be left unturned.

As the due diligence work in a deal nears completion, the focus
turns to getting the i's dotted and the t's crossed in all of the documentation. There is an old saying to the effect that work will always
expand to fill the time available. This is certainly the case with preparing and filing a registration statement with the SEC. Generally at the
last possible moment, the filing package destined for the SEC is bound
together, accompanying exhibits are assembled, requisite checks to
various government agencies are written, and the printer's courier is
thrown into a car for the mad dash to the airport. It's *always* this way,
and the Global Brands offering was no different. As always, though,
the courier successfully delivered the materials to Washington where
they were handed over to the SEC. At this point in a securities offering, an important transformation takes place: The pace of the offering's progress is no longer determined by the company and its advisors but rather by the U.S. government. The SEC will assign an
examiner to the registration statement who will review it in due
course—which may mean anywhere from 2 to 6 weeks before any kind
of response is received. Patience becomes a virtue at this point in the
process because badgering the SEC examiner for an expedited
response can do far more harm than good. Meanwhile, market conditions will assuredly change from day to day, which will have a major
impact on the pricing—and possibly even the success or failure—of a
securities offering.

October 8
The next 48 hours were a round-the-clock vigil at the financial printers
for the entire group working on the Global Brands offering. Seemingly
endless hours were spent editing and refining text in the prospectus.
Details were filled in, figures were proofed, and meaningless phrases were
fought over ruthlessly. Only a veteran of these drafting sessions could
believe that grown men and women would fight over words such as these
versus those, *will* versus *shall be, and* the leading *versus* leader.
Ultimately, these battles become a test of stamina since around four
o'clock in the morning one of the contestants would generally throw in the
towel out of sheer fatigue.

The third—and most gratifying—stage in a securities offering is the marketing process, but it can only begin in earnest once the due diligence phase has been completed and the registration statement has been filed with the SEC. Otherwise, unanticipated or unanswerable issues may arise during the marketing process which can quickly kill a deal and make everyone involved look stupid—or worse. However, if the underwriting team has properly done its job and the company is able to stand up to the scrutiny of thorough due diligence, marketing the deal is the most enjoyable stage of the whole transaction.

One of the paradoxes of public securities offerings is the fact that despite all of the endless hours which go into the preparation of a lengthy, detailed prospectus and registration statement, the deal is ultimately sold from a one-page internal memorandum, a 20-minute slide show presentation from company management, and some pithy commentary by the underwriter's research analyst who follows the company. These things are what truly *sell* the deal; in fact, an old axiom on Wall Street says that "securities are sold, not bought." Nevertheless, it is important to keep in mind that the prospectus is a carefully constructed legal document that, based on its content, will either hang or defend the company and its underwriters in the event that the stock performs poorly after the offering. Thus, real conflict often arises in securities offerings between the desire to achieve both full and fair disclosure *and* the right dose of "sizzle" in a company's story.

October 12
Things were really starting to come together in the Global Brands offering. My team had prepared a set of marketing documents relating to the offering which would be distributed to our sales force immediately after the registration statement was filed with the SEC. My firm's brokers would use these internal marketing documents—which were vastly simplified summaries of the underlying registration documents—to market the deal to their customers. Because brokers are generally following dozens of stocks and securities offerings at any one time, these marketing documents needed to be concise, to the point, and above all, easy to understand.

Too much cannot be made of the importance of a well-done road show. A poorly done, poorly timed, poorly attended, or poorly received road show can spell disaster for any securities offering. At a minimum, it will have a nasty effect on the ultimate price and quantity of the securities sold. For this reason, a company going public and its investment bankers will put a great deal of effort and energy into the preparation of the road show and its rehearsal. In this particular transaction, we were fortunate to have a senior management team that possessed an excellent ability to speak publicly and to clearly communicate the attractiveness of their business to prospective investors. The Global Brands road show went remarkably well, and as positive feedback spread throughout the investing community, the offering gathered momentum as it rolled from city to city. A few larger institutions expressed preliminary interest in the stock and gave the underwriters their preliminary pricing parameters. These preliminary "indications of interest" are an important part of the negotiations which will ultimately determine the price of the securities being sold. Larger institutions, acting as "price leaders," indicate a price above which they are not prepared to buy the stock. Smaller institutions and retail investors more typically act as "price followers" in that they simply buy at the same price that these larger institutions are willing to pay. From the perspective of the company and the underwriters, a greater number of investors willing to pay a higher price for the stock will generally result in a higher offering price per share and/or more shares being sold on the offering.

October 24
While the SEC review process was taking place, the senior management of Global Brands and their investment bankers were crisscrossing the United States and Europe during a grueling road show. Familiar stops on any road show—New York, Chicago, San Francisco, Dallas, London, Paris, and Edinburgh to name a few—were covered on this particular one. Roughly a dozen major institutions had requested one-on-one sessions where they could meet with the company's management privately for an hour or so. Naturally, these invitations were gladly accepted since each of these prospective investors could easily purchase 10 percent of the total offering. Equally important was the fact that smaller institutions and retail investors would take their cues from the interest shown by these major institutions in terms of price and overall appetite for the offering.

Once the marketing stage of a securities offering has been completed, the fourth—and final—stage of any deal begins, which is simply getting it closed. It is often the most difficult stage of the deal. Time pressures become quite short, unexpected crises are nerve wracking, and everyone involved in the deal feels an acute sense of nervous anticipation. Many things can kill a deal overnight. A deterioration in overall market conditions. A sudden change in the company's fortunes. Irreconcilable differences of opinion over price. Other unforeseen risks best described simply as acts of God. Fortunately, the Global Brands offering sailed through these and other potential problems without any serious glitches.

October 26
After all of the preceding months which led up to this point, this was the big day: pricing the Global Brands offering. The SEC and all other regula-

tory authorities had responded with their comments on the company's reg-istration statement, and the offering had cleared all necessary hurdles in order to commence the sale to the public. The pricing session was set for 4:30 p.m. EST in order to follow the close of trading on the major stock exchanges. In a session such as this, the syndicate manager of the invest-ment banking firm reviewed "the book" of all expressions of interest from institutional investors, retail investors, and other brokerage firms. All in all, the marketing campaign for the Global Brands offering had been suc-cessful: When the marketing effort began, we had hoped to sell 2 million shares at a price somewhere between $16 and $18 per share. Because of the widespread interest in the offering generated during the road show, my firm was able to offer the company pricing terms of $19 per share on a total offering size of 2.5 million shares. Senior management of the company, after huddling among themselves and consulting with their Board of Directors, approved the deal. Not a surprise. Once again, Wall Street had added to the ranks of America's multimillionaires, but it was achieved after many months of hard work and a fair amount of good luck as well.

This initial public offering for Global Brands was, indeed, a success-ful offering. Not all offerings end on a positive note, however. Occasionally, an offering will be cut in size and price or, worst of all, postponed or canceled. Other deals become disasters months or even years after their completion. The Global Brands offering traded extremely well in the months following the initial offering. The com-pany lived up to its earlier predictions of financial performance, which made everyone involved in the offering look smart. In fact, in an inter-esting postscript to this transaction, the company returned to the pub-lic market approximately 1 year later and completed a follow-up offer-ing of 3 million shares at a price of $25 per share. Their ability to complete this second offering so soon after the initial public offering and on such attractive terms was a feather in everyone's cap.

Commonly Asked Questions About a Career in Investment Banking

What Tasks Do You Do Most Often?

The investment banking business is incredibly competitive, and far too many bankers are always aggressively competing for the same clients and the same deals. As a result, the most constant part of an investment banker's career is the pursuit of new business. This usually means flying all over the country to make presentations to existing and prospective clients, entertaining these same people, and constantly getting your name in front of them by mail, by phone, or however else possible.

Furthermore, since most CEOs and CFOs of target companies are extremely busy people, an investment banker cannot take up their valuable time to simply shoot the breeze or talk about the weather. Doing so runs the risk of appearing to be an "empty suit." Effective meetings or presentations in the investment banking business usually focus on a specific—and, it is hoped, appropriate—financial concept, acquisition idea, or the like.

How Much Work Do You Do with People? Numbers? Computers?

The pattern of time spent in each of these ways closely tracks an investment banker's experience in the business. In the entry-level position (an associate 1 to 3 years out of business school), investment bankers may spend most of their time cranking out new business presentations and generating detailed financial models on the computer. Deadlines are usually tight, so this type of work often must be done on an around-the-clock or weekend basis. I shudder to think how many presentations and analyses I put together during my first 3 years in the business, only to attend the meeting with a client too tired or timid to even mutter a word.

In the years which follow, however, when investment bankers become officers in their firm, the detailed analyses are generally delegated to more junior professionals, and most, if not all, of their time is spent directly with clients. What this pattern really illustrates is the fact that a young, inexperienced banker can do much of the technical investment banking work, whereas the ability to generate business and manage relationships is almost always left to more senior and highly paid bankers—often referred to as "rainmakers."

How Much Time Do You Spend in Meetings? Writing? Other?

Here again, the pattern of involvement in these things depends on one's tenure in the business. Senior—and more productive—investment bankers probably spend 5 to 6 hours each day in meetings with clients or prospects. The balance of their time is probably spent on the phone, with little more than 1 or 2 hours available in an average day to read or engage in other required forms of information gathering. The more junior investment bankers probably spend 8 to 10 hours each day putting together presentations or drafting transaction documents.

This type of work is often extremely tedious, which probably explains the high burn-out rate in the industry.

It is also important to point out that the travel requirements of an investment banker are brutal. They tend to travel 3 or more days each week visiting clients and prospects. Certain types of transactions and projects—such as the road show for an initial public offering—require constant travel for weeks at a time. Someone who is not comfortable with air travel and long, unpredictable hours should probably consider another profession.

What Skills Do You Use Most Often?

The ability to juggle several projects at once is absolutely essential. At any time, an investment banker may be working on a half dozen or more active deals. Naturally, all clients think that their transactions are the most important. Moreover, most investment banking transactions involve the sale of securities, a merger or acquisition, or something of strategic importance to the company, so the stakes can get pretty high. Thus, errors and oversights tend to be costly.

Another important skill is the ability to work well under extreme time pressure and deadlines. Quite frequently, a client or transaction will require a great deal of work to be completed in a short period of time, which may mean working over the course of a weekend or around the clock for a day or two. These experiences are quite common, and an investment banker needs to expect them from time to time.

Finally—and probably most important—an investment banker must have good people skills and good selling skills. This requires, in more practical terms, the ability to make a good impression when meeting a new prospect for the first time and the ability to communicate clearly. An investment banker must inspire trust and confidence in a client or prospect. Again, it is important to bear in mind that the investment banking industry is *extremely* competitive, and one must be able to effectively understand complex issues and articulate ideas in a clear and convincing manner in order to successfully get a piece of business in the face of this level of competition.

What Training, Education, and/or Experience Are the Best Preparation for This Career?

Since financial analysis is usually numerical in nature, a background in accounting can be helpful for an investment banking career. Similarly, the credit analysis skills developed in commercial banking and direct selling experience can also be of use. Beyond this, however, a specific educational background or prior work experience is often not all that valuable or important. This is because the tasks performed in the early years of an investment banking career—detailed spread sheet comparisons, valuation analyses, surveying other transactions in the marketplace, compiling new business presentations, etc.—are really unique to the profession. Only in later years does prior work experience become extremely valuable in enhancing a banker's understanding of a particular industry and his or her ability to comprehend the strategic and day-to-day operating requirements of a particular client.

How Do Most People Get Their Jobs in This Career?

The entry-level position in investment banking is that of an associate. These positions are almost exclusively reserved for graduating M.B.A. students, and the competition for these positions is extreme. There is a more junior professional position in the industry—the analyst position—which is a 2-year assignment reserved for undergraduates. Typically, these individuals work for 2 years and then return to business school, although many have stayed with their firms and been promoted to the associate position.

It is interesting to note that there is remarkably little movement into investment banking from other functional areas within a securities firm. In my 13 years in the business, I can recall fewer than a dozen colleagues who made a lateral move into investment banking from other areas such as sales and trading, research, or retail brokerage. Certainly these opportunities exist, and there are examples of individuals who have successfully made such a transition. However, there are far more examples of individuals who have spent their entire careers in the brokerage industry within one particular functional area such as investment banking. Perhaps this is because all of the functional areas mentioned above have significantly different cultures, and the type of work therein differs greatly. While it would be a mistake to give anyone the impression that such moves across functional lines are not possible, they are certainly the exception rather than the norm.

What Do People in This Career Have in Common?

Because of the competition, long hours, constant travel requirements, and frequent time pressures in investment banking, people in the business are often type-A personalities and extremely competitive. Unfortunately, it is also a business filled with workaholics, many of whom woefully neglect their personal and family lives. The compensation aspects of the business attract individuals who are strongly motivated by money. The deal or transaction nature of the business also attracts people who like working on projects with a clear beginning and an end.

How Much Are You Paid?

Investment bankers are typically paid a base salary with a year-end bonus. During the first several years in an investment banking career, base salary ranges anywhere from $50,000 to $80,000, generally in line with what other bankers with similar years of experience are paid. Bonuses in early years are determined similarly and can reach 50 percent and more, but bonuses may vary from firm to firm based on the firms' profitability. Individual performance is always important but not to the same degree as it is in later years, at which time a banker's bonus is directly tied to the volume of business (and profits) which he or she brings to the firm.

What Is the Salary or Compensation Potential?

Given the salary and bonus structure described above, compensation in the early years of an investment banking career tends to be competitive with other career paths, and overall compensation generally rises with a certain degree of predictability—particularly when overall business conditions on Wall Street are good. In later years, however, a banker's compensation can rise and fall dramatically from year to year based on individual performance. A senior investment banker's base salary may be a modest six figures, but his or her bonus, which is always directly tied to the volume of business (and profits) which he or she brings to the firm, can be a multiple of 5 times or greater. Thus, bonuses for senior and productive investment bankers are typically large and may be hundreds of thousands—or even millions—of dollars in a single year.

What Are the Short- and Long-Term Career Opportunities?

One of the most appealing aspects of a career in investment banking is that a person gets to work with many different companies and is exposed to many incredibly talented people along the way. Certainly the chance to work closely with the leaders of many different companies is of great value. An investment banker can get a first-hand view of the important strategic issues facing all types of companies today, as well as different management styles, industries, functional disciplines, and corporate cultures. All of this can give rise to a wide range of contacts and potential career opportunities down the road. There are many examples today of individuals who have left successful careers in investment banking to purchase a company, join their clients' companies, or start companies of their own. These types of long-range possibilities are some of the most appealing aspects of a career in investment banking.

What Is the Range of Jobs in This Career?

This is an important question which can be addressed in several ways. First of all, during the 1980s, most of the higher-profile opportunities in investment banking were in new types of products and services: junk bonds, hostile takeovers, leveraged buyouts, merchant banking, mergers and acquisitions, closed-end funds, and so forth. Today, the most obvious emerging opportunities are not in products and services (indeed, the range of products and services offered by many investment banks today is still shrinking) but in new industries and new geographic areas of opportunity. Several investment banking firms are opening up offices abroad in eastern Europe and Asia. As more and more countries around the world make the transition from a controlled to a free-market economy, they will certainly need the expertise of the investment banking community. In terms of emerging industries, such areas as telecommunications, health care, and environmental services have been prime areas for many new and rapidly growing companies in recent years which depend on the sources of capital and expertise to which the investment banker has the greatest access.

Another way to look at this question is in terms of the role of the specialist versus the generalist. This has always been an actively debated issue for people in the investment banking business. The advantage of a generalist background is that one is better prepared to move away from areas that are experiencing a low level of activity into those areas that are active and rapidly growing. Similarly, many people just prefer the different challenges associated with being a generalist and the chance to work with a wide range of clients and in a variety of functional roles. It is clear, however, that investment banking has become more specialized in recent years. This is because rapidly changing industries, technologies, and markets require an investment banker to have a solid background or expertise in a particular area.

Furthermore, the competition in investment banking is so keen today that it is simply less feasible for someone to survive as a "jack of all trades but master of none." For this reason, someone entering the investment banking business today should attempt to identify a particular area of interest as a career starting point or, at a minimum, should target those firms which can at some point offer the chance to specialize in an area of personal interest.

What Provides the Greatest Satisfaction? Frustration?

The greatest satisfaction in investment banking is seeing many months of your work and ideas culminate in a successfully completed financing or the birth of a new company. It is a great source of pride to know that your efforts have had a profound impact—financial and otherwise—on your client companies and the many people who work within them. Such is the powerful allure of the "deal business."

The greatest frustration in investment banking stems from the fact that it is, first and foremost, a service-oriented profession. I can't count how many vacations and other well-laid personal plans were suddenly shredded by conflicting career demands in investment banking. Clients who are paying their investment bankers millions of dollars in fees or seeking advice on matters where the stakes are many millions or even billions of dollars don't want to hear about canceled weekend plans, birthday parties, and the like. For every investment banker—particularly the more productive ones—these simply become occupational hazards that never go away.

What Is the Biggest Misconception About the Job?

That it is a glamorous and powerful career. Investment banking is really anything but glamorous, unless a person is enamored with red-eye transcontinental flights, all-night drafting sessions, and carry-out Chinese food.

What Is the One Thing You Would Have Wanted Someone to Tell You About This Career?

I would have really benefited early in my career from knowing that Wall Street is and always has been a very cyclical business. This would have been helpful in tempering my naive enthusiasm in the bull-market years of the early and mid-1980s and lessening my anxieties in the postcrash years of the late 1980s and the recession years of the early 1990s. Only now do I really have confidence in knowing that the investment banking business is always changing and what is true in the business today may be the farthest thing from the truth down the road.

What Three Pieces of Advice or Wisdom Would You Give Someone Thinking About This Career?

1. *Choosing this career.* Don't just focus on the industry's compensation or prestige factors. Spend a lot of time thinking about what you *really* want to do with your life and what will give you the greatest amount of career satisfaction. Think carefully about where you want your career to be in 5, 10, or 15 years—not just today. Will this career get you there? Think about the people you will be working with in your job or career. Are you that type of person? Adequately address the negative aspects of this career. Finally, and perhaps most importantly, honestly assess your own qualifications for this career. Are you really cut out for it?

2. *Succeeding on the job.* Don't let the small disappointments that will inevitably come up from time to time cloud your overall feelings about your job. These are to be expected and don't warrant overreaction. Always take on a manageable work load. While it is good to be as productive as possible, the investment banker who can juggle five things at the same time very well will be more highly regarded than the person who juggles ten things poorly. Try to develop or carve out your own area of expertise. This will give you a sense of uniqueness within the organization and will make you more valuable to it in the long run. Make sure that what you are doing or what the group or department you are working in is doing is really important to the overall organization.

3. *Managing your personal life.* In any career, a person must have a life away from the job. Will this career enable or prevent you from achieving a fulfilling personal life outside of the office? Will it enable you to fulfill your outside dreams and responsibilities? Will it help you become a happier and more self-respecting person? Don't ever underestimate the significance of these questions.

12

Life Insurance

David L. Crane
*Senior Vice President, Glass Financial/
John Hancock*

One Month in the Career of a Life Insurance Agent

An insurance agent is often viewed as a salesperson who will do anything to sell you something you hope you never have to need. In reality, insurance is also a people business. Agents who are very professional in what they do are experts in learning as much as possible
about their clients—to the extent that they become almost a member of
each of their client's families. I think the reason for this is that it is the
job of insurance agents to discuss difficult subjects with people (death
and disability) in a manner that makes them open up and reveal their
innermost thoughts about their mortality. Once clients have discussed
such a sensitive topic and come to a conclusion about it, they will then
(over time) talk about all types of problems not necessarily related to
insurance. While that doesn't seem like a productive exercise, letting
clients talk about something like a problem child of theirs can be the
glue that binds the relationship.

> *A client expressed to me, at the beginning of our relationship, an over-
> whelming desire to preserve what was a significant asset base. That is a
> normal desire, but something in his tone of voice led me to question why
> he felt this way. Upon further discussion it was revealed that he had a
> mentally disabled child who would have to be cared for with those assets
> for the child's lifetime. This opened up a discussion not only of invest-
> ments for that purpose but also of the client's desire to buy additional life
> insurance to add to the assets available upon his death.*

In another instance, I worked with a couple who felt very insecure about their future. They were underinsured, had poor retirement planning—you name the problem, they had it. Upon looking into the reasons for this situation, they admitted to having never been able to balance their checkbook or make out a simple budget. When I helped them with this, they suddenly found all kinds of money to start taking care of the goals they had expressed—adequate insurance, retirement planning—the list went on and continues to this day. An insurance agent has to be more than a salesperson.

Insurance agents need to continually prospect for more (and better) clients—people who have insurance needs of all types. This can be accomplished in many different ways—direct mail, letters, telephone, referrals from present clients—the list is endless. Most agents *hate* using the telephone, but in the 1990s and beyond, good telephone skills will be critical in this business. Insurance agents often get rejected on the telephone, even when they have good skills. It's not because people don't like an agent (how could they know anyway from a telephone call?) but because most of them are underinsured—and they know it. A *good* agent will show them the logic behind adding to their coverage—and never get the sale. A *great* agent will do that *and* address the emotional part of the decision—and get the sale. Buying insurance is an emotional decision grounded in protecting someone or something the client cares about. Too many agents have lost sight of that fact and have instead gotten caught up in the world of computer illustrations—trying to get people to buy based purely on numbers. *It doesn't work*—believe me, I've tried it.

The same process applies with all potential clients, whether they are business owners, professional, corporate executives, etc. At the first meeting agents explain what they do, the issues they will address for the clients, and how they will be compensated (commissions). Agents then tell the prospects that it is their job to help the prospects minimize or eliminate the problems during their lifetimes (and at death) that can result in far less money being available to their families when they need it most. This explanation does not require more than 20 to 30 minutes. It is then decision time for the prospect—proceed or don't proceed. Assuming the client agrees, the next thing agents do is ask him or her a lot of questions. Good questioning should take an hour— maybe more depending upon how much the client wants to talk (don't cut clients short—their words will reveal to you what they want to accomplish). To be successful in this particular area, agents must become experts at asking "open-ended" questions—ones that cannot be answered with yes, no, or a number. This is a little more difficult than it sounds because you have to become a very active *and* effective listener at the same time to avoid misinterpreting the information you are given.

> *One of the best questions you can ask is, "Tell me what you want your life insurance to do for you." This is a very effective question because not only is the response not yes or no, but you learn a lot about how clients feel about their families. This is also a question that startles clients, so they might ask, "What do you mean?" Now it is your job to paint a mental picture, so you can say, "Well, if your spouse was coming to my office in 15 minutes to pick up a check for your life insurance proceeds (because you died last week), what questions would he or she be likely to ask me? Will I be asked about debts? What do you want to provide with that check?" I had a client actually start crying in my office when I asked him this series of questions because he realized there was a major gap between what he wanted to provide and what he had actually provided for. Fortunately, the story had a happy ending and he was able to "shore up" what had been a major weakness in his planning.*
>
> *Other clients will respond to that question with, "My wife will go back to work," figuring that will take care of continuing income. In many cases when clients have said that to me, I point out to them that if their spouse has been out of the work force for a while, making decent money could be hard without spending money for additional training. Also, child care costs can go up if day care or a babysitter is required. Most clients do not think about these things, so it is my job to point them out.*

Having gleaned the information an agent needs to help the client make a decision, the next step is to put together a package of information that matches the client's needs. In this effort, the agent might have to deal with several different insurance companies (depending upon the client situation) to come up with the right answer for the client. Once this has been done, the agent goes back to see the client and presents his or her recommendations. If the right questions have been asked at the previous meeting, this will simply be a confirming meeting and completing necessary paperwork. Since the sale that is being made is an "intangible" sale, an agent needs to reinforce at this point that the client is making the right decision.

Once the client's policy is issued, the agent will have to service the client's future business—buying more insurance, changing the existing insurance, changing beneficiaries, etc. This activity helps to further cement the client relationship and helps an agent get referrals to people the clients may know. This is a great way to build the business. A good agent also spends a fair amount of time getting continually educated. With changes in tax laws, new products, changes in old products, new planning ideas, and marketing seminars, agents will have to spend probably 4 full days each month in various meetings that cover the above subjects. The primary reason for doing this is to be in a position to give prospects and clients the best possible information and recommendations. The other reason is that some amount of continuing education is required by each state in order to maintain an insurance license. Keeping up with developments through these classes and seminars gives an agent a lot more than the required number of hours for license continuation.

Time management in this business is critical because agents can be subjected to a never-ending stream of interruptions and/or crises (telephone calls, client deaths, etc.) as they try to do the job they are supposed to—namely, generating new clients. The idea is to keep these interruptions to a manageable level by managing time; it is very easy to shuffle papers or sit down in front of a computer to play with insurance illustrations—both of which keep agents away from the nitty gritty work of making telephone calls to prospects for appointments and, eventually, more business. It's a truism in this business that the successful people do the things that unsuccessful people are unwilling to do. If an agent makes appointments, sees people, gets facts, makes presentations, and closes business on a regular basis, he or she makes money. If you do enough of that, you can basically make *unlimited* money—exercising complete control over your income.

It is critical in the time management process to also pay close attention to detail. An agent can get to the point where he or she has too many clients to keep up with. This is a paperwork-intensive business, and you have to follow up on everything to be successful. Missing a detail (like forgetting to change a beneficiary) can not only lose a client, but it can cause a lawsuit, too. Can you imagine, on the death of a client, the insurance money being paid to the wrong person?

A typical month is a never-ending series of phone calls, appointments, seminars, and paperwork. It is a cycle that repeats itself over and over again each week. Usually nobody tells agents what hours to work, at least if they are beyond their second or third year in the business. However, it is a good habit to work regular hours anyway. Another critical habit is persistence. People by nature are procrastinators (particularly when being asked to buy life insurance), so an agent must be persistent. Several additional phone calls and meetings may be required before someone finally decides to buy. An agent must keep asking because this shows people that he or she cares enough about them to keep following up. Statistics show that most clients only will buy after three of their objections are answered. The good agent will have the tenacity and patience to continue.

I had one client whom I met with five times over a period of 6 months. After purchasing what I had recommended, she said that the reason she bought *from me rather than another agent was that I had hung in with her through-out her thought process. She ended up purchasing a $2 million policy, and I earned a $35,000 commission. Patience, like virtue, has its own reward.*

Commonly Asked Questions About a Career as a Life Insurance Agent

What Tasks Do You Do the Most Often?

The insurance agent performs a variety of tasks, but the primary task is building the client relationship. This involves meeting people, telling them what you do, finding out the particulars about their situations, and then customizing insurance (or investment) programs tailored to the clients' needs. This involves selling them the products that satisfy the needs.

How Much Work Do You Do with People? Numbers? Computers?

The majority of the work in this business is dealing with people—their personalities, problems, and potential. Much of an agent's time is spent (or should be spent) in face-to-face contact with prospects or clients—or on the telephone with either group. People look to you for advice in a lot of different areas. When it comes to insurance planning, they will want input on the insurance company, estate taxes, income taxes, and a whole host of related issues—not the least of which is the premium.

If you are discussing life insurance that builds cash value, it is likely there will be some conversation about retirement planning. You will then have to be in a position to discuss IRAs, Keoghs, 401-(k) plans, and all other retirement accumulation vehicles that may be available. As part of that, you may also need to perform a present value analysis on the future retirement plans they have. This helps to point out what must be invested today in order to make it to the future.

Computers help you in this regard not only for doing present value calculations but in presenting insurance projections, doing graphs for investments—a myriad of things that would take incredible amounts of time to do by hand. You therefore have to be somewhat computer literate (but not a computer expert by any means) in order to effectively work with clients.

How Much Time Do You Spend In Meetings? Writing? Others?

Insurance agents generally spend very little time in office meetings compared to salespeople in a corporate environment. Initially there is a significant amount of time spent each week (6 to 10 hours) in formal classroom training and meetings. After the first several months, this declines dramatically and is usually replaced by going out to see new clients and prospects. Meetings with clients or prospects—on the telephone or in person—typically consume 70 percent of an agent's time. Many insurance agents today do little or no writing since there are staff people to perform word processing in a typical agency. You must be able to compose a good business letter, though.

There is a significant amount of reading that must be done during an insurance agent's entire career. Initially this reading is focused primarily on building product expertise; thereafter it is focused on industry developments and new planning techniques.

What Skills Do You Use Most Often?

The skills used most often by an agent are concentrated in the communication area—making effective use of telephone time, eliciting information from prospects through proper questioning techniques, and effective listening skills. People skills are what set the superior agent apart from the mediocre agent. Agents must also have some sales ability, which translates to the ability to persuade people to take action. That is a valuable skill because most people are natural procrastinators.

What Training, Education, and/or Experience Are the Best Preparation for This Career?

This is an unusual career in that people with a myriad of backgrounds and training can enter it and be successful quickly. The best candidates are generally:

1. Those who have been in high-volume, commission-driven sales positions requiring significant prospecting time—and have been successful performing in such an environment. Examples would be stockbrokers, pharmaceutical salespeople, and realtors.

2. Those coming to the career with a background in a related field that has given them some related technical expertise. Examples would

be banking, accounting, law, and other financial services (fee-only financial planners).

Generally speaking, formal training or background in communications is extremely valuable due to the amount of time spent face to face with clients and prospects.

Once you are in the business, there are many licenses you have to obtain. The first is an insurance license that allows you to do business in the areas you will concentrate on—typically life insurance and disability insurance. You must pass a test in order to obtain the license; this is usually preceded by 40 hours of classroom work. The next license is a securities license, which will allow you to sell various investment products. There are different levels of securities licenses you can obtain that allow you to sell progressively more products; each one has its own test that must be passed prior to approval, as well as a state securities test. The knowledge for this test can be achieved through self-study or in a classroom setting. Additionally, there are insurance products that have their own licensing requirements over and above a basic license—variable life and variable annuities. Each of these has its own separate exam and classroom requirements that vary by state. These licenses and classes, while they do consume time, put you in a position of being able to assist clients in many different areas.

Once you have achieved all of the base licenses required, the next level of education classroom work and exams is in obtaining professional designations. The common ones you see are

- Chartered life underwriter (CLU)
- Chartered financial consultant (ChFC)
- Certified financial planner (CFP)
- Master of science financial services (MSFS)

Keep in mind that all of this time must be spent at the same time that you are building your clientele to generate income.

How Do Most People Get Their Jobs in This Career?

Fortunately, this is not the type of career whose entry depends on "who you know." Most top-quality insurance companies continually seek "new blood" to add to their agent forces. Many times a simple telephone call to the head of an agency will generate an initial interview; beyond that point your success will be dictated by your ability to generate new clients.

Depending upon the initial training you need or desire, it is generally best to interview with one of the large insurance companies— Northwestern Mutual, for example—that has an extensive training program. Many of these companies run ads in the paper, recruit on college campuses, and participate in job fairs. They operate on the "general agency" system where people usually have a manager available to work with them.

This is the type of career that really does not give you a "job"—a word that connotates salary and a corporate environment. You are in business for yourself and are paid exclusively based on your productivity.

What Do People in This Career Have in Common?

The truly successful people in this career will have the following things in common:

- High level of social skills and personality
- Inner motivation to be a success and work the hours it takes
- Ability to persuade people to take action that is in their own best interests
- Thirst for additional knowledge to build their skills

How Much Are You Paid?

Most insurance agents starting out are paid under some sort of financing arrangement by their sponsoring insurance company, based in part upon the business they are able to generate. This helps to put a floor under a new agent's annual earnings (typically $18,000) but imposes no ceiling. It buys some time for an agent until a large number of clients is generated and renewal commissions begin at the start of the agent's second year.

After 5 or 10 years in the business, an agent who has done a good job of building clientele can expect to have an income in the range of $40,000 to $70,000—maybe more if the clients are generating a lot of business. At some point, most agents reach an income plateau for a variety of reasons: (1) They may need secretarial help because they are getting bogged down in administrative detail, (2) they do not improve their skills to be able to serve bigger and better clients, or(3) they stop going out and getting new clients (i.e., doing the things required to continue building their business). This plateau can be overcome by getting "back to the basics" or by becoming a specialist in one area—estate planning, for example.

What Is the Salary or Compensation Potential?

It is a rare career in which people have complete control over their earnings, but this career is exactly that. Your earnings potential is unlimited, depending upon how hard you want to work and the type of clientele you cultivate. Whenever you want to give yourself a raise, you just work a little harder. Nobody has the power to cut your territory or infringe on your earnings. There are several well-known agents who regularly earn high six figure incomes.

As an agent, you will earn your own commissions and be given various benefits at a reasonable cost. At some point in your career, you may decide to pursue a sales management position—helping other agents become more and more successful. Usually in a management role you will earn more money ($60,000 to $100,000); many agents are working for you and you receive some percentage of their written business as compensation for the time you spend with them. The trade-off is that your time is no longer your own because many people want a slice of it.

The ultimate in most insurance companies is to become a "general agent." This usually does not occur until you have significant experience in the business; once at this point, you will have several managers, many agents, and many staff people working for you. There is a lot of financial reward (typically $250,000 or more per year) and a lot of financial responsibility—you will own computers, furnishings, rent office space, etc. Some general agents, in fact, retire or resign and go back to being agents—simply because of the freedom it allows.

What Are the Short- and Long-Term Career Opportunities?

Initially, life insurance agents do nothing more than build their own clienteles. Because most thriving agencies are growing, sales management opportunities always exist, where an agent becomes responsible for training and managing new agents. The agent could at the same time continue to add to his or her own clientele and derive income from two sources. Beyond sales managers, agents could rise to become the head of their own agencies or even move into an insurance company home office in some capacity. Generally speaking, those who are money motivated will be happiest at the agent or sales manager level because that is where the money is.

What Is the Range of Jobs in This Career?

As discussed above, there is a wide range of jobs in this career. You begin as an agent, working to build a clientele. At some point, if you decide not to take advantage of sales management, you may have an opportunity to move into a position at the home office of the parent insurance company. This could be any number of positions—marketing, product development, training—the list is extensive. Making such a move usually requires a physical move (unless you live in the city where the home office is) and a change from commission to salary. Moving into areas in the home office such as underwriting or actuarial services is rare because the income offered is usually less than one can earn as an agent.

What Provides the Greatest Satisfaction? Frustration?

The greatest satisfaction in the career of a life insurance agent is in helping clients improve their financial situations through the purchase of properly designed insurance plans. This can help people educate children, supplement retirement income, pay estate taxes, and cover a host of other situations. The look on clients' faces when they see their plans coming to fruition and they express gratitude is the greatest reward.

The greatest frustration is getting people to change old habits or ideas about their life insurance and the resistance to change (otherwise known as procrastination). Clients will always tell you they want certain things, but they are unwilling to "pay the price" to obtain them. This is very common, so as an agent you have to get used to this; your best reaction is to hone your skills of persuasion to minimize the procrastination you will certainly face.

What Is the Biggest Misconception About the Job?

By far the biggest misconception about the job is the stereotype of a policy-pushing, fast-talking, marginally ethical agent. The majority of life insurance agents act much more in the role of an advisor—asking lots of questions and then designing an insurance program that fits the needs of the client. The ability to do this requires ongoing education on the part of the agent so that he or she keeps up with new product developments and planning techniques and develops an understanding of client needs.

What Is the One Thing You Would Have Wanted Someone to Tell You About This Career?

I would have wanted someone to say that this can be the most satisfying yet at the same moment the most frustrating career there can be. The moment when a client thanks you for the help you have given him or her can give you a feeling far better than receiving a big commission check because you know you are doing something worthwhile. Then the very next client, with bigger problems than the one who just thanked you, refuses to take action (even in part) to correct a problem. The emotional peaks and valleys that result from this can destroy your motivation if you let it.

What Three Pieces of Advice or Wisdom Would You Give Someone Thinking About This Career?

Three critical pieces of advice for this career would be:

1. Establish good basic habits at the very start (hours worked, telephoning, etc.) and *stick with them* your entire career. There is no substitute for hard work and meaningful sales activity—knowledge without exercise ceases to exist.

2. Develop the ability to present your information succinctly and to ask probing questions. People do not care what you know until they know you care (about them). Great questions create dialogue and will tell you what a client wants (or doesn't want).

3. Always serve the client first and yourself second. This may initially mean lower commission income, but the word will spread that you have high integrity. You will then begin to make more money then you ever dreamed possible because clients will refer you to other people. Clients who have been "sold," rather than deciding to buy, will seldom mention your name to others.

13

Management Consulting

Mark Howorth
Consultant, Bain & Company

David Sanderson
Manager, Bain & Company

Fred Studier
Manager, Bain & Company

One Month in the Career of a Management Consultant

No one can really describe what it is we do...the only way you can under-stand what a management consultant does is to experience it," said a partner of a large management consulting firm. My firm, Bain and Company, had been hired by a high-tech company (I'll call them "Tech-co"—the names and numbers have been changed to protect the innocent) that was involved in making storage devices for computers. Things had been going pretty well for Tech-co for several years. We had three different case teams working in different areas of the company and had been work-ing with the client for about 9 months.

The division that I was working on used a new storage technology that had not yet become the industry standard. Tech-co had purchased this division as an "insurance" policy in case the new technology became the hot wave of the future for computer storage. Unfortunately, this "insur-ance" policy was losing $50 million per year and requiring a capital investment of $25 million per year. This had gone on for 3 years, and the CEO was finally starting to realize that this cash flow situation was a real problem. He had asked us to help figure out what the best course of action *was for this division. This was a very important piece of work for the future of the company since it had a large impact on their financial results and would have an impact on the types of development activity that would occur over the next few years. I guess a $75 million annual investment would affect any company.*

In the consulting industry there are a wide range of firms, each focused on helping clients with different types of issues. At one end of the spectrum there are consulting firms which focus on very specific, technical issues, like information technology or automobile manufacturing, and at the other end are firms with the most general approach, strategy consultants. If you are like most people, "strategy management consulting" tells you very little about what we really do. One reason that those words aren't very specific is because we do just about everything when it comes to helping organizations solve problems.

Management consultants get hired to do whatever helps a client's bottom line. Clients range from companies which are on the cutting edge of their industries and want help in staying ahead to companies who are in trouble and need help staying afloat. Most often they are somewhere in between and want an objective outsider's view of what they can do to beat their competition. Given the range of capabilities of clients and the variety of situations which they face, the role of a management consultant can vary from "business fitness trainer" to "business psychologist" to "business doctor." Sometimes a consultant's work involves very short term tactical tasks like helping to launch a new product, while other times we will help a client to develop a 5-year strategy.

Given the range of things consultants work on, there is no "typical" month. The only constants are that consultants work as a member of a case team, that case team will be working on very difficult issues (which is one reason consultants are paid well), and the expectations for the performance of each team member are very high.

Our first job was to understand Tech-co's current business. To do this the case team (which consisted of two associate consultants, a consultant, and a manager) went to the client's headquarters and spent 2 days interviewing all of the senior managers, but before we did that we spent a few days doing general library research on the computer storage device industry. From this research we learned who the major competitors were, how the technology worked, and what the current trends were. That enabled us to ask reasonably smart questions when we got to Tech-co. While there, we asked questions about the current business mix, current spending on research and development, and the dynamics of their industry. Between our initial research and the management interviews, we were able to make some educated guesses about why this division was losing so much money.

It turned out they were deliberately selling the product below cost in order to increase demand. They were doing this because the technology was very new, and many of their competitors had similar products. They assumed that if enough customers chose their product now, it would become the "industry standard" later (like VHS in video tape), and then they could charge normal prices. The question then became: Did they have a realistic chance of becoming the industry standard? Not an easy question to answer.

A typical consulting case team will consist of a few associate consultants (people who have a bachelor's or maybe a nonbusiness master's degree from the nation's top colleges), a few consultants (M.B.A.s who typically come from top business schools like Harvard and Stanford), a manager, and a vice president. Each problem is broken down into tasks, and each member of the team has responsibility for his or her own piece of work. In addition to the members of the team already described, there is also a large support staff which consists of an information services department, a graphics department, case team assistants, training, data processing and clerical support.

In order to answer the question of future industry standards, we had to go talk to people who were currently buying the technology and people who might be likely to buy it in the future. I designed a simple interview guide and reviewed it with my boss, who made some revisions. We then took it to our client who also made some revisions. While the revisions were taking place, I was madly trying to schedule customer interviews. Scheduling interviews is tough work because the people you are trying to talk to don't really want to spend time with "another management consultant." However, with much persistence, I finally managed to get them scheduled. Then the case team hit the road.

Traveling around the country and interviewing people at high-tech firms may seem like glamorous work, but let me assure you it gets old very quickly. The allure of travel wears off when you are stuck for 2 days in Huntsville, Alabama, and it is about 1000 degrees outside with 99 percent humidity. Also asking people the same questions every day can get pretty boring. Pretty soon you realize that there's a real cost for all those frequent flyer miles. We would talk to people all day long and then spend the evening summarizing what we learned over room service at the local Marriott. At the end of 3 weeks we had a pretty good understanding of what the customers thought.

You might wonder why Tech-co simply couldn't have gotten this information for themselves. There are two answers. One is that customers (and potential customers) will tell us what they really think because they don't know who we work for, whereas they are more likely to tell Tech-co what they think they want to hear. The other reason is that the people at Tech-co simply didn't have the time to spend 3 weeks flying all over the country.

In order for companies to justify consultants' fees, they typically hire them to focus only on those issues where they can have a large financial impact on the client's performance. They also have to feel that they would have a very hard time solving those problems without the help of consultants. As a result, the issues that consultants work on tend to be very complex and critical to the company's future. Clearly, most organizations would prefer to solve their own problems rather than bring in outsiders. They bring in consultants when they have difficulty solving problems themselves. This creates a challenging task for the consultant since they often don't know the clients' industries as well as the client does. What consultants bring are approaches to solving problems that have been developed over decades and which have been proven in hundreds of industries around the world.

Another reason companies will bring in consultants is that they value an outside opinion. Because consultants are outsiders and have experience looking at a wide range of companies, it is often easier for a consultant to sort through the organizational politics to understand clients' businesses than it is for the client, being a part of it. The last reason that clients tend to hire consultants is that it is often easier to have an outsider help make a difficult decision. For example, if a client suspects that cost cutting may be required (especially when it may involve people's jobs), they might bring in consultants to get an independent perspective on a tough business decision.

My next task was to summarize the information that I had gathered into a presentation. My presentation showed that Tech-co's product had some technological advantages over the competition but that its reliability was very poor. In addition, many people were afraid to buy Tech-co's product because they questioned their financial strength to stay in the market over the long run. Potential customers didn't want to choose a product and then have their supplier exit the market.

In addition to summarizing the customer perspectives, I also had to predict how quickly the market was going to grow. In order to do that I built a "model," or computer spread sheet (we use Lotus 1-2-3), to predict what the future growth of the market would be in terms of units sold and dollar volumes. The model was based on a variety of assumptions about competitive dynamics, growth rates, and developments in the industry. The model is a very important tool because it allows us to change our assumptions (like how quickly prices would drop) and see what impact that would have on the size of the market. The model I built showed that the market was going to grow at a very healthy rate, but that Tech-co was unlikely to get a big part of it. We presented the interim results to Tech-co management, and the results were not surprising. They initially made a bunch of excuses about why their performance was so poor and challenged our conclusions. During that meeting and over the course of the next few weeks, we patiently took them through all of our background information and assumptions, and they finally agreed that their situation was more serious than they had originally thought. They then asked the key question: "So, what should we do?" This is the stage in a case where it really gets interesting because you have an opportunity to create real change.

Consultants are analysts and advisors of business. They are generally responsible for gathering, analyzing, and presenting information to help solve clients' problems. Initially, they do a lot of research (with sources like annual reports and survey results), interview people, build financial models, and present the results of their work. Consultants work with general management of companies to help them understand their recommendations and to help them implement solutions.

My part of coming up with the solution was to figure out how we could change the customer perception that Tech-co's products were unreliable. To do this I had to understand why they had that perception. After interviewing some more people in Tech-co, I discovered that their manufacturing process was not very good. Much of the equipment that they were using was relatively old, and they had a problem keeping skilled employees. In addition, quality control was not very thorough. I then built another model. This time I tried to calculate what it would cost the client to get higher quality. This would have included buying new equipment, hiring more highly skilled employees, and putting in a more detailed quality control process. I spent several weeks determining what this would cost. My work involved talking with people at Tech-co and then interviewing other companies who made similar products but whose quality was high. Most of these outside conversations took place on the phone, which was fine by me since I was sick of traveling. I also realized that just having high quality was not enough. Since Tech-co already had a reputation for being unreliable, we would have to take some action to turn that around. Therefore, I had to create a marketing strategy to convince potential customers that Tech-co's products were reliable. This marketing strategy involved things like advertising, participating at trade shows, and even giving away some free units. When I totaled up all of my calculations, I found that the cost of getting high quality was very expensive. This made sense since if it were cheap, the client probably would have already done it. Tech-co managers had always known that it would be expensive, but until I showed them my analysis, they never had hard numbers telling them what it would cost.

Associate consultants (ACs) come from the top schools in the nation. Consulting jobs are typically one of the most sought after jobs on college campuses because students are attracted to the idea of getting exposure to a wide range of different industries, working on a variety of issues, and getting paid well while doing it. Some consulting firms hire a substantial number of ACs each year, so the incoming AC is in a very large peer group, which creates an almost "collegial" atmosphere. Most ACs leave their firms after 2 to 4 years and a high percentage go on to top M.B.A. programs. The best consulting firms make a major investment in training, so art history and business administration majors are put on relatively equal footing after completing training. At Bain & Company, AC training is a veritable "boot camp" that starts with 6 weeks of book learning and culminates in 2 weeks of 16-hour days on Cape Cod.

For all reasons just described, a career in management consulting seems like a pretty good place to start a career in business, yet it isn't free. Consultants work pretty long hours. The average consultant probably works 55 to 60 hours a week, and during the first year that may get closer to 70 hours a week. There are even times when consultants can work 100 hours in a week. During those kinds of weeks, people have been known to check into a downtown hotel rather than go home at night. At such times the salary and the perks of free dinners and taxi rides home seem like little reward. The consultant's job can be stressful in that the work that a consultant is asked to do is very difficult. It is a far cry from college "problem sets" to try to figure out why a client's competitor can produce widgets at half the cost of the client. There are no answers at the back of the book.

Despite all of this, consultant's consistently rise to the challenge. Over time they build a confidence that comes from learning to take the toughest problems that the business world can throw at them and still come back for more.

Of course, while I was working on my part of the solution, the rest of the team was working on other issues. One member was trying to understand how much it would cost to keep ahead of the competition in terms of technology. It turns out that it took a huge amount of money to stay competitive. (To put it in perspective, some Japanese competitors were investing $150 million per year in technology while Tech-co was investing $25 million. Another team member was trying to figure out if there were new types of customers that the client could focus on. There were some other customer segments (my client was focused primarily on the government market), but it turned out some of the other competitors made products which better met their needs. Pulling all of these things together, we were able to build a comprehensive recommendation. This recommendation for Tech-co consisted of a few choices. They could either increase the investment in the business by about $25 million per year or sell the business to another competitor. Another alternative would have been to shut it down since it was losing so much money, but the Tech-co senior management *(who had hired us) were unwilling to take a write-off. It was a gloomy day when we presented our final recommendations to the divisional managers, but they had helped us develop the solution all along, so they agreed with it. We then took the recommendation back to senior management. After much discussion the parent company decided that they didn't want to invest $25 million per year in an "insurance policy" for their base business, and they decided to sell the business.*

This case is a typical example of what a management consultant at a large strategy management consulting firm does. As a consultant, I did basic research, client interviews, customer interviews, computer modeling, and presentations and participated as a critical member in developing what "the answer" was. It should be noted that many consulting firms get involved in all kinds of cases. Each of those types of work carries a different set of day-to-day activities for the case team members. Consultants often work on multiple cases at once. At the time I worked for Tech co, I was also working with a troubled S&L. At the S&L, I was helping to cut costs, particularly in their branches. Needless to say my experiences there were totally different from the case I described. Since most consultants come to the industry to learn about business, working on multiple cases helps ensure that you get exposed to many different situations.

To sum up, consulting offers one of the best opportunities that a person interested in business can take after graduating. It offers the opportunity to learn, to take on responsibility, to have an impact, and to mature professionally (and it also pays very well).

Commonly Asked Questions About a Career as a Management Consultant

What Tasks Do You Do Most Often?

The tasks that a management consultant performs vary widely based on the problem that is being tackled and what part of that problem the consultant is helping to solve. Consultants collect information from client sources and external market research. This often requires extensive interviewing of client personnel, customers, and industry experts. They then help analyze the problem and develop a plan for solving it.

Consultants work with middle- and senior-level management executives to build consensus on the analysis and recommendations. This requires developing presentations that are clear, concise, and persuasive. In addition, consultants often lead client task forces that are commissioned to implement the recommendations developed.

In almost all circumstances, consultants work on a case team. The case team as a whole has the responsibility for creating value for the client. As a part of the case team, the individual contributes in brainstorming sessions and hypothesis generation.

How Much Do You Work with People? Numbers? Computers?

Consulting provides an excellent balance between working with people and working individually on analytical challenges. Ultimately we are in the business of helping people and that means frequent interaction. Over half of the consultant's time is spent either working directly with the client or with other case team members. Typically, management consultants spend from 1 to 4 or 5 days a week working with the client at their facility. Activities could include task force meetings, presentations, joint analyses, client interviews, data gathering, and fact-finding missions. Consultants often find themselves working very closely with other case team members on tackling difficult problems, conducting external interviews, or just trading ideas and thoughts.

The time not spent with the client or with the case team is spent on individual analyses. The type of analysis that consultants conduct varies widely and is based on whatever is required to tackle the problem. Frequent activities include interviewing, fact finding, data gathering, external market research, and financial modeling. A consultant does not need to be a computer or numbers jock. Computers and numbers are tools and are used only to the extent that they help the case team "crack the case."

How Much Time Is Spent in Meetings? Writing? Other?

Since working with clients and operating in a case team setting is such an integral part of the job, meetings are essential. However, the meetings tend to be smaller and less formal than you may find in other jobs. The meetings are usually working forums for brainstorming, discussing new approaches to tackling a problem, and sharing your work with other case team members or with the client. That means that consultants usually take a very active role in all meetings they attend. Some consulting firms summarize their recommendations into written form, so writing is often a critical part of the job. Most consulting firms also communicate results through slide presentations.

What Skills Do You Use Most Often?

To be successful, consultants must be exceptional both analytically and interpersonally. Analytically, they should possess superior problem-solving skills, linear-logical thinking, and strong presentation development skills. Great analysis is not enough; consultants need to be very effective listeners and be able to clearly, concisely, and persuasively communicate their findings to a wide range of people with differing backgrounds and needs. Finally, because of the case team structure of most consulting firms, it is important to be a good "team player."

What Training, Education, and/or Experience Are the Best Preparation for This Career?

Fresh thinking about difficult problems, origination of new ideas and generation of keen insights are critical to success in this career; therefore many backgrounds are valued; the only constant is that consultants all performed exceptionally well at college. A business major is not required; in fact at many firms, business majors from undergraduate colleges are probably a minority. College graduates with political science, engineering, math, English, history, economics, biology, and other majors have all proved successful as management consultants. Most career consultants are people who have returned to business school for M.B.A.s.

How Do Most People Get Their Jobs in This Career?

It is extremely difficult to get consulting jobs, but it's well worth it. The typical way for people to enter this field is through top-tier college or graduate school placement offices. Many firms hire at two different entry-level positions. An associate consultant or analyst is usually hired from an undergraduate program or from a nonbusiness graduate program. A consultant is hired from the very best M.B.A. programs from around the world. The recruiting process is quite rigorous. It starts with a review of résumé, transcripts, and test scores. The applicant is then interviewed by six to eight people and often asked to solve difficult business cases on the spot. It is not unusual for a consulting firm to receive 50 to 100 applicants for each job offer.

What Do People in This Career Have in Common?

People who enter and thrive in management consulting usually are exceptional, both analytically and interpersonally. They have been educated at the top universities, are young and energetic, and often tend to enjoy working very hard. Typical consultants have chosen the job because they see it as a good learning experience. They enjoy challenges and get a thrill out of cracking the most difficult business problems. Finally, they enjoy working with others and thrive in a team environment.

How Much Are You Paid and What Is the Salary or Compensation Potential?

Management consultants are paid at the top of the range for graduating seniors and M.B.A.s. Compensation is made up of salary, a signing bonus, and a year-end bonus. In addition, there is a fast trajectory in compensation for those who are successful. While there is a wide range across firms and specialty area, total compensation for starting M.B.A.s often tops $100K, and graduating college seniors make between $30K and $50K. Pay at both levels can increase up to 20 percent a year.

What Are the Short- and Long-Term Career Opportunities?

Working in consulting prepares you for a wide variety of opportunities both in and outside of consulting. Because of the constant learning and challenges and wide range of experiences in consulting, other industries value this background very highly. In fact, some people feel that 1 year in a consulting firm can be worth several years on the outside. In addition to careers working in their clients' industries, many consultants successfully pursue entrepreneurial opportunities.

Within the consulting industry there are opportunities to become managers and then partners (or vice presidents) of prestigious firms. Some senior management consulting executives are among the most respected thinkers in their areas of expertise.

What Is the Range of Jobs in This Career?

There are primarily four types of consulting positions: associate consultant (or analyst), consultant, manager, and vice president. An associate consultant usually starts immediately after college or from a non-business graduate school. They work between 2 and 4 years and then attend a top M.B.A. program. A consultant is usually hired directly from a top M.B.A. program and typically has had work experience prior to business school. From consultant, the career track has a fast trajectory to manager and then vice president (partner).

What Provides the Greatest Satisfaction? Frustration?

The greatest satisfaction in this job comes from hearing the CEO of your $10 billion client firm say that "our company could not have survived without your help" or reading in the *Wall Street Journal* about the breakthrough strategy that your case team developed for the client. A close second is seeing your client implement your recommendation and actually seeing the results of your and your case team's efforts. This is a double-edged sword though. The biggest frustration occurs when you are not able to see the results of your work. This happens when results of long-term strategies sometimes take between 2 and 3 years to manifest themselves (and you're not around to share in the excitement).

What Is the Biggest Misconception About the Job?

The biggest misconception about this job is that it is a "corporate" environment and that the people are homogeneous. Many consulting environments are made up of young, energetic individuals and that's where the similarities stop. At one top firm, in addition to the gray suits, there are male consultants with ponytails and earrings and a female vice president with purple tinted hair. While this is not the norm, the environment allows people to be individuals.

What Is the One Thing You Would Have Wanted Someone to Tell You About This Career?

While working in consulting is a great experience and prepares you for a multitude of opportunities, it is also a very fun place to work. Because so many of the people are young and energetic, firms often consciously look for fun people in the recruiting process. Some firms have case team events, where teams get together quarterly to go sailing or wine-tasting, or to take cooking lessons. There is a wide range of formal and informal events that can make consulting firms fun places to work.

What Three Pieces of Advice or Wisdom Would You Give Someone Thinking About This Career?

1. Being a consultant is not a 9 to 5 job. It requires dedication and commitment to get the job done. This may mean a red-eye from coast to coast to deliver a presentation to the board of directors or an all night crunch to complete the due diligence for an impending client acquisition.

2. You need to love challenges to enjoy this job. As a consultant, you will be challenged constantly in a variety of ways. The challenge could come from an analytic problem, an unhappy case team member you are supervising, or a client that just does not agree with your findings.

3. You must enjoy working with the "best of the best." Management consulting firms hire the best graduates from the top schools from around the world. You need a mix of confidence and humility to fit in and be successful in this environment.

14
Marketing

Sally Cohen
Chain Marketing Manager, Coca-Cola, USA

Sarah Salant
Brand Manager, Kraft-General Foods

One Month in the Career of a Marketing Manager

> *Even though I've been in the business for 6 years and have been to count-less product shoots, I am still amazed by the number of highly trained peo-ple it takes to photograph one little plate of spaghetti. It strikes me as funny that I am paid to sit here for several hours, watching a woman in an apron using a pair of tweezers to move a strand of spaghetti around a plate and a paintbrush to apply extra tomato sauce while several assistants, pho-tographers, and advertising agency executives hover nearby. We refer to the plate of spaghetti as the "hero" and have just spent several hours set-ting up lights using a different plate of spaghetti as the "stand-in." All of these people—and one little plate of food. And all of these people will look to me for the final nod before the camera starts flashing. And if the spaghetti doesn't look good, no one will buy it. For this I got an M.B.A.!*

For almost every product in the store, there is a person who cares more intimately about that product than anyone else in the world, a person who may have helped that product to reach the shelves and decided to give it that name, provided it with those flavors, made the package that color, advertised it with that commercial, and priced it at that amount. In many instances there is one individual whose liveli-hood and personal satisfaction are dependent on the ups and downs of that product—that individual is known as the brand manager.

Brand managers (also called product or marketing managers in some companies) like to think of themselves as mini-business owners. Their products, whether they are cereals or lines of hair conditioners, are the businesses and they are the general managers. The theory behind the development of brand managers, which is often attributed to Procter and Gamble, is that if one person or one team of people can focus on all aspects of a specific product or product line, it ensures maximized sales and profits. The job is often described as being "at the hub of a wheel"—the brand manager is at the center and at the end of each spoke is a function required to keep a brand solvent: finance, research, sales, advertising, manufacturing, packaging, etc. The brand manager taps into each resource as needed, and coordinates all the efforts to deliver the bottom line.

> *I am brand manager of DiGiorno Pastas and Sauces—a new product under development at Kraft-General Foods in Glenview, Illinois. The line of fresh pastas and sauces is sold in the refrigerated section of the grocery store, which has traditionally been a stronghold of the Kraft sales force. However, because these new products have such a short shelf life, DiGiorno has required the development of entirely new distribution and inventory management systems. Although the product has been in development for a number of years, this month the wheel of development needs to get its spokes to turn together into a presentation to introduce the product to the sales force.*
>
> *DiGiorno had been tried out in test markets for over a year, and the results looked very promising. We were now ready to start "rolling it out" across the country—getting the product into distribution in a number of markets all at once. The first step in doing that is to brief the sales force: give them all the information and tools it takes to enable them to sell it into grocery stores in their regions. We were only a month away from the first round of presentations, and we had to finish all the sales, materials, produce the commercial, prepare the slides and—last but not least—get manufacturing to deliver a final product formulation.*

The development of brochures is usually handled by an assistant brand manager, who is the second step in the brand management ladder. Generally, freshly minted M.B.A.s enter as brand assistants—doing much of the analysis and more tactical work (getting artwork developed and approved, handling promotions, tracking data, etc.). After a minimum of a year, they are promoted to assistant brand managers (ABMs) and take on more and more responsibility until deemed seasoned enough to be promoted to a full brand manager. New products groups tend to have more ABMs and fewer brand assistants—since the work tends to be somewhat more complex and requires more strategic skills. However, as a new product, like DiGiorno, gets closer to being "rolled out" (introduced into the marketplace), the need for a lot of executional work arises and a brand assistant is frequently enlisted.

> *I am reviewing the layouts and copy put together by an outside agency for the sales brochure. This is the second go-around. The first time, the design was poor and the copy unreadable. The ABM came up with the concept in the first place and then had to rewrite everything. We pay these agencies a great deal of money for this work, but we stay very involved every step of the way.*

Assisting the ABM in the preparation of the materials are the professionals who do the consumer and market research. These people have similar backgrounds to the brand managers (often M.B.A.s) but tend to have had more quantitative training. In general, almost anything that could affect sales (packaging, advertising, flavors, etc.) is run past consumers in the form of a test, prior to introduction. Once much of the product research—such as taste tests and in home trial tests—has been completed, the research staff works with the ABM to condense the mountains of findings into a few bullet points that will help convince grocers to stock the new product. At the same time, the research manager works with the brand manager to run some "focus groups" to fine tune the brand positioning.

> *I am sitting in a darkened room behind a two-way mirror watching a dozen women reveal their innermost feelings about pasta. I can see and hear them perfectly, but they don't even know I am here. They usually can't hear me either, unless one of the others watching the groups with me (people from our research group and the ad agency) makes a particularly raucous comment and we all burst out into loud, uncontrolled laughter. Every half hour or so a helpful woman comes in with a fresh bowl of M & Ms or some other snack for us to entertain ourselves with as we listen to these women describe what freshness and convenience mean to them.*
>
> *We are trying to decide what main message we want to communicate: Is it taste? Convenience? Variety? The women in the focus groups all agree that taste is the number 1 concern—"If my husband doesn't like it, then who cares if it's so easy to make," one lady points out.*

Focus group findings are used to help formulate the next round of commercials. The first TV spot to introduce DiGiorno is already in preproduction. A cartoon version of the commercial (called an animatic) has been through consumer testing to determine its ability to motivate consumers into trying the product. The brand manager is in New York meeting with the ad agency, the director for the commercial, and the production staff to plan out the actual shooting of the commercial, which is slated for the next week.

There we are arguing about which pasta and sauce should we show. If we do the white alfredo sauce on the white pasta, it won't show up. How about a red sauce on a green pasta? A red sauce on a white pasta? Once we decide that, we'll move on to the equally critical questions—what should the cast be wearing? What color tablecloth? What pictures should be hung on the background wall? Every element that will show up in the final commercial needs to be discussed. Even though the background elements may not help sell one more carton of sauce, you don't want to distract the consumer from the message you are trying to convey. When you consider how much a 30-second commercial costs to produce (usually well over $100,000), you can see why we sweat over each detail.

While the battle is raging over what serving implements will appear in the commercial, the ABM is struggling through the sales materials back in Glenview. Several layers of management have reviewed the brochure—most importantly the category manager to whom the brand manager reports and the vice president of the division (boss to the category manager). Now on the fifth copy revision of the brochure, the ABM has progressed to commissioning the photography and artwork to be included. The food shots shown will be done in Kraft's studios right in the building and a mini-preproduction session (not unlike the one prior to the commercial shoot) has been held with the photographer and food stylist. The artwork will be done by an outside illustrator.

In the meantime, the entire brand group labors away with paper and calculators to estimate the profit contribution of DiGiorno to the grocers, the sales force, and to Kraft. The brand manger is interacting daily with the finance staff, manufacturing, and sales. The days tend to be loaded with nonstop back-to-back meetings. Each presentation on each aspect is worked and reworked to ensure that the sales force, and ultimately, the grocer and the consumer, become enthusiastic. Since the day is devoted to meetings, the DiGiorno brand group tends to do its work, respond to memos, return phone calls, and sit around to discuss ideas before 8 in the morning and after 5 at night. Frequent long hours and weekends in the office are unavoidable.

We were getting pasta samples from the factory every few days. As we were getting closer to the deadline for the sales samples to be produced (packages of the pasta and sauces to be handed out at the sales meetings and made available to the sales force to use with the grocers), we would come in on Saturdays to taste the latest batch. One day we were getting a little punchy, so we did the classic cooking test for pasta—we threw it against the wall to see if it would stick. It did.

Testing the samples takes place in the Tech Center, located down the street from the headquarters' office. The laboratories in the center look like Frankenstein meets Julia Child—industrial-sized mixers and giant aluminum racks of pasta are tended by scientists in white coats, with advanced degrees in food technology. The product is still going through last minute formula revisions and some of the pasta samples are not quite right. It is agreed that a quick visit to the plant manufacturing the product is needed.

> You have to put on a set of "whites" (white cotton slacks and shirt), a hair net, and heavy shoes and remove all of your jewelry. Then you stand around and look knowledgeable while waiting for the latest batch of tortellini to come off the line. As it comes off, I take a look at its appearance—are the holes the right size, is the color right—and I feel the dough to make sure it's the right consistency.
>
> As the brand manager, I really keep an eye on the product from start to finish. I pay particular attention to the packaging line. Is the label on straight? Is the code date right? How does the product look in the package? All of this could have an impact on how well it sells.

The brand manager takes several of the plastic cartons of pasta back up to Glenview and deposits some with the "kitchens" located on the ground floor of the building. Staffed by home economists, each kitchen resembles a cozy, but state-of-the-art, home kitchen—complete with ovens, microwaves, and refrigerators. The home economists work on recipe development and package instructions.

> This month they have arranged it so all of our tastings are at lunch time. That is a great help—it's hard to taste fettucini alfredo at 9 in the morning. Even though my tastebuds are no different from the average consumer, I am asked to taste things and pass judgment on them regularly. Admittedly, I eat my product so often that I know when it tastes right or wrong, but it is incredible the amount I get to eat on the job—sometimes I'm not sure whether it's a benefit or a hazard of the job.

The product manager has also returned to Glenview to be greeted by disturbing news: the vice president wants to be assured that the plastic packaging is the best possible and has asked for a last-minute competitive packaging test. The packaging experts, the brand group, and the research manager meet in an emergency session to plan how to meet the VP's request. A test plan is put together to ensure a 2-week turnaround, providing a comfort level before the sales presentations.

Two weeks before the sales presentations are to begin, the brand manager heads off for 2 days of a commercial shoot in New York. Filming takes place in an old warehouse in Brooklyn, and the time passes slowly as lighting is adjusted and the actors provide different readings for each of the few lines of copy.

When we were casting the commercial, the agency sent us a reel of actors, with a recommended choice and several alternatives. One of their recommendations was a Swedish actor, which caused some amusement since the spot focused on an Italian meal. We ended up casting an Italian actor instead.

We had a few disagreements on the set. I didn't like the way some of the lines were being read. You have to be careful that the delivery does not denigrate your product in any way. As the brand manager, you ensure that the product you are trying to sell is always the most important element in any shot. It has to look fantastic so that the consumers will want to try it. For example, I also did not like the black background used in the closing shot. The background color had not been specified in the preproduction session, so we ended up shooting it against black with the understanding that if it wasn't the best background color for the pasta shot, we would change it.

The ABM has in the meantime reviewed all the proofs for the brochure and 10,000 copies are being produced by a local printer. Specification sheets are likewise in production—pages which describe the dimensions of the cases of product, provide relevant code numbers, outline the flavors, etc. The actual presentation has been written and rewritten several times and the typed-up pages have been sent down to the graphics department at Kraft to be turned into high-quality color slides (that fit into a carousel projector). The ABM is also putting together a "Jeopardy" game to be played at the meetings. The game will add some fun to the presentations and will reinforce important sales information.

The brand group and research staff gather to hear a presentation from the person (called a moderator) who conducted the positioning focus groups. The moderator reviews the overall findings of the discussion and makes some key recommendations on how the brand group should address some of the consumers' concerns. Although the group has not yet even seen the "rough cuts" (early versions) of the current commercial, they are thinking about the next round of creative—the input into commercials.

Whether you work on an established brand or a new product, you are always thinking of how to modify your advertising. You are always tinkering with your positioning. Are you saying the most motivating things about your product, or is there something more compelling to say? You also know that after a certain amount of viewings, there is consumer "wearout"—consumers are tired of seeing the commercial and are no longer influenced by it. When you develop a new commercial, you hope it will become "campaignable," that is, you can produce new spots, but they stick with the original theme or tone to create an advertising campaign—rather than a single individual spot. These are the advertising issues that you are constantly grappling with and that keep the advertising agencies busy.

One week before the presentation, the group is running through its checklist of what needs to be done before the meetings. A few minor details have not been taken care of due to some uncooperative staff groups. This requires the brand manager to spend some time "coaching" one of the ABMs to determine the best way to get the final tasks completed.

I spend 70 percent of my time managing people. Each of the people who reports to me has a different personality, is at a different career point, and has different needs—so different ways are needed to manage them. It all requires a huge amount of energy. I have to keep my energy up and give everyone the best of my ability. The ABM working on the brochure is very senior and is very independent. I can give her broad areas of responsibility and know she can handle them. My discussions with her these days are either to help her solve a particularly tough problem or to map out what additional skills she needs to develop before she can be promoted to a brand manager.

A few days before the first presentation, the results have come back from the packaging test. Good news, the current packaging is the most durable and cost effective, and no change is needed. The brand group collectively sighs in relief and notifies the plant to make sure that the product samples are shipping on schedule. Airline tickets have been delivered, hotel reservations have been made, and several rehearsals of the presentation have been scheduled.

The flight is booked for the evening before the presentation, which begins early the next morning. The group goes through a final checklist. They have confirmed that all of the brochures and other selling materials as well as the product samples have made it to the regional office where the presentation will be made. The slides have been reviewed and packed carefully into a briefcase along with the animatic copy of the TV spot (the final commercial is not done yet), and the presentation is as rehearsed as it can be. As the brand manager and the ABM head out the door for the waiting taxi to take them to the airport, the brand manager stuffs the mound of paper filling her in-basket into her bag to look at on the plane. The hectic activities of the last month have prevented her from sorting through the pile of memos, reports, and copies of *Advertising Age* on her desk.

We are set for this meeting, but after it's over, we'll go on to the next. This job never lets up and there are constant demands on my time. But

*when I see DiGiorno on the shelves or catch the commercial on TV, I
know that it has been worth all the trouble.*

Commonly Asked Questions About a Career as a Marketing Manager

What Tasks Do You Do Most Often?

Successful brand managers are better defined by the volume of tasks
they *don't* do, as opposed to what few they do. That is, brand managers spend their time trying to get others to do the work that needs to
be done to keep a product line solvent. In terms of tasks, that translates into an inordinate amount of time on the phone, in meetings, or
developing plans and presentations. It is a career built on interacting
with people from a range of functions, communicating with those people, and convincing them to do what is required on the brand. It is
coaching subordinates, coaxing staff groups, haranguing agency executives, and presenting to senior management.

How Much Do You Work with People? Numbers? Computers?

Even in small packaged goods companies, brand managers interact
with people constantly. The nature of the job is that all business is conducted through others. Brand managers in large companies working
on major brands may also have a number of direct reports to help
them conduct business. Working with ABMs and brand assistants can
take up 60 percent of the brand managers' time.

A brand manager, as a mini-general manager, is supposed to be well
versed in his or her "numbers." The specific numbers tend to be volume, spending, and margin. The most junior members of the brand
teams are usually responsible for analyzing all the volumes, keeping
the budgets, and doing any relevant share or competitive analysis, so
by the time they make brand manager, they are comfortable with the
needed numbers.

Students pursuing studies in marketing at business school are often
perceived as less quantitative than their finance-bound colleagues. No
doubt it's because much more time *is* spent in creative areas such as
advertising or package design, and the practice of marketing itself is

not an exact science. In reality, you have to be able to handle pretty basic business analysis and statistics and to take large quantities of data and condense them down into a usable form. To facilitate the analysis, there have been great strides in building databases to help brand managers manage their business. More and more computer equipment is making its way into brand managers' hands. However, it is the more junior people—marketing assistants—who spend more time in front of the screen, doing the routine analysis (also known as grunt work) necessary to track the business.

How Much Time Do You Spend in Meetings? Writing? Other?

A glimpse of a brand manager's date book usually reveals a bewildering display of room numbers, times, and large pieces of days slashed through with swipes of a pencil. It is hard to reach a brand manager by phone during the normal course of the day, and forget trying to invite one to lunch with anything less than 2-weeks' notice. Brand managers dash from meeting to meeting and from building to building. At Kraft, the progression of meetings can begin as early as 7 a.m. and have been known to run late into the night. They are held in one of headquarters' myriad small conference rooms, at the technical center down the street, at the advertising agency downtown, or even in the atrium cafeteria which dominates the center of the building. Because so much of the brand manager's work is dependent on the coordinated actions of a number of people, meetings are the accepted way to get those people acting in sync.

Needless to say, each of those meetings requires some preparation, presentation, and follow-up. There is quite a bit of documentation and report writing on a regular basis. Although much of the persuasion happens in the meetings, there is almost an equal amount happening on paper. You may guess that since the day is spent on the meetings, the writing often occurs before 8 in the morning, after 5 at night, or on weekends. And concomitant with a volume of writing is a lot of reading other's writings.

What Skills Do You Use Most Often?

The power to persuade is what ensures a brand manager a livelihood. Whether on the phone, in a formal presentation, in a written proposal, or in casual conversation in the hall, the brand manager is constantly convincing people to do things. Negotiating with junior assistants or senior management, with outside vendors or internal staff groups, with agencies or food scientists—in every case the success of the brand manager depends on success in getting everyone else to contribute.

Along with the need for the ability to persuade, political savvy is an important skill for the brand manager. Brand management tends to evolve into resource allocation issues—there are limited marketing dollars and staff resources to be allocated over a number of products. The better the brand manager is at office politics, the more resources and support that may come his or her way.

What Training, Education, and/or Experience Are the Best Preparation for This Career?

Brand managers at the top packaged goods companies usually have M.B.A.s and experience at other packaged goods companies. It is hard to break into the field without prior experience or without starting at the bottom as a marketing assistant and working up. There are a few other fields that occasionally succeed in bucking the system—consulting, advertising, or sales—but you have to be truly exceptional to make the change. Brand managers are expected to start contributing on day 1, and skills such as understanding research, media, etc., are built up over time.

There are a number of companies that are known as "training grounds"—notably Procter and Gamble, Quaker Oats, and General Mills. Those three companies pick the cream of the M.B.A.s (P & G will also take extremely talented B.A.s) and train them in the rudiments of brand management.

How Do Most People Get Jobs in This Career?

The easiest, most direct way to start in brand management is to be recruited out of an M.B.A. program by one of the brand management companies. However, given the limited number of companies which are training grounds for brand managers, there are numerous other ways to get jobs in brand management. It is fairly common, for example, for people with advertising agency experience to have the knowledge-base and connections to find jobs in brand management. Once in brand management, the easiest way to find jobs is through executive recruiters. There are a number of firms that specialize in filling marketing positions, and it is usual for a larger marketing company to use recruiters to find brand managers. Networking and using connections helps in finding brand management jobs; ads in specific trade publications such as *Advertising Age* might also pan out. It is unlikely that a brand manager will find a job through a newspaper ad.

What Do People in This Career Have in Common?

Good brand managers come from all walks of life; however, they universally have a good deal of energy and enthusiasm (necessary for motivating a range of people). A trait they all share is that they tend to get wrapped up in their product—whatever it is. You find consummate brand managers looking forward to trips to the grocery store or drugstore, and they will frequently plant themselves in front of their products' shelves or roam the aisles looking at new products. While not all brand managers are creative, they do seem more interested in, and critical of, advertising and media in general. In fact, when brand managers happen to share a Sunday newspaper—they fight over who gets to look at the FSIs (free-standing inserts, aka, coupon pages) first.

How Much Are You Paid?

Competition for talent at the business schools has pushed up starting salaries for brand assistants at the top packaged goods companies to high $40s or low $50s. Current brand managers, despite their years of experience, have watched the differential between their salary and starting assistant's salaries be squeezed by this competitive activity. Brand managers at many of the larger firms make between $60,000 and $75,000 base plus a bonus. Bonuses can range from 5 percent to the 20 percent range—usually dependent on a combination of company, division, and individual performance.

Smaller companies pay substantially less—particularly for entry-level positions or for non-M.B.A.s. Salaries for recent college graduates with no prior experience could be in the $20s, with experienced brand managers making more in the $45,000 to $50,000 range.

What Is the Salary or Compensation Potential?

Although annual increases for brand managers tend to be small, they can increase their salaries by switching firms or being promoted to the next level. Directors and marketing VPs at the big packaged goods companies can have compensation packages well into the six figures.

What Are the Short- and Long-Term Career Opportunities?

Brand managers often fall into several classes: those who are doing it as a step to other careers and those who want to do it for life. Most packaged goods companies are indelibly hierarchical. You crawl your way up from assistant to manager to director to VP over many years. You may switch brands, but you are still a brand manager. You generally are in marketing the whole time, there is only a small amount of movement across functions, and such movement is often viewed with suspicion. Consequently, in the short term you work as hard as possible with the hope of eventually climbing to the next step.

In order to accelerate the movement, brand managers can switch companies, leveraging past experience into a higher-ranking, higher-paid position in a different organization. Some decide to use their general management training and start businesses of their own. Others go to smaller companies or work for suppliers to the world of brand management. But the majority hop from company to company, staying in packaged goods marketing for the bulk of their careers.

What Is the Range of Jobs in This Career?

Brand managers can either climb the brand management track or pursue a related or more specialized field. For instance, a brand manager could take over a promotions department, marketing services division, or account management in an advertising agency. Depending on the company or department structure and as more and more companies develop regionalized structures, a marketing professional may opt for a "field" job as opposed to a headquarters job. Some marketing positions are increasingly more sales related, and it is not unusual to see one vice president over a sales and marketing department. In every case, the jobs can range substantially—a function of the orientation, size, and resources of the organization.

What Provides Greatest Satisfaction? Frustration?

One of the great thrills of being a brand manager is seeing your product on the shelves, your ad on TV, or your coupon insert in the newspaper. There are very tangible results to be seen, and you can have a great deal of impact on the business. Most brand managers get a kick from knowing that thousands of people are exposed to their work daily.

The joy of, say, seeing your new package design hit the shelves is somewhat tempered by the long and arduous process it took to get there. For the most part, changes to formulas or packaging, new flavors, and new advertising have long lead times, which means there are ample opportunities for changes, revisions, and even termination of a project. In reality, the brand manager does not have final say, and all too often a great idea or the brand manager's pet project can be eliminated by the next level up. Often, brand managers have moved on to other brands before their projects are completed. The final product may differ dramatically from the original brand manager's concept.

What Is the Biggest Misconception About the Job?

Few people truly understand what a brand manager does, so misconceptions are plentiful. "Do you write the ads?" No—the advertising agency does. "Do you develop the formula for the product?" No—trained food technicians do that. "Do you come up with the coupons?" Well, sometimes, but it is usually on advice from the promotions department. "Do you have the final say on everything?" No—the brand manager is there to guide the brand, but usually there are VPs and other more senior managers who have enormous veto power. "Do you sell the product?" No—the sales force is there to get the product onto the grocers' shelves. The brand manager is responsible for getting the consumer to buy the product from the shelves.

In other words, the brand manager gets involved with everything, is master of nothing, but is still ultimately responsible for the rise or fall of the brand.

What Is the One Thing You Would Have Wanted Someone to Tell You About This Career?

The brand management track can be fast or slow—but in the majority of cases it is the latter. There are usually very few vice presidents in the larger consumer products companies, and it takes an unpredictable blend of luck, skill, and politics to get there. Consequently, titles and salaries tend to be somewhat suppressed—particularly compared to investment banking (salaries and titles) or even advertising (everyone is a vice president). If you look for positive reinforcement in that form, there is a high probability of disappointment.

What Three Pieces of Advice or Wisdom Would You Give Someone Thinking About This Career?

1. At some point, be sure to work in a company that has a good reputation in its field for marketing. That will help build credibility in your résumé, ensure that you work for people who understand marketing, and help you network later in your career.

2. Be willing to give up some of your free time in the early stages of your career but don't make it a permanent part of your work ethic. Brand management can take a huge commitment of time and energy—there are always more things to do on the brand and more pieces of data to analyze. Many managers get caught up in perpetual long hours and weekends at work. Ultimately, they burn out or lose perspective. You have to be able to set priorities and sort out the things that need to be done which will have a real impact on the brand's success. Everything else is just busy work.

3. Many industries tend to be incestuous—so never burn any bridges. "Incestuous" means that there are a relatively small number of people doing marketing in a given industry, and they all seem to know each other. There is a fair amount of movement across companies, so there is always a high probability that a colleague you didn't care for may show up in a company you want to move to.

15
Production

Scott Springer
Former Plant Manager, Dixie Yarns

One Month in the Career of a Production Manager

Where to start the day? As a plant, or production, manager, everything needs doing right now. Not later, but right now. Today, I start by focusing on the numbers. Managing a plant is primarily a "people" job, but somehow it always comes back to the numbers. If what you do with people doesn't eventually affect the bottom line—well, that's the ultimate feedback, isn't it?

It has been a tough month. The numbers are discouraging. Somehow, some way, we have managed to have only 30 percent of what was supposed to be ready this week actually ready. What are we doing wrong? Is it scheduling? Is it manufacturing? If so, which part of the process? Is it our sourcing? We need to ship 175,000 pounds of fabric this week, but only 55,000 of it is ready. I can imagine what our customers are thinking about us and about their reorders. We have some serious detective work to do in the next few weeks.

A mini-general manager. Always looking for any way to get just a little better or even a lot better. Plant managers have tremendously broad responsibilities and an equally broad choice of options to make things happen. How do they know if they are being effective and if their methods are working? Was the plan as good as it sounded a year ago? To dig out the answers to these and other ponderous questions, plant managers inevitably have to look to the numbers. The trick is choosing the right ones.

Plant managers spend much of their time wondering what is going wrong. Of course, if everything always went right, you really wouldn't need a plant manager. There are enough problems in almost any plant that plant managers must train staff members to be adept at true detective work. Coaching, teaching, guiding—all are critical elements of molding a staff so that problems get solved quickly. Ideally, plant managers train their people so well that problems get solved *before* they get started (or at least before they get serious).

> *When in doubt, form a task team. A cop-out? Hardly—one thing that a good plant manager learns is the value of the collective knowledge within the plant. Give people a chance to solve a problem, and it's extraordinary how many will come through. Progress is not always as fast as I like (have you ever tried to get a group of people with regular, important jobs together for yet another responsibility?); but once you get past the initial problem of coordinating schedules, response is enthusiastic, and results are almost guaranteed. In this kickoff meeting, even the VP of manufacturing (my boss) came down to emphasize the importance of the team. "Get our deliveries on time, or we go out of business," he crows. We meet for 2 solid hours and decide that the first problem we have to fix is the "late report" itself; its accuracy is highly questionable, and we need a good feedback tool to tell us whether we are doing any good or not. Somehow I don't think this is going to be a quick fix.*

The people working for a plant manager tend to be a diverse group of individuals. What are they good at? Can they handle more supervisory responsibility, or would that play to their weakness? Should they be given a shot anyway—after all, the best rewards (at least monetarily) come to effective people managers, those who can take the extra responsibility and get an organization rocking. But if they fail, it is terribly difficult to take them backward to positions of lower responsibility (and pay). So do you really want to promote an outstanding mechanic to shift supervisor? You lose a great mechanic and gain an unknown manager. Despite this, someone has to step up to the plate and show some leadership. One solution is going outside the organization for an "outsider" to fill empty slots, but that is not generally good for morale. So plant managers must choose more carefully than stock pickers, cultivate their assets better than venture capitalists, have more patience than bond traders, and take bigger leaps of faith than consumer products brand managers (well, maybe not that). But in the end, most people succeed, given a little coaching and time.

> *One morning I plan to arrive at 6:00 a.m. to visit with third shift. They work until 8:00, so I should have a good 2 hours to "shoot the bull" with the graveyard operators—they always have a different perspective of what's going on than our more "normal" first-shifters.*

But things are not going as I expected. Overnight torrential downpours have just flooded our yarn warehouse, where over $1 million in inventory sits waiting to be ruined. This, of course, is the first time in 35 years of operations that we've actually had a flood inside the building. I race back to the warehouse, expecting to see a disaster in the making. Instead, I see a situation which, in retrospect, should not have surprised me. My warehouse manager and maintenance superintendent, two dedicated men with a work ethic you may not believe still exists, have already conscripted half the knitting work force to get the yarn off the floor. Damage would be minimal. People in this plant really care about what happens, and they pulled together in this emergency to make the best of a potentially devastating situation. And these two managers made an impression on me which I would not soon forget.

Fortunately, not all is crisis management at the plant level. Real planning and long-term change are critical to staying competitive. The plant manager will get a true chance to practice budgeting, strategic planning, competitor analysis, product planning, process flow, cost reduction, and team building. There never seems to be a good time to partake of any of these luxuries, but if you don't, you won't be in business next year. Nothing is standing still, so planning for the future keeps everything in perspective. To be quite honest, sometimes the planning seems like so much drudgery, and the manager almost longs for a crisis to interrupt the deliberate pace of planning. Parts of the plant manager's job are addictively exciting.

Quality numbers have slipped a bit this month. Our reworks are up to 7 percent. Fortunately, internal QA caught most of the substandard product before it got out the back door, so our reputation is still intact. But what an expensive way to be the industry's high-quality producer.

Everyone in the plant has received at least 4 hours of training in a high-profile "quality first" program. The expense is staggering—over $300,000 in direct and indirect costs. But we lost that much in 3 months due to quality problems, so payoff should be high, if people don't blow this program off as just more tinkering by management. The key to long-term success in quality is getting everyone believing in it, believing that they can make a difference, and believing that management will let them make a difference. Our Quality Improvement team, created to lead the effort in long-term quality advances, gets people involved directly in taking up quality as a personal issue. I could have led the team, but that defeats the purpose of participatory management. Instead, I chose my best department manager to head the team and made sure we included line operators from several areas. They're the ones who really know what is going on—as managers, our job is to get them to use their insight to make improvements.

It would be easy to assume that all a plant manager needs to do is run the plant. But in the position as "top dog" in the mill, the manager also gets to represent the plant to all sorts of visitors. Everyone from customers to graduating high school seniors want to see the operation—of course, the plant manager wants to keep the plant in showcase condition just for these occasions. Actually, many of these visits can be the most enjoyable part of the job. Put on the charm, get the floors gleaming, make the management staff put on ties, and have some fun showing off. A 2-hour tour, if done well, will leave the toughest customers feeling that their supply source is in good hands.

Once a month, the plant goes through an exercise in frustration called physical inventory. I recall a day, fresh out of business school, when I was called a "bean counter" by a plant manager (who didn't foresee my manufacturing-based future). Now, as a plant manager myself, I see how much a good bean counter can mean to a plant. It seems so simple—count your raw materials and products as they go in or come out and then at the end of the month double-check your math. Throw in a little pixie dust, and you can fly, too.

Somehow, the process takes 100 people most of Saturday just to count boxes of yarn, rolls of finished fabric, and everything in between. After I spend an hour working on a problem in the yarn warehouse, I walk down to see how the finished goods inventory is going. My hopes of going home at a reasonable hour vanish quickly as I approach the warehouse and detect hints of mass chaos. Several customers held up taking the fabric they ordered, so the warehouse is dangerously overfull, a condition which makes finding specific rolls exceedingly difficult. Now I have 60 people, each with a desire to spend the afternoon with family, frustrated and disorganized and ready to give up. I gather the four people who know the most about the whole process, and we change it in midstream. Management on the fly—not the best plan, but sometimes the only way to lead. Almost everyone got out by 4:00 p.m., and another crisis was averted. However, the next Monday, when our numbers showed over 400 adjustments to be made in the inventory records, I started wishing for a little pixie dust.

Plant managers must keep the configuration of machinery at the right level. New equipment is expensive and not always necessary. But they simply cannot let their plants slip behind the competition in critical technologies without ending up with crippling cost disadvantages or several quality limitations. To achieve this balance, they have a cast of would-be advisors to assist them. Least among them are vendors selling the new machinery—rarely do they admit any deficiencies in their equipment. However, they do serve the role of keeping various technologies in view, giving a general feel of the current state. Most organizations devote one or more engineers or product development specialists to scan the technology horizon and make assessments.

But the ultimate responsibility (right to the bottom line) rests with plant managers.

Technology, the "savior" of U.S. manufacturing, plays a very effective role as a double-edged sword. As technologies come along, decisions must be made: Is this the right machine? What if a much better one comes along? Do you buy the proven machine (which some of your competitors already have) or go with the unproven, high-risk/reward prototype? How much time, management energy, labor, and product will you really waste during the startup of a machine, and is it worth it?

> *Our new prototype is just not working. We spent over a million dollars on this mass of steel, computers, and gas pipes which make up a continuous fabric dryer. Fabric from this machine, when it comes out well, is very, very good. Unfortunately, we have enough fabric coming out poorly that this has already been an excessively expensive experiment. Every day that we don't get the dryer running costs us in capital and lost opportunity. I spend the afternoon with my department manager and a team from the dryer manufacturer, analyzing dozens of trials, searching for the cause of the problems. The data is fuzzy, like watching HBO without a descrambler, so we end up with some pretty weak hypotheses. But at least we have some direction, so we set up another series of tests. How long will it take until we get it right?*

The old computer saying goes "garbage in, garbage out." This probably started out as a manufacturing axiom. The beginning of making a product right starts at the beginning—the raw materials. If a plant gets junk from its suppliers, it's awfully difficult to make a quality product. One of those painful manufacturing dilemmas is how to achieve the Toyota-revered model of perfect suppliers with just-in-time delivery. Any operational manager will tell you that this is much tougher than it sounds. The "book" answer is to establish long-term relationships with win-win arrangements. This definitely works—in the long run. However, to get to that point, much pain must be endured (probably builds great character). Short-term, marrying a plant to one or two suppliers for each major component can cause plant managers to start thinking about updating their resumés. Learning how to work together, even when the supplier is a vertical element of the same company, requires agonizing months (years?) of adapting. Once there, however, the payoff is worth it.

> *It's my knitting manager on the phone. Yet another disaster has struck— the shipment of yarn we just received, 30,000 pounds of raw materials, is bad. Ouch. I call an emergency meeting of my key managers, hoping we*

can find a way out of this one. Otherwise, our late position is going to get much worse, wiping out all the gains we sweated for.

The session starts with three key floor managers, the QA manager, and the production control manager. The knitting manager rattles off the laboratory analysis of the yarn and pulls out a few yards of fabric to show the extent of the problem. Is there any way we can use this yarn selectively? Some colors hide this particular problem fairly well. Can finishing the fabric with certain chemicals help us? Are there any less-discriminating customers who won't care about this problem? After an hour of heated discussion, we conclude that this really is a bad lot of yarn. Well, there go our deliveries. We'll return the yarn to the supplier, order some more, and start calling customers to advise them of yet more later orders. Will we ever get ahead? More importantly, will my managers ever believe that just-in-time deliveries can work, or will they insist on holding large safety stocks because they know there will always be problems with the yarn?

Communicating with other parts of the company seems easy enough. Most operations managers get a wonderful "opportunity" to improve this communication every month, in a formal review. Depending on the structure of the company, anyone from the CEO down to the VP of manufacturing can be the reviewer. When the story is good, or at least if it holds no bad surprises, the review is not overly arduous. Otherwise....

Everything is fair game for scrutiny. How much money did the plant make? What are the budget variances (which tell how much was left on the table)? Were deliveries on time? How does the plant rate on safety issues? Although the exercise often seems senseless, it is an excellent tool for forcing people to look critically at their operations. Even good managers may think their departments are running well, but if they are forced to analyze the data, they are often surprised by the room for improvement. Then they get on track for making improvement, something they never would have done without the review process.

The monthly review has become quite a production. Just a year ago, each manager presented questionable numbers on hard-to-read overheads just because they had to do something. They put minimal effort into the reviews because they felt their real job was out on the floor, keeping the operation running smoothly. Now the review is a battleground for who has the best, most accurate numbers and who can present them with the most style. Productivity is up 35 percent, largely because we hired a new industrial engineer who fixed the numbers. Before he came, we didn't even know how much our process loss was in any area in the plant. He was one of the best hires I ever made. With their eyes open to reality, and with confidence in the feedback, the managers attacked the task of improving productivity with a vengeance. Standing in front of one's peers and looking like the laggard is not fun. Not only are the numbers better, but every manager now knows how to use Lotus 1-2-3 and Harvard Graphics, so the slides are works of art. What giant strides in just a year.

Have you ever been impressed by someone who remembered your name when you didn't think he or she would? Or, have you ever been truly embarrassed by not remembering someone's name when you know you should? When production managers have perhaps hundreds of people working for them, the embarrassment opportunities are numerous. However, so are the opportunities to impress someone with your astounding powers of recall. The key to it all is to get out and get involved with as many people in the plant as you can. Plant managers spend hours every month talking to anyone they can, everywhere in the plant. They create situations just to be able to interact with operators; they go out of their way to find ways to get to know people better. Then, when managers walk the floor, they can call people by name and also can ask about their family, their hobbies, and other personal issues—a touch that lets people know the manager cares about them.

Before the plant review, we have scheduled a presentation by one of our quality circles. The circles, all 10 of them, take on several projects each year aimed at improving quality in the plant. When they have recommendations, they present them formally to management. The plant review, with division staff present, is a perfect time to have a quality circle presentation nothing like an hourly worker making recommendations to the division president.

Quality is vastly underrated. And undervalued. But when you get the front-line associates, the ones who get paid the least, to put pride in quality first, only then will you get the benefit of any quality effort. The quality circle program, although a carryover from another decade, still works as a way to get the commitment of very bright people who can and do make a difference. Today's presentation is by one of the best groups, six knitting machine operators with only 50 years of education, but also over 50 years experience, between them. What assets they are. Their idea, although simple, is one which will make a big difference in the way their department operates. And giving them a chance to present the idea to their boss's boss's boss, knowing that he will make sure their idea is implemented quickly, gives them a feeling of total involvement. We have never not implemented a quality circle idea in the time I have been in this plant.

As a superb side benefit of the presentation, we all get to know some wonderful human beings a little better. These six knitters are not just associates, but they are mothers and cub scout leaders, wives and choir members, real people with interesting lives. It's an opportunity that no manager should pass up.

A famous strategist once said, "No matter how good your strategy may be, you will lose if you cannot control costs." The converse of that is also true, but plant managers spend a *lot* more time working on lowering costs than on deciding strategy. Every day, every week, they must concentrate their efforts on finding better, more cost-effective ways of operating their plant. Bureaucratic law, which is enforced more strongly than any criminal law, clearly states that organizations will get as fat as you allow them to get. This law holds right down to each and every department. Cutting fat is difficult for anyone to do—it implies that they let the fat get there to begin with, which can be an ego-bashing admission for any manager. The operations manager must create a supportive environment that rewards cost cutting. But even this noble goal must have constraints: Never sacrifice quality or customer service, but cut costs to the bone right up to the very limit.

> *How in the world do they do it? The consultant's report shows that our competitor's costs are 35 percent lower than ours. We pushed and pushed for the last year, but the target just keeps moving. Productivity is up 20 percent over last year, but we obviously have more work ahead of us.*
>
> *The biggest opportunity lies in gaining better control over our material loss. The plant industrial engineer, working closely with the consultants, detailed our measurable waste at 6 percent, which is much better than a few months ago but still way too high. Even more distressing, our "invisible" waste (material loss we can't explain—what a concept) is at 5 percent, an absurdly high number. The I.E. commits to finding out where all this invisible loss is going, and I know he will succeed, at least partially. But he will need the consultants a few months longer, an expense I had hoped to cut out next month. But with the lean staff we run, we must rely on outside experts for extra projects such as this.*
>
> *The other element of controllable cost (corporate and division allocations, unfortunately, are not controllable by the plant manager) is labor. Productivity is up but still lags industry averages. One of our biggest problems is the lack of a usable cost system. Ours measures costs extremely well in yarn mills but was adapted to attempt to cost product in a knitting-dyeing/finishing plant—and it just doesn't work. Fortunately, we have an excellent financial manager on board now, one who has a solid plan for attacking this gaping hole. I hope she can make it work fast; good feedback will definitely strengthen the decisions of my managers and supervisors.*

Plant managers get to make an image choice, one which will be made consciously or made by default. Are they managers who will roll up their sleeves and get out on the floor where the real work is done? Or are they managers who sit up front, a bit afraid to get their hands dirty? This decision not only affects how the people in the plant view the manager, but it also influences the depth of the manager's understanding about how the plant runs. Getting out and trying a few tasks in the plant can give someone a real appreciation for the people who do those tasks day in and day out.

> Expediting *is one of those words that needs to be outlawed. It's a poor way of making up for either inadequate planning or sloppy execution or both. But when an important order for an important customer ends up late, we jump through hoops to get it out fast (without compromising quality, of course). The problem is, all sales account executives believe (understandably) that their customers are the most important, and the plant needs to jump the highest for them. Take my word, it is physically impossible to expedite every order that is overdue—we tried once or twice and just ended up with a big mess. The trick is to not be late in the first place (whoops, there goes another operations cliché).*
>
> *Today, I get to have some fun expediting myself. Although not something a plant manager can devote much time to, expediting can be exhilarating (particularly if you succeed at it). A big catalog retailer needs some fabric right now, and getting it out for them will lead to a big reorder. That's a nice carrot to have out there. I hover over the collar knitting machines as the last ones come off, sling them over my shoulder, and rush over to the finishing department. We slip the collars in between a couple of "normal" lots and watch in satisfaction as they come out the back end of the resin-applying frame. Then I hurry over to the shipping dock, where I get to help throw over 100 forty-pound rolls of cloth onto the truck. Now, if my chief scheduler succeeds in expediting the paperwork (a more daunting challenge than expediting on the manufacturing floor), we'll get the order out. What a rush of adrenaline when you succeed in such a high-payoff, make or break task. All in all, looks like just another day in the life of a plant manager.*

Commonly Asked Questions About a Career as a Production Manager

What Tasks Do You Do Most Often?

Strangely enough, the task a plant manager does the most often is setting priorities. In a plant, there is an endless number of things you could be doing—but which one to do now is the real trick. The plant manager motto is the same as that for most consultants: Don't do everything right, do the right thing. Finding some quiet time, with nobody interrupting, allows managers to focus on their task lists, pushing those myriad "could do's" and "should do's" out and deciding which are the "must do's."

The other absolutely critical task for a plant manager seems simple enough—just showing his or her face around the plant. Walking the floor seems frustratingly unproductive—there are so many other things that should be done—but nothing could be more important. And this means all three shifts. If you don't have enough time to show the "grave" shift people you care about them, too, getting their respect is a lost cause. By getting out, managers get to know the people who really make the product. Everyone in the front office is just overhead, but that machine operator makes things. Who is the truly important person in a plant?

Besides talking with people, a manager gets to know first-hand what is going on in the mill by walking and observing. What's broken today? Who is serious about housekeeping? Are safety rules being enforced? How much inventory has piled up behind various machines? Reports supposedly tell you all these things, but no reports can give you a sense of what is happening like a quick walk in the morning can.

How Much Do You Work with People? Numbers? Computers?

In a plant, people may not be everything, but they're damn close. Fully 90 percent of the time is spent dealing with people, either face to face or on the all-intrusive phone. And in a plant manager's position, a strong obligation exists to be as available to as many people as you possibly can be. Short term, this becomes a near fatal philosophy. When you are available to everyone, and you mean it, people figure it out and actually start to take advantage of that fact. A plant manager may cringe when it's 9:50, there is an hourly associate in his or her office complaining about unfair treatment, three department managers are outside the door with major production and quality problems, and the division president is due at 10:00. But plant managers must listen to people, or they will simply blow them off as idiots who never listen to the ones who know what's really going on. And they do, too, so listening pays off.

Numbers, on the other hand, reveal either a great deal in a very short time or get ignored. There simply is not enough time left to analyze numbers—they must be presented already analyzed so that the plant manager can act upon them. Despite this caveat, the right numbers are imperative for running the plant well. Off-quality percentages, unit costs, budget baselines, capital expenditures, turnover, and (watched with intense, if misplaced, interest) weekly shipments get scrutinized feverishly but never for long portions of the day.

For many plant managers, working with a computer is a near-impossible task to find time for. They rely on others to do computer work for them, which is sometimes like Mario Andretti riding in the back seat. Managers may want to do some work on a computer, but others can do that. What they get paid for is leadership and decision making. Some plants, however, have installed some very sophisticated PC-based decision-aid systems; managers there can use a PC to get current information on plant status, order performance, cost, or other high-impact data. But again, the plant manager is using the computer to receive timely data, not to analyze data with complex spread sheets.

How Much Time Do You Spend in Meetings? Writing? Other?

If vulnerable to "the meeting trap," a plant manager could end up in meetings from dusk till dawn. People, if given the chance, want someone with authority to be at any meeting where decisions are made. If you don't show up for a meeting, you run the risk of making the subject seem less important. Customer meetings are important, quality meetings are important, production meetings are important, crises are important, supplier reviews are important, et cetera, et cetera. Thus, choosing the right meetings to attend will make or break a day. Plant managers must save some time to actually work rather than to meet. Overall, most plant managers probably spend one-third of each day in meetings, but quite a few days end up being one nonstop stream of meetings.

Writing comes in spurts. Once a month, the CEO may require a report from each plant manager detailing the past month's profits and activities. That can be an interesting report to write. Good months are easy to write, but bad months take forever.

Performance evaluations of all the plant staff are due periodically. These are not long in verbiage but take very careful thought and preparation. Other miscellaneous memos make up the bulk of the remaining writing a plant manager can expect to do; overall, writing skills tend to rest most of the time, with notably extreme interruptions.

Perhaps the most underrecognized activity for a plant manager is talking on the phone. Everyone wants to talk to you: customers who want to talk to "whoever's in charge"; the division VP of manufacturing passing along information or demanding action; the VP of sales wanting to know why an order is so late; and, most annoying of all, unknown vendors wanting to know when it would be convenient to "drop by" to see you (answer? never). Smart plant managers train their secretaries to screen their calls so that they can get some things done. Even the CEO should have difficulty getting the manager then!

What Skills Do You Use Most Often?

Three primary skills can make a plant manager. First, an ability to motivate people is absolutely critical. That involves recognizing what motivates those people and the ability to follow through. Short-term motivation often is the focus, but long-term motivation really makes the plant hum. A subset of this skill would be team-building, getting people to work hard together. Getting people to work hard is fairly easy; getting them to work hard toward a common goal—instead of stabbing each other in the back to get ahead—is a real trick.

Second, plant managers must be able to constantly evaluate people's true capabilities. This skill enables them to put together teams with the right people. A recent U.S. president only survived because he had some very sharp people around him to allow him to effectively delegate (some may argue that abdicate is a more appropriate term). Similarly, until plant managers know they can trust individuals to do a job well, they will find delegation a very difficult thing to do. But since they can't do everything by themselves, finding the right people becomes crucial.

Finally, basic communication skills round out a plant manager's primary skill set. As the pivotal "person in the middle," he or she cannot afford to communicate poorly in any direction. Managers understand the strategic and tactical directions under which their companies operate; they must persuade the people with the purse strings that their projects are more important than other plants' projects contending for the same limited dollars, and they must realistically convey plant performance to avoid surprises.

Within the plan, poor communications cause chaos—everyone perceives a different objective. Enforcing discipline while encouraging stronger teamwork and commitment calls for sharp communication skills. With customers, a plant manager's ability to communicate well can make the difference in whether they believe in the products or just write the plant off as another one full of hot air and promises.

What Training, Education, and/or Experience Are the Best Preparation for This Career?

Anything dealing with general problem-solving, identifying cause and effect, will help prepare for this career. A basic understanding of finance and accounting certainly helps for understanding the numbers which will be thrown at a plant manager. Any kind of public speaking can give the confidence needed to be at ease making presentations to the CEO—of your own company or of a key customer. A military background provides a great deal of self-confidence, and many plant managers seem to have a military stint in their résumés. Overall, experience which enhances leadership and decision making will be invaluable for a plant manager.

How Do Most People Get Their Jobs in This Career?

Most people work their way up through the ranks to get to this job. That does not mean they do this with just one company—most do not. Once you reach a certain level within a company, moving up to plant manager means either replacing your boss or someone like your boss in another company plant. That is a very limited set of opportunities, while opportunities in the "outside world" are numerous. Additionally, some bias seems to exist against internal talent. If a plant manager is not doing a job well, replacing him or her with someone from the outside often seems more appealing—"the grass is always greener." But even with company-hopping, most plant managers start out as shift supervisors (usually on third shift) and work their way to the top.

What Do People in This Career Have in Common?

Most plant managers have astounding dedication. That plant is his or her baby, and a plant manager is on call 24 hours a day to protect that baby. Workaholic hours are the rule, tremendous energy is the norm, all because there is always more to be done. A less-dedicated plant manager might be able to keep the boss from knowing, but the people in the plant cannot be fooled. And they take their cue on how dedicated to be from their boss.

Another seemingly trivial commonality is an elephantine memory for names. With hundreds of people working at most plants, knowing individual names really lets them know you care. Some plant managers know not only all the names of their employees, but the names of family members as well.

How Much Are You Paid?

Compared to many M.B.A. peers, plant managers are not paid much. To get rich quick, find a job in consulting or investment banking. Most people choose this career for the impact they can have on real people in real manufacturing, but extravagant pay is not the norm. In general, plant managers earn from $60,000 to $150,000, depending on the industry and size of plant they are running. Many companies will hire an M.B.A. to start out as a shift supervisor. This is an outstanding way to learn some fundamentals of manufacturing, but compensation will start in the low $30,000 range.

What Is the Salary or Compensation Potential?

The end-point of this career path, for those with ambition, is general manager of the company (or division). Along that career path, a plant manager in some companies can earn well into the low six figures. A step up, as vice president of manufacturing, could earn from $100,000 to $250,000, again depending on the company. General managers can go well up from there, but that's beyond the scope of the plant manager job description.

One trend which is dramatically influencing the compensation of plant managers is the growing predominance of large incentive and bonus programs. Some companies allow plant managers to more than double their pay by achieving preset goals for quality, cost, service, or some other objective. In companies offering these plans, the guaranteed pay is lower, but the upside can be much higher.

What Are the Short- and Long-Term Career Opportunities?

Short term, keeping your own job can be a real challenge. Plant managers lead a dangerous life, so doing well in current responsibilities, keeps their attention. Upward mobility presents itself in three forms: a bigger plant to manage, a vice presidency in manufacturing, or a cushy position in division or corporate staff. One former plant manager I know now peddles wares he used to make—he's trying his hand as a salesperson. Many plant managers are doing just what they want to do for the rest of their career—but that can be a precarious attitude. Ultimately, most plant managers are potential candidates for top leadership in the company—they are general managers in their own right, so moving on to top management is a natural progression.

What Is the Range of Jobs in
This Career?

As a plant manager, an individual could be working anywhere from third-shift supervisor to vice president for manufacturing. Typical steps, some of which don't exist in many companies, could include department manager, superintendent of manufacturing, assistant plant manager, and plant manager. Each step encompasses broader responsibility, more authority to fix all the problems that were so frustrating back on third shift, and, unfortunately, greater distance from the great people on the line who are making the plant run so well.

What Provides the Greatest
Satisfaction? Frustration?

Satisfaction comes from watching a "plan come together." Plants set goals for improvement in many areas—and when they achieve these goals, there often is quite a celebration. As goals are reached, plant managers will see the abilities and confidence of their people grow. Getting the whole plant pulling together as a team generates strong loyalty, which can be tremendously satisfying.

Another great satisfaction comes from actually making high-impact decisions. Time and again, consultants bemoan the fact that they can only advise, not make decisions for an operation. The plant manager makes those decisions and can be the one who causes improvements; this is a wonderful feeling to experience.

But the frustration comes from the constant focus on instant results. What were the shipments this week? The profits this month? When things are going great, these pressures are easy to brush off; when times are tough, these pressures seem awfully dangerous to long-term success. But balancing long- and short-term pressures, tough though it may be, is an essential of business today.

Other frustrations are born of the many failures. Not everything works, but the plant manager can't stop trying. Worst of the failures are people failures—someone who did not perform well and does not seem to be capable of improving. Letting someone go is even harder than it sounds.

Finally, events beyond your control can be painfully frustrating to a plant manager. Events such as floods in the warehouse and losing power due to the river overflowing can severely set back on-time deliveries to unsympathetic customers. Catching up is tough enough without Mother Nature intervening.

What Is the Biggest
Misconception About the Job?

The biggest misconceptions are that plant managers operate with iron-fists, what they say is what gets done, loyalties are built by strong paternalistic management, managers know more about manufacturing than people on the line, autocratic management is the best way—don't bother listening to anyone else. Yeah, right.

What Is the One Thing You Would
Have Wanted Someone to Tell You
About This Career?

I would have liked to know how consuming this career can be. Problems and opportunities abound, and a plant manager's mind has to stay in high gear all the time, always afraid of missing that extra edge you need to succeed. What can be done to improve yields, to compress throughput times, to better the safety conditions? The job is never "done," so it is difficult to put it away. Early hours, late hours, weekends, you always feel the need to give more. Being responsible for the financial future of hundreds of people makes that pressure even more intense. But this same pressure is what bears the most satisfaction when things actually work—you know that you have made a difference in a lot of lives.

What Three Pieces of Wisdom or
Advice Would You Give to
Someone Thinking About This
Career?

First, be prepared to be a participant more than a boss. Get your people working with you, not for you, and you will succeed much better. Every example of autocratic management I have seen, at every level of operations management, has failed.

Second, don't be someone who is "better" than others. If you treat people who earn an hourly wage as somehow lesser than those who receive a salary, you cannot ever get them to respect you. You will have injured their dignity, a fatal mistake. Don't enter this career field if you have some innate idea that M.B.A.s are more important than dedicated individuals who dropped out of high school.

Finally, don't take up this career unless you want to do something which really adds value—to individual people, to U.S. manufacturing, and to your own sense of self. Plant managers seem to be able to live with themselves better than people in many other careers can.

16
Property Management

Patricia S. Connolly

Property Manager, LaSalle Partners, Ltd.

One Month in the Career of a Property Manager

My husband and I had been away for the weekend. Another member of the management team was on call—finally a weekend away. Upon returning home, there were several cryptic messages on my answering machine. I contacted the management person on call only to find out that a defective sprinkler head had let go on one of our newly renovated floors at the smaller historic building. The water leaked through five floors of various tenants' spaces. Rather than getting to bed at a reasonable hour and being refreshed for another week of work, we drove to the building to take account of the damage.

We met our newest tenant at "ground zero" as it was warmly referred to. She was also taking account of the damage and was rather good humored (thankfully). She had purchased rain hats, rubber ducks, and carpet deodorizers for all those employees whose offices had been "rained" upon. The general contractor who had helped me build-out the space 5 months ago had been there earlier with the sprinkler fitter. The head was identified as being defective. A number of similar incidents had been reported in the city, and the sprinkler head manufacturer had already taken full responsibility for the damage.

I spent the next month coordinating woodwork, computer repairs, and carpet replacement among the affected tenants and the general contractor. All seemed to be going smoothly until the sprinkler head manufacturer's insurance company subcontracted the claim to an out-of-state appraiser who threatened subrogation unless we all cooperated. (Since we all had been cooperating with one another, this threat came as somewhat of a surprise.) I suddenly became the mediator but was soon forced to contact the State Insurance Bureau to file a complaint because the appraiser became too busy to process the claims for damage. Another learning experience.

A property manager is responsible for everything that goes on concerning the property. Sometimes it is just managing the normal flow of activities, such as leasing, building maintenance, and so forth, but it also can involve a crisis situation. As a property manager, it is important to know how to do everything and keep in the loop on everything, yet to do as little as possible so the next "crises" can be handled. Theoretically this works well if all of the people working at the property pay attention to all the details, catch everything that may potentially fall through the cracks, know all the ins and outs of every task, and never get sick, take vacation, or care about what time of night they get home. But actually, a property manager is involved in everything and sometimes in order to get things done he or she needs to roll his or her sleeves up and "do" something. For people who thrive on being able to accomplish a hundred things at once and still appear cool, calm, and collected, property management is the perfect occupation.

The job of the property manager includes but is not limited to leasing, building operations, accounting, administration, renovations, and everything in between. In larger buildings, some of these functions may be handled by a specialist such as a leasing associate. In smaller buildings, you're it. And Murphy's second law that anything that can go wrong will probably was written with a property manager in mind.

Our computerized preventative maintenance program assists us in anticipating building problems. Because the electrical distribution system is 25 years old, we decided to conduct a thorough examination of the entire system. We have recently hired a new chief engineer who has greater building-specific experience than the past chief. Once again he comes to my office with his stories of doom and gloom. This time, I am forced to listen as he shows me pictures of bus bars within centimeters of each other. Stories of the building down the street come to mind. They had lost their electrical distribution system and had to close the building for a week. Tenants were suing the owner and the management company for negligence.

We hired the best electrical consultant in town and began to detail the problems with the electrical distribution system. We concluded that we had no other choice but to replace the entire system. With a plan in place, we presented our ideas to the owner. With his approval, we presented the plan to the tenants. The project would take 8 months to complete with 13 weekend electrical shutdowns. (If we didn't have any tenants, the project could have been completed in 6 weeks—of course, then we would have an empty building and none of us would be working.) Many of our tenants had little idea of the magnitude of the project. Our major tenant assigned an electrical engineer to attend all of the coordination meetings.

With the assistance of our electrical consultant, we completed the project on time and $200,000 under budget. Our in-house electrician was given a bonus and special recognition at our annual Christmas party. I'm convinced that no one other than those of us at the coordination meetings had any ideas what the risks were associated with this project. This I owe to the in-house electrician.

It is incredible how litigious society has become. Some crazy claims don't get very far (like the person who caught his head between the elevator doors), and then there are some which require that we drop everything. Lawsuits and lawyers mean money and therefore require attention. Since property managers represent the owners, they must respond to legal action. Sooner or later, all property managers get a crash course in the law, whether they want to or not.

I am sitting in a small warm conference room with five attorneys: ours, the owner's, the plaintiff's, the general contractor's, and our maintenance contractor's. Three out of the five were at the last deposition. However, they each have the opportunity to ask more questions. I have been identified as the person who knows the most about the details of the alleged (I have learned to use this word specifically) incident. The alleged incident occurred almost 3 years ago now. We were first notified about 6 months after it allegedly occurred. An employee of a subcontractor to our general contractor allegedly slipped on the garage ramp. This ramp is the entry way to the garage leased by our major tenant. We had hired the special services division of our janitorial maintenance contractor to clear the ramp of snow and ice during the winter months. The contractor would have reported to the building upon the request of our director of security. As a result, many parties are involved due to indemnification language within each of the contracts involved. Our security records show no report of this particular incident. Yet there is a report of a similar slipping incident. The ramp is clearly posted "pedestrians prohibited" and enters the building next to our tenant's security office. I am asked to recall details of snow clearance procedures, construction guidelines, and my interpretation of contract language. Six hours later, the deposition is over.

I return to the building and document everything to ensure that all the interested parties are kept in the loop: the owner, our in-house legal counsel, our in-house risk manager, and those who will still be at the property a year from now when I will be located at another project in another state.

Collecting the rent or other payments is easy. Rent is due on the first or fifteenth of each month, while utility charges usually are billed as incurred. Sounds pretty cut and dry. Not really. When companies get in trouble, the rent is usually one of the first things to slide because eviction is a drawn out process. Other payments also may not be so clear-cut. Property managers can be bill collectors, unpleasant as that may be.

> *Approximately one-third of our operating budget is made up of utility expenses. As a result, energy savings is one way to get major points with the owner. After doing the traditional energy-saving projects (installation of energy-efficient lighting, variable-frequency drives on motors, etc.), it becomes a little more difficult to squeeze out those energy dollars without affecting tenant comfort. As we reviewed the electrical utility bills for the year, we determined that a portion of the building meter consumption could not be accounted for. It seems that during tenant construction, there wasn't enough power to the tenant panel for all of the tenant's power requirements. Rather than asking for direction, the electrical subcontractor wired the tenant equipment to the building meter. From a practical standpoint, the issue was simply resolved: install a meter and back charge the tenant for consumption on a month-to-month basis.*
>
> *I informed the tenant of the subcontractor's mistake, quoted lease language stating that the tenant was in fact responsible for the electrical utility costs, and informed the tenant that a meter would be installed. Issue resolved—I thought. The tenant informed me that although the lease clearly stated his obligations, that was not the "intent" of the lease.*
>
> *Unfortunately, precedents had been set where "intent" did make a difference. I needed to demonstrate patience with the tenant although the owner would not allow us to give in on this issue. This particular tenant heads up a very successful insurance agency. He travels around the world and is rarely in his office. I spend several weeks leaving cryptic messages on his voice mail and with his secretary. The last thing he wants to deal with is lease language and electrical utility charges. However, his accountant won't pay the utility-related charges without specific authorization from him.*
>
> *I set up an appointment with him. He apologizes because he has been unable to focus on the issue and has misplaced my letters. I politely offer him the additional copies I made for his reference. He reviews the information and suggests that he take the opportunity to review the information with his accountant. I insist that the balance must be paid as soon as possible. He commits to authorizing payment within the next week.*
>
> *Business completed, I am prepared to bid the gentleman a good evening. However, this gentleman is in a relationship-building business, and I reconsider the idea of leaving just yet. I notice a dated wedding photo and ask the gentleman if this photograph is of him and his wife. After listening to the gentleman talk about his family for about 45 minutes, my job is complete. The following morning, he contacts me to inform me that a check will be cut that afternoon.*

Property management is people management. A good manager is only as good as his or her people. Therefore any opportunity to demonstrate social leadership should be seized. This involves constant

meetings, informal talks, and continued observation. It is also important to get people together for formal "good" times.

*It's the holiday season again. Each week at the staff meeting, the adminis-
trative staff member assigned to lead the Christmas party task force
updates us all on the upcoming affair. Last year we decided to have the
party at a local hotel rather than at one of the properties—an opportunity
to get away from the work environment. Our theory is that people will be
more relaxed and more apt to have a good time. The day after last year's
gathering, we booked the same room for this year's festivities.*

*During the month, we're involved in signing Christmas cards to be
sent to vendors, tenants, and other business associates. Because we believe
in the personal touch, we commit to personally signing each card—all 200
of them. We use the lunch hour over a 2- to 3-day period to sit around the
conference room table and sign the cards. Team members goof on me
because I have wished our tenant's security director a "secure" new year.
All of this may sound frivolous, but we consider it a good team-building
experience.*

*The night of the Christmas party is finally here. My husband and I
arrive early at the hotel and check in (we intend to demonstrate our social
leadership well into the evening). We arrive at the party relatively early so
that we may greet people as they come through the doors of the ballroom.
People are well dressed and in the holiday spirit. As the time approaches
to make the employee awards, one of the management team members
dresses up as Santa to give out the awards. Another opportunity for the
property team to poke fun at the property managers.*

*The nominations for employee of the fourth quarter are read by the
respective supervisors. It is my job to get people up out of their seats and
up on stage. The honor (a dinner for two) is awarded, and Santa
announces the employee of the year award (dinner and a show). I and the
other managers read the nominations and the award is presented. This
kicks off the disc jockey's dance music. Much to my chagrin, the general
consensus is that the crowd hasn't yet warmed up. The other managers
and I request the music for the latest line dance and dare to make fools of
ourselves once again. After stepping on several toes, I finally pick up the
step. We wave out to the crowd and beg them to join us. We are successful
and the dancing continues until the disc jockey packs up his equipment.
Another successful team building experience.*

The job of the property manager is never done. It's like having to
deal with all the problems associated with owning a home, only multi-
plied by a factor of 100. Little things which often can be resolved easily
in other situations become major problems for a property manager
because of the number of parties who are usually involved. Tenants
and suppliers are just two examples. This makes every situation a
challenge or management opportunity depending on your perspective.

Back at the office on Monday, it is 4 days until the Christmas holiday. Like all other month-ends, it is time to make sure that all of our accounting is in order and tenants are billed on their monthly statements. We review the accounting reports and find everything to be in order with the exception of the utility meter readings. Every once in a while, I need to take a walk to the engineering floor and beat the chief engineer's door down to get the meter readings. After speaking with the chief, we determine that the readings were being held up because one of the meters had been miscalibrated. This was one of those last minute details which slipped through the cracks. He and I make several telephone calls and are able to get the manufacturer's representative in this afternoon. We will use last month's meter reading as a proxy for billing purposes.

Back in the office, I make telephone calls to the contractor completing the punch list on one of our construction projects. He admits that he's falling behind, so I inform the accountant that the dollars retained on the project won't be paid for another week. The accountant puts the invoice aside for future processing. Just another little detail that needs to be tracked.

Commonly Asked Questions About a Career as a Property Manager

What Tasks Do You Do Most Often?

The tasks of a property manager can be split into two distinct parts: those completed during normal business hours and those done after hours. Normal business hours are when the average tenant in the building is working. After hours is anything after 5:00 p.m. during the week and any time during the weekend (fortunately weekend work is minimal after the first year as a management associate).

During normal business hours almost all of the tasks involve working with people. This means making telephone calls, conducting meetings, and walking around the building with a number of different individuals, including the client, a tenant (happy or otherwise), legal counsel, an employee, a contractor, or a salesperson. In this vein, a property manager must delegate, provide direction or answers, present solutions, coordinate activities, and sometimes "harass" contractors and employees who are closing in on milestone dates.

Other work gets the attention of a property manager after hours. After-hours tasks include approving purchase orders, commenting on a variety of letters and documents written by members of the staff, and writing a few letters and reports. Other tasks depend on what's happening in the building or the time of year. The property manager may be working on the budget for the following operating year, updating the most recent quarter's year-end projection, developing a financial model for the building, tightening up contract language for maintenance, writing performance evaluations that can't be delegated, or thinking through the strategy for resolving any one of a number of building concerns. After-hours has also been the time for meeting with the busy tenant executive, discussing strategy with the client, or entertaining corporate personnel (in hopes that we'll win their favor in the future).

How Much Work Do You Do with People? Numbers? Computers?

When starting out as a property management associate, time allocations are 10 percent people, 50 percent numbers, and 40 percent computers. This is necessary to pay your dues. With a promotion to assistant general manager and general manager, a good portion of the number crunching is delegated to subordinates; then the split becomes 60 percent people, 20 percent numbers, and 20 percent computers. The key is to hire and develop people who can do this stuff for you. Then, the property staff affectionately will refer to you as "merely a figurehead."

How Much Time Do You Spend in Meetings? Writing? Other?

Most property managers are accused of always being in meetings. The term *meeting* is used somewhat loosely. A meeting may be a formal coordination meeting scheduled weeks or months in advance or an informal meeting with an employee who stops by the office to "discuss a few things."

Some days are better than others; 30 percent of the time is spent in formal meetings. However, one begins to learn which meetings really require a manager's attendance and which meetings a representative may be sent to. Another 30 percent of the time is used up by informal meetings. A lot of this depends on the management style of the manager. An "open door" policy invites people to meet. It is better to spend the time answering someone's questions or providing direction up-front than to fix a problem after the fact because questions weren't asked or insufficient direction was provided. The more an employee knows, the better he or she will be able to accomplish the task at hand.

Some discussions with employees may be classified as "gripe" sessions. However, constructive listening helps to build rapport. This can be helpful when you need to persuade people to assist you.

A good portion of the rest of a property manager's time is spent responding to the action plan developed during meetings or preparing for the next meeting. This may mean more informal meetings or preparing something in written form. Anything which requires interaction with people generally occurs during normal business hours. Tasks which require a significant amount of thought or dedication are accomplished after hours.

What Skills Do You Use Most Often?

People-management skills are used most often by a property manager. The building operates most efficiently when the entire property management team works together. It is the property manager's job to make sure that each of the individual teams work in harmony to provide quality tenant services on a consistent basis. The project manager must take the heat when things don't work as efficiently as desired. As a result, a good amount of time is spent making sure everyone has what is needed in terms of information to maintain smooth operations.

People-management skills consist of the art of negotiation and persuasion, good listening and communication, basic understanding, and politics. There are a number of tasks required of a property management team which are not considered glamorous. Building operating budgets provide constraints on staffing. The client's capital is also limited. Resources and support depend on office politics and reciprocal relationships.

What Training, Education, and/or Experience Are the Best Preparation for This Career?

In general, professional property management firms consider an M.B.A. and supervisory experience as prerequisites. Because of the operating budget constraints on staffing levels, a property manager is expected to hit the ground running. Others have landed in property management with different skills in addition to their M.B.A.s and have taken a different career path. For example, a recent management associate I knew had banking experience. Initially, he focused on the financial analysis of prospective tenants and moved into more of a leasing role (in contrast to an operations role).

An M.B.A., supervisory experience, strong financial skills, and a high level of confidence are mandatory. A number of people possess these skills. The deciding factor then becomes "personal chemistry." In the people-management business, it becomes very important that one fits in well with the rest of the team.

How Do Most People Get Their Jobs in This Career?

The cliche "It's not who you know... " rings true in the real estate business. Many of the professional property management firms recruit management associates directly out of business schools. Some firms make a practice of recruiting at the nation's top business schools and tend to look for people who possess good general business skills but aren't afraid to get involved in the details when they have to.

Each property manager is responsible for maintaining the proper staffing level at his or her property. Often times when assistant property managers are promoted to manage their own properties, property managers can't wait for corporate's annual business school recruitment. This means that the property manager must search for his or her own candidates. In that case, property managers look for someone with a strong operations background and someone who is willing to "pay his or her dues." Over the past 3 years I have been the person to follow up on all the details. We're looking for that same personality trait. Corporations also use the local properties to screen local candidates who are willing to relocate. These candidates are recommended by management professionals nationwide. Many people have been personal friends of other professionals in the firm. They have the basic skills (M.B.A., supervisory experience, financial skills, confidence); receiving the personal recommendation of another professional within the firm theoretically means that the person also possesses the right "chemistry."

What Do People in This Career Have in Common?

People working with a professional property management firm have a number of characteristics in common, not the least of which is that they are highly motivated individuals with a desire to operate their own "business." These people are challenged by the opportunity to wear a number of different hats in the course of a day. They aren't afraid to get involved and get their hands dirty. They have the ability to work with people of varying abilities and personalities to solve problems on a routine basis.

Successful people pursuing a career in professional property management demonstrate a high degree of patience and tend to take things in stride. Strong financial skills, supervisory experience, political savvy, assertive behavior, and a high level of confidence contribute to this success.

How Much Are You Paid?

A property manager's compensation package consists of an annual salary and a performance bonus which start at $30,000 and go up from there depending on experience, responsibilities, location, etc. Bonuses depend on achieving management objectives which are set at the beginning of the fiscal year. However, salary should not be the only criteria in selecting a career in property management.

What Is Salary or Compensation Potential?

Even though real estate has taken a battering in many markets, the salary or compensation is still good (not great but good). We are in the midst of surviving a tough economy. Despite the failure of a number of property management firms and the return of property management groups within large institutional investment firms, some firms have done very well, although cost cutting, including cutting bonuses may be necessary. Nonetheless, there is the potential to be earning six figures within a 5- to 7-year time frame. For top performers, there is also the opportunity to invest in the firm as an "equity vice president." Dedication, hard work, and making moves which are in the best interest of the firm are how one gets there.

What Are the Short- and Long-Term Career Opportunities?

Career opportunities in property management are good, even in a sluggish market. Through good times and bad, there is always a need for someone to manage properties. In leaner times, there is a greater need for innovation and good tenant service. People are just beginning to realize that the better one manages an asset, the greater the tenant retention and tenant attraction.

Career opportunities are varied depending on an individual's specific skills and the specific needs within a property. Traditionally, an individual starts out as a management associate. In this role, associates pay their dues. By this I mean that they have the opportunity to get involved with the gory details—the number crunching, the bidding out of contracts, the cold calling of prospective tenants, etc. Depending on the size of the project and the size of the management and property teams, the period of time one remains a management associate could range from 3 to 12 months, with 8 months being the average. Relative to working for a large company, this is a short period of time.

Traditionally, one moves from being a management associate to an assistant property manager and then to a property manager. Some take these steps at a single property. More often than not, a relocation is necessary to become property manager. This generally occurs within 3 to 5 years. Longer term, one is a property manager at a number of properties. The firm relocates managers in order to take advantage of specific skills.

The hierarchy is fairly flat. Some property managers become area managers in cities where there are a number of managed properties. Others become regional managers. Still others make a transition into other parts of our business, including client capital, acquisition, investment development, and corporate relocation (to name a few).

What Is the Range of Jobs in This Career?

The range of jobs is equal to the range of property types. Office buildings, retail shopping malls, warehouses, and parking garages all need to be managed. In addition to types of property, there's also the location. The management of a high-rise downtown office building is much different from that of a suburban corporate office park. Once you determine what type of asset you would like to manage, there are a number of areas of expertise to pursue, including but not limited to engineering, construction, accounting, leasing, and administration. One can use any of these areas as a starting point. The strategy is to master each and become a true "general" manager.

What Provides the Greatest Satisfaction? Frustration?

Team work or lack thereof. Hearing from tenants that they really enjoy working in the building and that the team anticipates their needs is very satisfying. This means we're doing a number of things right and that we've developed the rapport and respect that is needed to get a job done efficiently. Building tenants don't want to have to worry about anything but their businesses. If that's all they're concerned about, the property manager has succeeded.

Property managers need to work as part of a team to get a job done efficiently. When, despite our knowledge and experience, we mess up and aggravate a tenant, that's frustrating. As property managers, we don't want to get on the bad side of the tenant, especially a large sophisticated tenant. Large sophisticated tenants can make a property manager's life miserable if they want to. Each time we mess up, we take a look at the problem to determine what we could have done to avoid the confrontation. Often times it comes down to lack of communication and team work—not rocket science. Once the property team is established, frustrations are minimized.

What Is the Biggest Misconception About the Job?

The biggest misconception about property management is that it's not a professional career. I personally held this belief prior to attending business school. I had worked for two large corporations that had very strong professional cultures. I was a snob about real estate. I felt it was something I would dabble with in my spare time. Once I went to business school, I joined the real estate club and determined that a number of firms took a professional approach to property management. Our firm refers to the business as "asset management" in order to move away from the stigma attached to property management. As I interviewed for property management positions, I was amazed at how many people from *Fortune* 500 companies had made the career change to "run their own business" as an asset or property manager.

Another misconception is that as a property manager, one sits and reads the newspaper in his or her office all day waiting for something to happen. Every morning I drive into work trying to anticipate what might occur during the ensuing hours. Every once in a while I'll think I can get some personal task out of the way during the day. Rarely am I successful. I hit the ground running every day and suddenly realize that the day has ended.

What Is the One Thing You Would Have Wanted Someone to Tell You About This Career?

Many people told me that their decision to pursue a career in property management was a "quality of life" decision. I now say the same thing to people looking to pursue such a career, but then I define what I mean by quality of life.

Many people define quality of life as a balance between work and family. The quality that I was looking for was a quality of life at work. To a certain degree, I was looking for a firm and a job where I could feel good about the people I work with. Not that I hadn't felt good about the people at other companies, but there wasn't the same personal "we're in this together" type of feeling. Every day in property management there is a new challenge, and the feeling that there is a team made up of individuals who would support me in resolving a problem provides a quality of work life I will always look for in a company. I like knowing who I'm working with, their families, and what makes them tick. Things can get very hectic. When you can relate to an individual on a personal level, it makes the job go a lot more smoothly.

Many people will interpret quality of life as working only 8 to 10 hours a day. This job requires more than that. My average day is 10 to 12 hours long, and I always bring my work home with me (at least mentally). When it snows, I'm not only concerned about my driveway at home, but I'm also concerned about the plaza and the garage ramp at the building. This job becomes your life. What makes it all easier is that the property team spends a good amount of social time together. Each of our spouses is an integral part of the team, too. When there's a tough job to get done, it makes things a lot easier when your spouse knows who you're working with and understands what the process is. The "balance" between work and family then becomes a lot easier.

What Three Pieces of Advice or Wisdom Would You Give Someone Thinking About This Career?

First, if you're thinking about a career in property management, you must be honest about how involved you want to become in your job. Similar to running one's own business, this job can become your life. If you enjoy being concerned about a property and the individuals who help you pull it all together, from a quality of life standpoint, this career will work for you long term.

Second, "never let them see you sweat." Often times I will tell people that all one needs is common sense to efficiently manage a property. People will look to you for the answers. Sometimes things get pretty hectic. Know how to keep your cool. The biggest problem of the day will be small by comparison when looking at the list of issues resolved over the past month. The secret is maintaining your cool, thinking through the issues logically, and not being afraid to ask for assistance every now and then.

Third, ask questions and share information. You will be expected to be the expert on just about everything. In order to become the "guru" of property management, you need to learn from everyone working with you and in the industry. Much of this expertise will be based upon experience. If you haven't had the experience, ask someone who has. The people in this business are great for sharing "war stories" because of the status one derives from resolving major building issues.

17
Real Estate

Harriet Hinson
Broker Associate, Re/max Achievers

One Month in the Career of a Realtor

An ideal month would consist of prospecting every day from 8:00 a.m. to noon, lunch from noon to 1:00 p.m., previewing or showing property from 1:00 to 3:00 p.m., solving problems and following up with phone calls and leads from 3:00 to 5:00 p.m., dinner from 5:00 to 6:00 p.m., listing appointments, negotiating contracts, or prospecting from 7:00 to 10:00 p.m. with Thursdays and Sundays as days off.

Well as long as I have been in real estate I have never had an ideal month. Real estate is an emotional roller coaster, and you are in for the ride of your life. People buy and sell residential real estate on emotion. It has nothing to do with logic. Real estate agents are usually dealing with the largest single investment that people make. Purchasers want to make sure it is the right home for them. Realtors are actually a part of the family for the period it takes the purchasers to find the right home. There is great satisfaction when the home closes and everyone is so happy to move on with the next step in their lives. It's a great feeling and the realtor made it happen.

> *Imagine getting to the office at 8 a.m. and expecting an ideal day. I'm on the phone prospecting, and an emergency call comes in. I quickly take the call and find the purchaser crying hysterically on the other end. After calming her down, I find out that she has just discovered thousands and thousands of honeybees in her new home. The honeybees have built a nest between the first two floors of the home the purchaser is supposed to be*

buying in 2 days. I have been over to this particular home many times and have never seen any honeybees. The honeybee nest was hidden and the purchaser just happened to walk around the back of the home before she went to work one morning and saw bees flying in and out through a tiny hole between the first and second floor on the back of the house. The lender will not lend any money on the home until the honeybees are removed. That means, I'm not going to be closing on this home until the bees are gone. I stop what I am doing and find a honeybee specialist to go over and remove the bees. Once I have found the specialist and have gone over to let him into the home, I wait for him to get the bees out and find out it is a 3-day process. That means going over to the house at least three times to unlock the door, let him in to do the work, and then make sure the door is locked when he leaves. I have to do it because there is no one else to solve the problem. After thinking I have solved the problem, more problems creep up. Who is going to pay for this honeybee specialist and when is the closing going to take place? The closing will have to be postponed because this transaction is supposed to take place in 2 days, and it will take 3 days to correct the honeybee problem. I have to make many phone calls to explain the situation to the present owner of the home and then to the lender. I have to get the closing attorney to postpone the closing, and then I have to solve all the problems related to the postponement of the closing. I have to keep all parties informed on the progress of the honeybees and the closing date. I have to work out the details of the payment to the honeybee specialist and reschedule the closing date so it is an acceptable time for all parties involved. This happened one morning when I was on track for my ideal day.

A realtor specializes in selling residential or commercial real estate. There are two ways to sell property: (1) working for the sellers to sell their properties to purchasers or (2) working for purchasers to find property for them to buy. Therefore, a real estate agent is constantly searching for people who want to sell and people who want to purchase real estate.

Most real estate agents work as independent contractors. As independent contractors, realtors work for themselves. They only get paid when they close a sale. Once a realtor has found the property and negotiated the details, it generally takes 30 to 45 days to close a sale. Therefore a realtor must have enough money to continue to sell other properties while waiting for the first one to close. As an independent contractor, realtors are responsible for their taxes and all their benefits. They have to keep track of all their expenses, making sure to pay their federal, state, FICA, and self-employment taxes.

Once a person decides to become a real estate agent, he or she is opening his or her own business—a business that is only as good as he or she makes it. In order to have a successful business, a realtor has to continuously prospect to find sellers, people who want to sell their property, and buyers, people who are ready to purchase property within a given time period.

There are millions of problems that arise out of real estate transactions. A real estate agent has to be a problem solver. No transaction is ever the same. No home is ever the same. There are unique circumstances that crop up on every transaction. Once realtors think they can't be surprised by any more unusual circumstances, watch out.

Some of the more common problems one is faced with as a realtor are: (1) home did not appraise, (2) home has termites, (3) spouse does not want to move, (4) work on home prior to closing is not completed, (5) purchasers were not qualified for the loan, (6) sellers worry why their house has not sold, and (7) purchasers worry why they cannot find the perfect home. One of the main things you have to remember is that there is no perfect home. No perfect home exists. There is always going to be at least one problem with every home. Purchasers and sellers always justify this problem in some way.

The purchaser wants a level back yard and a five-bedroom home but finds the perfect five-bedroom home with a steep yard. If the desire for this particular home outweighs the desire for the yard, the purchaser will justify the yard by saying that dirt can always be added to make it level.

When a realtor is working for the seller, the realtor's job is to market the seller's property and try to get the highest possible price in the least amount of time with as little inconvenience to the seller as possible. A realtor has to come up with some creative ideas to sell the property. Real estate agents have to spend a lot of time coming up with listing presentations and marketing plans. They are usually competing with other realtors and their marketing plans for the business. Real estate agents have to continuously update their listing presentations. The listing presentation usually includes (1) building rapport with the sellers, (2) asking questions about the home and financing, (3) viewing the property, (4) establishing a salable price for the home through a comparative market analysis, (5) company's benefits, (6) realtor's benefits, (7) marketing plan for the home, (8) reviewing contracts, and (9) closing the sale. A realtor usually has to be the best in order to get the listing on the seller's property.

After receiving the listing, the realtor is responsible for marketing the seller's property to the public and to other realtors until the home is sold or the listing expires. In marketing any home, one has to make sure the property is priced correctly in order for it to sell. Price is the key to selling one's listings. In order for realtors to price property correctly, they have to know the inventory. Learning the inventory takes a great deal of time and experience. Every market is different and any news can affect the salability of a home. If the interest rates go up, there will be fewer purchasers able to buy the property. Every time the interest rate goes up 1 percent on a loan of $100,000, the purchase is in effect buying $10,000 less home than before the interest rate went up. Realtors have to constantly be aware of the changes in the market so they can best inform the sellers.

In order to market the seller's home, a realtor has to get the seller's property in the best possible condition. This is called "staging a home." This means telling the sellers to (1) paint the front of the house, (2) pull up or replace the carpets if they are old, (3) get rid of unneeded items by having a yard sale or renting a storage unit, (4) clean the home thoroughly, (5) display fresh-cut flowers, (6) remove all pictures of family members, (7) turn the stereo to an easy listening station, and (8) put vanilla on the oven to give the aroma of freshly baked cookies. How the seller lives in the house is not necessarily how it will sell. The home has got to look as spacious as possible. It has got to smell good to appeal to the purchaser's senses. The purchasers have to mentally move all the seller's furnishings out of the house before they can move their furnishings and themselves into the seller's house and make it their new home. The purchasers will know in the first 15 seconds if this is their new home. Therefore, the seller's house has got to look good, or the seller has to be willing to take less for the property.

I listed a house for sale that had been on the market for 2 years before I got the listing. The seller was very discouraged because he felt the property was priced correctly and had not sold. Before I agreed to take the listing, I had to decide why this house had not sold. After seeing the property, it was obvious. This house had no curb appeal. It was painted a fluorescent yellow, the yard had not been worked on in months, there were no flowers or shrubs, and there were no shutters on the home. No one could get past the exterior of the home because it was so ugly. The owner agreed to paint the exterior, plant shrubs and flowers in the front yard, and put shutters on the home. I priced this house at the same price as the previous agent had. The house sold within a week, and the seller was so excited that he continues to send me referrals.

Once a realtor has been hired by the seller, there is lots of pertinent information that needs to be taken care of. Some of the paperwork that a realtor needs are the listing agreement, the first multiple listing service and the metro listing service computer profile sheets, loan information forms, the seller's disclosure forms, a copy of the survey, and a copy of the deed to secure debt. Realtors may need to take pictures of the property, get keys made, and put a lockbox and a sign on the property. Back in the office, the realtor has to input all the information into the computer and mail all the necessary paperwork.

In working for the seller, a realtor has to determine who is going to purchase this house and then focus the marketing efforts toward that market. This may include advertising the property to the public and to other realtors in the area, holding open houses, having theme luncheons, making a flyer on the property, and distributing flyers to the public and other realtors. Realtors have to create interest in the homes they are hired to sell.

On two different homes that I was hired to sell, I had to decide who was going to purchase these homes. I knew that both of the homes were close to a college. Knowing that students move in and out at the end of a semester, I knew I had to focus on the students' parents. They had the money to purchase property. It would be a good investment for them. It was likely that through appreciation the home would make money when their children were ready to graduate. I made some flyers and posted them at the student center and the housing office at Emory University. It was at the end of a semester. Parents came to get their children, saw the flyer, called me up, and bought the homes. In both instances, the parents were proud of their children for making good grades and wanted to reward them. The homes were also good investments for the parents.

Once a contract comes in on the property, a realtor is responsible for helping the seller negotiate the best possible price. Real estate agents have to know what the contracts say so that they can best advise the seller about the merits of the contract and explain their concerns if they have any. Realtors have to show the sellers how much money they would net after expenses when the homes closed. When receiving a contract, a seller can do one of three things: reject the contract, counter the contract, or accept the contract. As soon as the contract is accepted, all parties have to fulfill the obligations that were agreed upon in the contract before it can close.

Realtors who are working for purchasers must find their buyers the best homes at the lowest prices possible. Before showing anyone property, realtors should make sure that the purchasers are qualified to purchase the property or they are wasting their time. Once the purchasers have been prequalified by a loan officer, the search is on for their new home. Once that home is found, the realtor has to write a contract and hope it will be accepted. Usually, the seller counters the contract and the purchasers then decide if they want to accept, counter, or reject the offer. Once the contract has been accepted, the property is then under contract. Then the home must be inspected and the buyer must receive a clear termite letter, an appraisal, a home owner's insurance policy on the new residence, and finally the official loan approval before the closing can occur.

When I first started selling real estate, I had a purchaser who wanted this home very badly. She was prequalified to purchase the home although she could barely afford it. Her loan-to-value ratios were very tight. Loan-to-value ratios are the ratios lenders use to establish how much money they will lend a purchaser. Loan-to-value ratios are based upon the purchaser's income and debt. Finally the day came and the loan officer called to say the purchaser had final approval on her new home. The purchaser was so excited that she went out and bought $5000 worth of furniture for her new home. We went to closing less than a week later. The loan officer pulled up her credit report one last time to make sure her ratios were still in line. To make a long story short, she lost the house because she had bought the furniture. She had all this furniture and had nowhere to put it. I learned a good lesson that day. The purchasers I work with cannot make any major purchases until their home is closed.

An important clause for a realtor to write into contracts when working for the purchaser is one which makes the contract contingent upon an acceptable inspection. An inspection will tell the purchasers everything structural, mechanical, and electrical about the home they are purchasing. Inspectors are hired by the purchasers at a small fee. Inspectors check all the circuit breakers, the appliances which remain, the cooling and heating systems, and the roof for leaks; they also check for termites, wood rot, and radon. Inspectors go through the interior and exterior of houses with a fine tooth comb and then give the purchasers estimates of costs of items that need to be repaired or replaced. Home inspectors tell you how much longer roofs and systems in the home will last before the purchasers can expect to replace these items, and they tell purchasers how to maintain their homes.

Once I was showing property to a minister who wanted to purchase a brand new home for his wife and two children. He picked a lot and the house plan he wanted. The builder for this particular subdivision was very well known throughout the Atlanta area for building high-quality homes. We wrote the contract and the contract was accepted. It usually takes 4 months to build a new home. So for the next 4 months, the purchaser would go by every day or every other day and check on the progress of his new home. After 4 months went by, the home was completed, and everyone was ready to close on the home. The day before the closing was supposed to take place, the minister and I went by for a final walk through the home. We noticed some of the interior walls were starting to crack. We hired a structural engineer to inspect the home because we were concerned about the cracks. The structural engineer said that one of the main support beams under the home was missing. Over time the home could cave in. We showed this problem to the builder. He couldn't believe that his contractors overlooked this major support beam. He told us not to worry, that he would raise the house a couple of inches and install this support beam. Well, when he raised the house, all the exterior walls cracked. It was incredible. I had never seen this happen to a brand new home. The purchaser did not want a defective home, and he did not want to go through with the closing. We got him out of the contract and everything was fine. I learned a good lesson; even if a house is brand new, I will always recommend having an inspection on the home before it closes.

The process of working for the purchaser is a little different from working for the seller. If purchasers want a realtor to represent them in the transaction, they sign a buyer's broker agreement. It is very similar to the listing agreement signed by the seller. The purchasers are hiring a realtor to find them a home in a certain time frame and in a certain price range. The real estate agent is obligated to the purchasers to tell them all the information gathered that would influence their decision.

A realtor would then input all the information on the purchasers' ideal home into the computer and would preview the houses that the computer selected. After previewing these homes, the realtor would take the purchasers back to see the best ones.

Before previewing a piece of property, a realtor has to call the listing agent to make sure it is still available for sale and to tell the other agent that he or she would be representing the purchaser if he or she were to bring in an offer on the listing. The realtor must also give the owner of the property a courtesy call to say he or she will preview the home. It takes a long time to actually catch people in the office or at home just to let them know about plans to preview the seller's property.

After previewing the properties and selecting those that meet the purchasers' criteria, the realtor is ready to show them to the purchasers. Again, before showing the homes, the realtor has to call all the sellers to let them know he or she will be showing their homes to potential purchasers the next day. Usually, if a realtor is going to see a home for the second time, the owners will really spruce up the house. The owners are, of course, hoping that the realtor has the new purchasers who will buy their house. In most of the houses the realtor and the purchasers would see, the scene would be set, with every light on in the house, the stereo playing soft soothing music, the home filled with an aroma of freshly baked cookies, and everything organized in its proper place. Whenever a Realtor is showing property, it is always best for the homeowners to leave so the purchasers feel more comfortable. The purchasers have to feel comfortable opening the sellers' closet doors, looking underneath cabinets, and opening refrigerator and oven doors. It is hard for purchasers to do this if sellers are standing around watching them. If the purchasers don't feel comfortable, they will not buy the home. The purchasers will usually know immediately if this is going to be their next home.

> *Once I was showing property to a newlywed couple and we had already seen five homes. We were about to see the sixth home, I rang the doorbell and no one answered, I took the key that was in the lockbox and proceeded to open the front door. I yelled out, "Hello, this is Harriet Hinson with Re/Max Achievers here to show your home." Again, no one answered. I started showing the purchasers around the house. The home was really staged, it was beautiful. Well, I finished showing the purchasers the first floor; we walked upstairs to the second floor and there was a huge entertainment room that had glass windows overlooking a gorgeous pool. There was a waterfall coming out of the rocks above the pool spilling into the water. It was truly spectacular. We looked down at the pool and saw the sellers in the water skinny dipping. The sellers were not embarrassed in the least. They got out of the pool and wrapped towels around their bodies. The husband said, "We really have enjoyed the privacy of this backyard. Let my wife and I get out of your way so you can feel the freedom that we have had in this home." Well, the sellers got dressed and left the house. No sooner had the sellers left the house then the purchasers said, "We want this house. This is our new home." We went back to the office to write the contract, and they had the home under contract by the end of the night. I have never seen a home staged more than that one to this day. The newlywed couple now own this home and call frequently to tell me how much they are enjoying it.*

Before an offer can be presented, the real estate agent needs to find out the price the seller paid for the home, the improvements the seller has made, and what other homes are selling for that are comparable to this one in the same neighborhood. The purchasers can decide what they want to offer for the property. The prices, terms, and conditions have to be agreed upon by all parties involved.

The most important way to be successful in real estate is to prospect. There are many ways to do this. The secret is to continue to search for clients on a regular basis. Realtors get full-time clients to work with by calling those with "For Sale by Owners" signs, expired listings, a particular area out of the phone book, past customers and clients, absentee owners, and other realtors, especially out-of-state realtors. Realtors also walk door to door, meeting people face to face, to see if they have any real estate needs. The bulk of realtors' time should be spent prospecting if they want to stay in the real estate business.

Before prospecting, realtors have to be mentally prepared to be up, very confident, and enthusiastic. Their voices will reflect this feeling through the phone. Realtors have to be knowledgeable about real estate. Listening to real estate and motivation tapes in the car and watching real estate videos is a great way to find the motivation to prospect and to think about improving business. There is no such thing as a successful, unknown real estate agent. Realtors have to become household names in the areas they work in. This can be very expensive and very time consuming.

All real estate agents need business plans that identify their goals for the next year. They should always want to increase the number of transactions they do from year to year. They cannot measure how they are doing in the real estate industry by measuring sales volume. Sales volume fluctuates every year. They can only measure real estate by the item that remains constant, the number of transactions they actually close. The average real estate licensee sells around three homes a year. The average full-time real estate agent sells approximately seven homes per year. In order to be successful in real estate, one should strive to sell 50 homes per year. A realtor's business plan should include the following:

1. Objectives (what one wants to accomplish)
2. Plans for accomplishing these objectives
3. Financial goals (how many deals will be done?)
4. Office goals (how many people are going to be hired?)

Remember, real estate agents don't work for anyone, so they have to set their own business goals: the amount to spend on business expenses, the amount to invest back into the business, the number of homes that will be purchased this year, the amount to invest in health insurance and retirement fund, etc.

Once realtors have a business plan clearly defined and broken down to the last detail, they know how many hours they are going to have to work in order to accomplish their goal—and realtors are only working when they are face to face with qualified clients who are ready, willing, and able to sell or purchase homes. Remember, listings are the name of the game.

If a realtor gets a call from a realtor from California who knows some purchasers who are going to be moving to Atlanta and wants the realtor to find a home, of course, the realtor would be delighted to help them find their next home in Atlanta. They fly down and the realtor has to introduce them to Atlanta, then the different areas of Atlanta, so they can get a feel of what it is like living in different areas. It takes a week of driving them around all day for seven days, but finally they purchase a home. How many listings could the realtor have gotten that week? A real estate agent has to weigh each client every week. Which one do you want to work with? Real estate agents must control their time and their clients or someone else will.

Realtors should hire employees to work for them as soon as they can afford to. They should hire as many assistants as they need to handle work projects that will free up their time. With more time, realtors can afford to prospect more, get more sales, and ultimately have more closings. Real estate assistants should be able to handle incoming calls, computer work, input all information into the computer, make flyers, deliver documents, place lockboxes on doors, place signs in yards, place ads in papers, call other agents for feedback on properties shown, arrange all the realtor's luncheons, and basically keep the realtor organized. A real estate assistant should do everything that the real estate agent doesn't have time to do. Hiring an assistant frees up the agent's time to list more property, negotiate more contracts, prospect more, and show more property.

When realtors have other people working for them, they have to spend some time managing the office and keeping employees excited about the business's success. Managing employees becomes a little easier if they are self-motivated and they know what needs to be done every day.

With all the help I get from my assistants, nothing will ever replace the excitement that I feel once I have sold the seller's house or found the perfect home for the purchasers. Even though there are many problems to solve and details to work out, every day is different. There is no routine of repeating the exact same day because I am always working with different people with different personalities on different emotional levels. As a realtor, I have to wear many hats and relate to many types of people. I love meeting people and listening to their experiences, their viewpoints, and knowledge about life. It makes me see life through other people's eyes. When people share their lives with me, I am able to learn about their lifestyles and match them in the right locations and with the right homes. Real estate is a great business because everyone wants to own their own home; it's the American dream. I want to share their excitement and make their dreams come true.

Commonly Asked Questions About a Career as a Realtor

What Tasks Do You Do Most Often?

Most of my time as a realtor is spent on listing presentations, showing property, negotiating contracts, and prospecting. Listing presentations need to be constantly updated. Realtors need to read magazines and books and attend seminars and real estate courses to be knowledgeable about the current information in their areas. Showing property is a necessity in this business. People will not buy property until they have seen it. Negotiating contracts is critical in making all parties have the feeling of a win-win transaction. If purchasers and sellers don't have a meeting of minds and feel good about their decision, the whole transaction can go sour and a real estate agent will have a hard time ever making it to the closing. If realtors could choose only one task that they do most often, it would be prospecting. Prospecting is a realtor's livelihood. A realtor must constantly look for people who want to purchase or sell property within a given time frame and are ready, willing, and able to act on their decision.

How Much Work Do You Do with People? Numbers? Computers?

The real estate business is a service-oriented business. If realtors are not around people, they haven't got a chance to sell a seller's house or to sell the purchasers a home. Realtors are around people all the time. When realtors are with sellers and purchasers, they have to know how much the sellers are going to receive from the proceeds of their houses and how much the purchasers can invest in their new homes. That's where the numbers come in. Realtors have to be good with people and numbers.

As for computers, I have three of them. I don't know everything about how to run them, but my business revolves around computers in keeping up with prospects, letters, flyers, promotional items, advertising, business plan, graphs, and expenses. Computers are the way of the future; you need to own a personal computer in real estate.

About 7 years ago, one of my co-realtors got a personal computer. He was so excited about learning how to run the computer that he spent all day, every day at the office on his personal computer. He would read all the manuals, play with all the numbers, and tell all the other realtors in the office how they needed to invest in a computer. He spent so much time with his computer that he lost his focus on selling real estate. He is no longer in the real estate business.

I didn't want this to ever happen to me. So, I hired a computer expert to work for me. I know how to get around on the computer, but I don't know every program that I have. He does. So if you are getting into the real estate industry, spend most of your time with people not with your computer. Computers cannot buy or sell homes.

How Much Time Do You Spend in Meetings? Writing? Other?

Realtors do not spend a lot of their time in meetings or writing. The bulk of their time is spent with people who have real estate needs. When real estate agents meet purchasers and sellers, they usually spend 1 to 2 hours reviewing the process of the real estate transactions. Realtors need to explain the whole process of buying and selling a home. Everyone needs to be informed so that miscommunication will not occur. Realtors frequently meet with other agents to spread the news of their new listings on the market and their buyers' needs. Keeping a good rapport with other agents in the industry is important. It will help a realtor sell more property because other agents will be willing to work with them. Realtors need to attend real estate seminars to stay current with new laws that will have an effect on their business.

What Skills Do You Use Most Often?

The skills I use most often are writing and negotiating contracts, preparing and giving listing presentations, and showing people property.

What Training, Education, and/or Experience Are the Best Preparation for This Career?

I think in real estate, you have to be good with people, good at negotiations, good in math, good in business, and a very hard worker. There is no one background that realtors come from. All types of people are successful in the real estate industry because a realtor sells to all types of people. A college education is not required to become a real estate agent. Realtors who are not strong in one area, need to hire someone with strength in that area.

How Do Most People Get Their Jobs in This Career?

In order to become a licensed real estate agent, you must pass your state's real estate exam. To become a realtor, you must pass your local real estate board's exam and promise to abide by the Rules and Regulations and the Code of Ethics.

After becoming a licensed real estate agent, research the companies, interview with different managing brokers, and pick the one that offers you the greatest benefits for your needs. It is a mutual decision. You are interviewing the company as much as the company is interviewing you. The company makes more money by having more agents. You will be an asset to them.

What Do People in This Career Have in Common?

There is no one trait that people have in common in the real estate industry. Realtors have to enjoy selling property and to be able to withstand a lot of rejection. Realtors have to be flexible with their time and have to be well organized. Realtors have to have empathy for their clients' situations and never forget that buying and selling homes is an emotional transaction. It is probably the biggest investment clients have made. Providing professional service and having empathy for your clients is probably the most important trait successful realtors have in common.

How Much Are You Paid?

The average full-time realtor makes approximately $12,000 a year. Who in their right mind would want to be a realtor? Well, real estate is a business that builds on itself. The longer realtors are in the business, the more they will make. A realtor works really hard to get a paycheck. Most agents are paid a percentage of the sales price as their fee. The company's pay scale determines how much of this fee the realtor will actually receive. All companies have different fee structures.

In most companies the company gets 50 percent and the agent receives 50 percent of all income (fees) that the agent generates. If the company gets a percentage of an agent's fee, it usually pays for some of the agent's overhead, which usually includes signs, marketing tools, training, and some advertising. An agent's income usually increases with a higher percentage going to the agent and a smaller percentage to the company after the agent has increased production in transactions closed.

Real estate companies that do not get a percentage of the agent's fee receive a monthly payment from the agent. Real estate companies that pay 100 percent of the fee to their agents usually attract more experienced agents who are inclined to sell more. These agents usually treat real estate as a business. Real estate companies that pay 100 percent do not provide training to new agents.

What Is the Salary or Compensation Potential?

Your salary is only limited by yourself. What you sell is what you make. You can make as much as you want. It is all a mindset. You are what your mind believes you are. Napoleon Hill said, "What mind can conceive, your heart can believe, you can achieve." I believe this.

When I first got into real estate a co-realtor of mine asked me what I thought a good income for me would be. I thought about it and I said, "$30,000." At that time I was 23 years old, and $30,000 was a lot of money. He said, "You are limiting yourself to $30,000, and you will never make over this because your mind is limiting you." I decided at that point in my life that I was going to restructure my thinking. Top agents can make a million dollars a year and more.

What Are the Short- and Long-Term Career Opportunities?

I have been offered many jobs since I have been in real estate. Once people see you at work, they know you are dedicated to provide them with the best service you can. This is a good quality for any business.

If you get burned out in selling real estate, which has not happened to me, you can always become a managing broker or maybe even open your own real estate company.

What Is the Range of Jobs in This Career?

There are many jobs in the real estate industry. You could sell commercial real estate; manage office buildings; manage residential real estate; manage investment property for people; become a leasing agent for apartments, offices, or homes; or become a real estate speaker, an appraiser of property, a loan officer, or interior designer specializing in staging homes. The jobs in this industry are limitless.

What Provides the Greatest Satisfaction? Frustration?

The greatest satisfaction in being a realtor is negotiating the deal. It is a wonderful high when you have gotten the best deal for your client. The other party doesn't know that your purchaser would have paid more for the home or your seller would have taken less for the property. In negotiating, all parties leave the transaction thinking it is win, win, win. Inside, you and your client know they have gotten the best deal of all.

The biggest frustration in being a realtor is that it is a hard business to get away from. Your clients don't want you to leave town if you are working for them. They are afraid that something might happen, and you will not be there. You are the cement that holds this emotional transaction together. If you are not there holding their hands, they think everything will crumble. Therefore, your clients want you to be there for them all the time.

What Is the Biggest Misconception About the Job?

Most people see real estate as a part-time job. I see real estate as a business and as my profession. People think if an agent sells a house or two a year, or if they see the check an agent receives at a closing, that the real estate agent is getting paid too much. People don't realize that real estate agents only get a portion of that check and that the check has to be reinvested back into the business to pay gas, marketing tools, employees' salaries, and just create more business. The public perception is that anyone can become a real estate agent or that a real estate agent has an easy job. This irritates me.

What Is the One Thing You Would Have Wanted Someone to Tell You About This Career?

You are married to this business. It gets in your blood and doesn't let go. Real estate can be the hardest job in the world to do with the least amount of money earned, or it can be the best job with the most money earned. You decide what you want it to be.

What Three Pieces of Advice or Wisdom Would You Give Someone Thinking About This Career?

1. *Concentrate on getting listings.* You could get five listings in one week, or you could spend a week working with one purchaser. Weigh the potential of a possible five homes sold to one home sold in 1 week. Which would you pick? You cannot get listings unless you prospect.

2. *Market yourself.* Spend the bulk of your advertising budget to promote yourself. If you don't promote yourself, no one else will

either. You want people to think of you every time they think of real estate.

3. *Learn the market.*   You will never be able to give good service unless you learn the market. You need to be able to walk into a home and know what it is worth. You need to be able to tell your sellers that their prices are too high if they are. You need to be able to tell the purchaser what the value of a home should be. Always be honest. If you lose your reputation, you are out of business. I think that every time you give good service to someone, they tell about 10 people. If you do give bad service to someone, they tell 250 people. Always, provide great service; your reputation depends on it.

18

Restaurant Management

Deborah Cashin
Vice President, SouthTrust Bank of Georgia

Jason Cashin
Restaurant Manager, Ernie's Steakhouse

One Month in the Career of a Restaurant Owner or Manager

Late Friday Night, 11:56 p.m.
It was a great night—one of the best ever. New sales records were broken, the customers were in a good mood, the staff was quick and efficient, and all the equipment was in good working order. To top it all off, clean-up was a breeze, so everyone was able to leave earlier than usual. I feel satisfied with the team's performance, and I'm looking forward to praises from the boss when she sees the nightly sales numbers.

Early Saturday Evening, 8:14 p.m.
What else can go wrong? The dishwasher broke down, one waiter never showed up and I can't find a replacement, two customers got into a rather loud argument at the bar, and efforts in the kitchen are disjointed. The worst-case scenario is unfolding—customers are getting tired of waiting and are migrating to the competition's establishment next door. No matter what I do or how hard I try this is not going to be a good night. There must be an easier way to make a living.

Every restaurant manager or owner knows that each day is different in the restaurant business. Unlike other businesses where projects can last for days, weeks, months, or even years, each day is a new project, start to finish, in the restaurant business. Good days follow bad days which follow good days, etc. While it is possible to do advance planning and preparation to ensure that a quality product is served efficiently by courteous staff, one minor thing like a broken refrigerator or a shortage of lettuce can slow down the entire flow of the restaurant. When problems arise, the manager's job shifts from overseer of what is largely a repetitive process to crisis manager. Flexibility and creativity are two attributes which serve the manager well during these inevitable crisis moments. The manager must never forget that this is a fast-paced environment where many decisions are made in mere moments, oftentimes right in the presence of the expectant customer. The manager's goal is to make it appear to the customer that he or she is running a clean, efficient, friendly restaurant—no matter what the circumstances might be. The restaurant business is fiercely competitive and customers can choose where they spend their hard-earned dollars. If customers sense (and they will) that the commitment is lacking, they will disappear quickly, putting the survival of the establishment—and the manager's job—in question.

In its purest form, the restaurant manager's job is to oversee a repetitive process. Organization is critical—all systems must be operating at peak levels to allow the manager and the staff to complete required tasks quickly and efficiently. The one caveat here is that curve balls are the rule rather than the exception; some are significant enough to derail the best-laid plans. Once managers accept that this is an inevitable part of the job, they develop the ability to recover quickly and thereby become transformed into seasoned, competent operators.

A typical day for an owner or manager of a restaurant might look something like this:

8:30 a.m.
I arrive at the restaurant to prepare for the lunch crowd, which usually starts to arrive at 11:30. The cooks, dishwashers, and waiters begin to arrive to assist me with this process. I hope the evening crew closed out the computer properly and cleaned up adequately or else I will be finishing their job now. That would be an undesirable situation because I have barely enough time to complete my own assigned tasks. I check the inventory for shortages—there should be adequate supplies on hand if inventory orders were placed appropriately. If we are short of any items, it may not be possible to serve everything on the menu. Fortunately, I work for a chain operation where I can "borrow" product from another location. I would be out of luck if I worked for a one-restaurant operation.

I begin to set up the kitchen, bar, and dining tables. While as the manager I am responsible for overseeing the entire process, the compressed

time schedule requires that I pitch in as well. If all scheduled personnel show up, this entire process should flow smoothly. At times, however, there will be no-shows, which will force me to scramble for replacements.
11:30 a.m.
The lunch crowd is beginning to arrive. At this time all stations should be ready for operation. My job is to make sure that everything runs smoothly to ensure that the customers get both good food and good service. As the overseer of the process, I will be moving around constantly—helping out in the kitchen, refilling empty water glasses, interacting with the customers, bussing tables. More importantly, I am there to manage situations before they turn into crises. A crisis is defined as any situation which results in a negative experience for the customer. This situation may be as indirect as a back-up in the kitchen caused by a broken dishwasher or as direct as a complaint about the attitude of the waiter. How well I handle the situation will determine whether or not people are satisfied, repeat customers as well as one-time visitors.
2:30 p.m.
The lunch crowd is just about gone. Now I will have a few hours to attend to administrative details before the dinner crowd arrives. These details include ordering food and beverage inventory, preparing the payroll, interviewing potential staff, meeting with vendors, preparing the weekly work schedule, meeting with health inspectors, and other miscellaneous projects. The pressure is off for a few hours—now is the time to get things in order to prepare for the next rush.

Most managers usually work one shift per day. For example, if the manager works the day shift, his or her hours might be 8:30 a.m. to 5:00 p.m. The evening shift would begin around 2:00 p.m. and finish after closing and clean-up. This is not a hard and fast rule since some shifts can be significantly longer, say 10:00 a.m. to 10:00 p.m. The restaurant owner or manager should expect to work well over 40 hours per week. The average work week is 50 to 60 hours, minimum. In general, restaurant personnel work the hardest when most others are not working. Eating out is something people do on their time off, typically lunchtime, dinnertime, weekends, and holidays. If the manager does get a day or two off during the week, it will rarely be a Friday or Saturday night since those evenings are generally the very busiest times.

No matter how good the food, no matter how courteous and efficient the service, factors outside of the manager's control can affect the level of traffic at the establishment. For example, if the home team is in a national playoff game, expect smaller crowds because people will order pizza and watch the game at home. A recession always affects the restaurant business because people are watching their expenses. Access is another issue. The customers must be able to find the restaurant and have access to it—many people knowledgeable about the industry say that success in the restaurant business can be summed up in three words: location, location, location.

5:00 p.m.

The dinner crowd is beginning to arrive. This is a repeat of the lunchtime drill with the exception being that the dinner and lunch crowd have different definitions of "good service." The critical element at lunchtime is speed of delivery. While the lunch crowd wants courteous service, they demand quick service so that they can get on with their day. This is especially true of office workers who usually get just an hour for lunch. It is also in my best interest to have a quick turnaround in order to maximize the number of customers served, which translates into additional revenue earned.

The dinner crowd is more interested in ambience than quick service. For most people it is the end of their work day, the time for relaxation and entertainment. The entire experience—food, service, atmosphere—is what the dinner crowd expects. I assume the role of "host" rather than "expediter," as is the case at lunchtime. My primary goal is to guarantee a pleasant experience for customers to ensure that they return.

11:00 p.m.

Assuming that I am not working for an establishment which remains open for 24 hours, now is about the time when I close for the evening. Typically, a handful of customers will be finishing up at closing time. I begin to supervise clean-up of the areas which are out of sight of the clientele, such as the kitchen and stock room. I also begin some of the lighter chores in the dining room area such as closing down the bar and running the computer tapes of the night's sales totals. After all of the customers have left, I can supervise the completion of the remaining chores such as vacuuming and mopping the floors, refilling the tabletop condiment containers, dusting, etc. My goal is to get ready for the morning crew so that they are not left to clean up anything from my shift. Normally, the close-down process takes 2 to 3 hours to complete. If major problems arise, the process can take significantly longer. Some example of major problems include register sales totals which are out of balance with individual customer checks, cash balances which do not equal the cash sales total, and inventory discrepancies such as the computer showing that we sold 10 steaks while the pantry inventory indicates that we sold 12. In these situations, I must exhaust all efforts to resolve the problem.

At this time congratulations are in order for all of the new managers who have just completed their first day on the job. How do they feel? They're probably bone tired because they spent most of the shift on their feet. In addition, they may have walked the equivalent of 4 to 5 miles on repeated trips between the kitchen, the dining room, the bar, and the pantry. Most now realize how physically and mentally demanding this career can be.

Recall that each day is an individual, discreet project in the restaurant business. In other words, what managers actually do better come darn close to what they are supposed to do. In many professions, tasks can be postponed or delayed if time runs out. Can you imagine postponing clean up of the restaurant for a few days? Or how about postponing the ordering of inventory? Postponing the lunch hour? OK, you are probably thinking that all businesses have tasks which cannot be postponed—what's different about the restaurant business? The difference is that it is the type of business where most of the tasks cannot be postponed beyond the target and point of the project (i.e., closing time).

Having said this, two constraints define how managers complete their work. These constraints are working with perishable items and the human factor. Both are extremely tricky elements to work with from managers' perspectives, oftentimes creating a gap between what they are supposed to do and what they actually do.

Managers work with perishable items as a natural consequence of this business—a restaurant is in business to serve food, which is a perishable item. Controlling this factor is critical to the manager's success. The consequences of running out of inventory are that all of the items offered on the menu cannot be served, which will displease the customers. If the problem persists, the restaurant will be hurt by a decline in traffic, which translates into a decline in revenue. The consequences of keeping too much inventory is spoilage. For example, the manager will want to avoid having a 2-week supply of steaks on hand. Since it would be unethical, as well as bad business practice, to serve spoiled food to customers, the only alternative is to dispose of the spoilage. If this becomes a chronic problem, operating expenses will soar and eat into profits. Most restaurants work on very thin profit margins and are not in a position to continually absorb expensive inventory mistakes. Costly errors must be avoided.

> *I must make fairly accurate weekly projections about what food items, and the quantity of these items, I will need to run the restaurant. While this is not an easy task, I have learned to use historical sales and purchase data as my guideline. Fortunately, I have established good working relationships with all of my purveyors, and I am comfortable discussing with them issues such as price, quality, delivery schedules, service expectations, and product availability. I've noticed that as they get to know my business better, they make helpful suggestions and offer workable solutions to my problems. Another important aspect of my job is cost containment. I must stay focused on ways to reduce my food and beverage costs. One time I ordered too much lettuce and ended up throwing out half of it. My expenses were really high that month. This mistake happened because*

I didn't listen to my head cook when he told me that we would never go through that much lettuce in 1 week. This illustrates a very important point—sometimes the best ideas come from my staff. Over the years I've learned to listen to their suggestions, and I make it a point to encourage all of my staff to participate in this activity.

The second constraint for managers, which is at the same time the most frustrating, the most rewarding, and certainly the most time consuming, is the human element. Many restaurant managers and owners say that roughly 99 percent of their time is spent managing the staff and the other 1 percent is reserved for all the other important tasks. A restaurant manager must be part psychologist and part parent to the staff. To understand this comment you must understand the motivations of the individuals who populate this business.

There are low barriers to entry in the restaurant business. With few exceptions, high school or college degrees are seldom required. This means that the labor supply is plentiful, which translates into low wages, oftentimes the minimum wage, for all but the managers and owners. Low barriers to entry mean that the manager will probably experience high turnover because there are many potential employers in the market. To succeed, the manager must be able to motivate a staff of people who are making low wages and have other options.

You would not believe how many people I've hired who have quit after a few weeks once they earned enough money to buy a leather jacket or a stereo system. I've watched many people pick up restaurant positions when they are in between jobs in their field. Actors seem to practice this quite often: They will keep the restaurant job to pay the bills until they can find another acting job, at which time they will quit. A day doesn't go by when I don't have some personnel problem. Yesterday I had to console one of my waitresses who was upset by a customer's rudeness. The other waitresses had to cover her station while she calmed down. Last week one of my cooks almost walked out after his girlfriend called to break up with him. Fortunately, I talked him into staying on the shift by convincing him that this job is his livelihood and should be just as important to him as an ex-girlfriend.

The successful manager must learn to deal with these and other situations when the staff performs at sub-par levels. Remember, the manager is responsible for the level of performance of the entire staff regardless of their moods or the personal issues affecting their lives. To consistently achieve superior results from employees, managers must discover the technique which motivates them to do their best—this will vary with each different individual. Some will want praise. Others will want sympathy. Some will be happy with the knowledge that the manager is available to listen to their problems. The manager will undoubtedly spend an inordinate amount of time both coaching and encouraging the staff. These are the people who make the process flow. While taking particular care of them is time consuming, this practice will ultimately make the manager's job as overseer of the process easier in the long run. Over time, most managers usually come to view human resource management as the source of their greatest challenges and greatest rewards. Many successful restaurant managers and owners have worked their way up through the ranks; accordingly, most view their participation in the staff's personal and professional growth as a source of great pride and make this one of their primary goals.

A typical month is made up of 20 to 30 of the typical days described earlier in this chapter. In most cases managers work varied shifts; thus, they may work the day shift on Sunday, Monday, and Thursday, the night shift on Friday and Saturday, and have Tuesday and Wednesday off. If they work for a restaurant chain, they may even work in different stores on a daily, weekly, or monthly basis. Turnover is prevalent, so managers might find themselves moved into different management or staff positions regularly. This statement may sound contradictory, but change is a constant in the restaurant business.

In addition to scheduled hours, managers must take a physical inventory of the stock at least once a month. Shrinkage is high in the restaurant business; responsible management practices dictate that physical inventories are taken at least monthly. Physical inventories are usually taken on the first of the month, and all managers are required to attend, regardless of whether or not it is their day off.

Finally, managers may be required to attend weekly or monthly management meetings to discuss events and issues affecting the establishment. Larger organizations tend to have regularly scheduled management meetings in order to keep the network informed. Smaller chains or single entities may meet infrequently, if at all.

Despite all of the hassles and frustrations which are part and parcel of the restaurant business, I really enjoy what I do. I have a great time working with people and relish the ever-changing, ever-present challenges of running a profitable, efficient operation. My moments of greatest satisfaction come from situations when I am called upon to "save the day." At times like these I muster all of my experience and resourcefulness to ensure that my customer is not disappointed. One time we were hosting a 50th anniversary party in our banquet hall. While we were serving the appetizers, the couple's daughter told me that the cake hadn't arrived yet. She was extremely distraught because she had been planning the party for months and wanted it to be perfect. Since there

*was no time to lose, I put my assistant manager in charge and called up
a friend who worked at a bakery. She quickly decorated one of their cakes
and delivered it to the restaurant in time for dessert. I saved the party,
and I felt good. The good feeling lasted at least until my next crisis at 10
a.m. the next morning.*

Commonly Asked Questions About a Career as a Restaurant Owner or Manager

What Tasks Do You Do Most Often?

Food and beverage preparation is the primary task of restaurant
owners or managers. Many of the tasks which they undertake are
related to this overall purpose. Managers are primarily overseers;
however, they must be ready to jump in to take on any task which
needs to be done. For example, they may be cooking hamburgers 1
minute and bussing tables another—whatever it takes to meet the
ever-present goal of providing quality food and beverage items to
the customers.

Another major task is clean-up. After a few weeks in the business,
most managers believe that all they ever do is clean up. They are
forced to do this by two different groups—customers and health
inspectors. Both are capable of shutting down the operation, although
each group uses different methods. Customers merely disappear;
health inspectors come armed with court orders. Cleanliness is a number 1 priority.

Finally, the most time-consuming task is management and motivation of the staff. To accomplish this, managers need good interpersonal
skills and a generous supply of patience.

How Much Work Do You Do with People? Numbers? Computers?

Roughly 85 percent of managers' time is spent working with people.
They must enjoy working with people if they hope to become successful restaurateurs. The two groups which are of critical importance are
the customers and the staff. Only slightly less important are the vendors and inspectors. Managers need to establish good working relationships with all of the individuals in these groups.

Approximately 10 percent of the time is spent crunching numbers. Managers are responsible for preparing the weekly work schedules and tabulating the regular and overtime hours for the payroll. Managers of smaller operations may be responsible for preparation of the company financial statements and tax returns. A larger operation would probably employ an outside CPA to do this work. Other numbers-oriented tasks relate to cash control and sales information. At the end of each day, managers must "balance the books" to see if the sales figure on the register tape matches the individual customer checks. They must be sure to pay particular attention to the cash sales figure to ensure that it agrees with the actual cash received. Recall that restaurants operate on thin margins: Managers cannot afford the consequences of poor financial controls.

Unless the manager is with a large, sophisticated company, 5 percent or less of his or her time is spent with computers. In many locations the registers are the only computerized items present. One rarely sees many personal computers with fancy software packages in the back office of a restaurant—they are too expensive to justify the type of work which they do.

How Much Time Do You Spend in Meetings? Writing? Other?

Depending upon the size of the company and its management philosophy, managers may find themselves in weekly, monthly, or annual meetings or in no meetings at all. Larger organizations tend to have more frequent meetings in order to keep the network informed about new ideas, issues, policies, etc. Smaller companies may meet once a month or less because the network is small enough to allow for information to be passed on person to person.

During any given week, managers probably find themselves in two to three meetings which include third parties such as vendors and inspectors. Vendors include food and beverage purveyors, fixture suppliers, and furniture salespeople, to name a few. Occasionally, managers are visited by the various inspectors who are there to ensure that the restaurant meets the required safety and cleanliness standards.

Unless managers work in a large organization (all of which seem to have an ongoing love affair with the interoffice memo), they spend very little time writing. The manager's most important form of communication is the spoken word. Writing takes up no more than 5 percent of the time, maximum.

What Skills Do You Use Most Often?

Many of the skills which managers must be able to employ have something to do with people. The restaurant business is a people business—managers must be prepared to spend the lion's share of their time at work in the public eye. Good interpersonal skills will serve them well as they interact with the staff and, most importantly, the customers. Regarding staff members, the manager is responsible for motivating each and every one of them to provide the highest level of customer service. Regarding customers, the old saying "the customer is always right" definitely applies to the restaurant business. As discussed earlier, the customers have many choices when deciding where to spend their entertainment dollars. Managers who win all of their arguments with the customers may end up losing overall as customers take their business elsewhere—permanently.

Other critical skills relate to flow management. Restaurant managers must be very organized to ensure that the food and beverage service flows smoothly at all times and particularly at peak times, namely, lunch and dinner. They must make sure that all the inputs are present and in good working order. Key inputs include people, food and beverage inventory, water and power, equipment, and service inventory such as plates, glasses, and silverware. In essence, all of the skills necessary for keeping the system and its required inputs in prime condition should be the top priorities.

What Training, Education, and/or Experience Are the Best Preparation for This Career?

Restaurateurs can rise to the top via many avenues. By and large, many owners and managers ascend the ranks after years of hard work and dedication—oftentimes without the benefit of an advanced degree. On-the-job training is critical in the restaurant business—arguably the most critical piece of any manager's training. It can be safely said that one of the reasons why the restaurant business is a popular career choice for so many is because formal education is not a must. In fact, the two qualities which a manager must have, common sense and good interpersonal skills, are gleaned more from life experience rather than from the classroom.

Having said this, two exceptions must be noted. Those who aspire to become chefs must be willing to attend a school which has a culinary arts program. Admission is competitive and the curriculum is grueling—the goal of these schools is to create the world's greatest chefs. After their formal education is completed, many aspiring chefs opt to apprentice with a master chef to hone their newly acquired skills. After this apprenticeship period is over, these individuals can move into the top slots at the world's finest restaurants where they are given both creative flexibility as well as a generous salary.

The second exception arises for those who set their sights on the top spot at a large restaurant chain. Many of the larger organizations have hundreds of locations; efficient management of an empire of this magnitude is achieved through the efforts of a highly skilled management team. Those competing for these spots probably possess a combination of formal education and hands-on work experience. In this circumstance a college or even an M.B.A. degree may become a necessary supplement to work experience.

How Do Most People Get Their Jobs in This Career?

Most restaurant employees simply walk in and apply for a job. Many career restaurateurs start in the business at an early age and stay with it, transforming what was originally a part-time job into a viable career. It is likely that you know many people who at one time worked at a restaurant. High school and college students pick up restaurant jobs to earn spending money. Contract workers such as actors or artists may hold down restaurant jobs to pay the bills between engagements. If all of the people who ever worked in a restaurant stayed in the business, there would be an oversupply of workers in this field. Most people, however, move on into other careers, thus ensuring that there is always room for new entrants into the industry.

What Do People in This Career Have in Common?

The restaurant business attracts people who are independent and entrepreneurial. Many enjoy the flexible work schedules which give them great freedom to pursue other interests. Many aspire to open their own restaurant someday. Most prefer the unstructured, congenial environment which tends to prevail in all but the most formalized operations.

It would be safe to say that at any given time many of the individuals who currently work in a restaurant are not planning to stay in the business for long. The restaurant industry is a very transient industry where annual job turnover rates of 100 percent or higher are not uncommon.

Most career restaurateurs are outgoing, extroverted individuals because so much of the job involves contact with others: customers, coworkers, bosses, vendors, and inspectors, to name a few. Anyone who believes that dealing with other people is either tedious or unenjoyable will not last in this business. As a consequence, the industry is populated by outgoing, sociable individuals who initiate a fun, upbeat working atmosphere at most establishments.

How Much Are You Paid and What Is the Salary or Compensation Potential?

There is an old saying in the restaurant business which goes something like this: To make $1,000,000 in the restaurant business, start with $2,000,000. This is a not-so-thinly veiled warning that the restaurant business is a risky one. More restaurants fail than survive. There are many reasons why restaurants fail: poor location, poor management, and weak operational practices and controls. Successful operators work hard and pay attention to the basics—the payoff is handsome financial rewards for their efforts. Realistically, an owner's annual salary potential can range from negative numbers to millions of dollars.

The chef's salary can range from $50,000 to a few hundred thousand annually. Many chefs aspire to own their own establishments. If they are successful, their salary potential can be significantly higher.

The annual salary for an assistant manager or manager can range from $20,000 to $60,000. Regional and divisional managers of chain operations can earn salaries ranging from $50,000 to $120,000.

Finally, waiters and waitresses can earn $12,000 to $50,000 annually. Many waiters and waitresses in the finer restaurants are highly skilled operators who have turned this job into a career. The lion's share of their salaries are derived from customer tips. Therefore, the higher the menu prices, the better the earnings potential. Positions of this caliber rarely turn over—people who land in these jobs tend to hang on to them. To reach this level, you must be willing to work hard and ascend through the ranks.

What Are the Short- and Long-Term Career Opportunities?

In the short term, here defined as 0 to 3 years, most individuals start out as dishwashers, table bussers, waiters, or waitresses as they learn the ropes. From these ground-floor positions, a dishwasher might be promoted to cook and a table busser to waiter or waitress. The high level of turnover characteristic of the restaurant business ensures that opportunities exist for those who want to move up. Occasionally, the opportunity to become a manager is presented early on in one's career. This is an unusual situation because as is the case in most businesses, turnover decreases as one moves up the ladder. Larger organizations naturally provide more advancement opportunities sooner than smaller organizations because they have more positions to fill. As a general rule, when thinking about the short term, be prepared to remain in the restaurant learning the details of operations.

In the long term, here defined as over 3 years, an individual may become a maître d' or manager. Larger organizations have more layers of management, including district or regional management positions. Individuals in these slots are in charge of a number of restaurants in the system. A cook may aspire to a management position or might opt to return to school to become a chef. The ambition of many in the business is to become an owner. This goal can be reached by those who work in both large and small operations, by those who work as managers or chefs. If restaurant ownership is your long-range goal, you should be able to reach this dream through hard work and determination.

Another long-term career path option involves entering other food-service-related fields. For example, on occasion restaurant employees are offered positions with one of the establishment's vendors as an account representative selling to other restaurants. The entire food-service industry is enormous—restaurant employees have many potential career choices, including retail establishments such as grocery stores, caterers, and supermarkets, wholesaling establishments responsible for getting the product from the manufacturers to the retailers, and product manufacturers. Each of these entities has human resource needs in sales, marketing, operations, and administration. The point here is that while a restaurant job can become a fine restaurant career, it is also a stepping stone to other food-service-related careers.

What Is the Range of Jobs in This Career?

Each individual restaurant must have the following positions filled in order to operate properly: waiter or waitress, dishwasher, cook, bartender, and manager. Many operations also have hosts to greet and seat the guests, and workers to help the waiters, waitresses, and bartenders with set-up, service, and clean-up. In some locations, due to the size and/or complexity of their menus, division of labor may occur within these functional positions. For example, a fine dining establishment may have a chef who specializes in the preparation of sauces, another who creates the desserts, and another who oversees the entire kitchen. Very often the management itself is delegated among two or three assistant managers who report to the general manager. Larger restaurant operations have positions such as district and regional managers to enhance management control in the organization. These managers may be responsible for as few as 5 restaurants or as many as 30, depending upon the nature of the operation. The degree of complexity of the operation dictates the amount of management resources required. Larger operations also require a significant amount of support staff; individuals in these jobs serve in various capacities such as financial management, human resource management, marketing, advertising, and new product development. Essentially, larger operations offer many job opportunities, some of which appear to be only remotely related to the operation of the restaurant.

What Provides the Greatest Satisfaction? Frustration

Most restaurant managers say that they get the greatest satisfaction when everything "clicks." Recall that managing a restaurant requires great coordination and organizational skills: The payoff for the painstaking attention to detail is a smooth, well-run system which gives the customer good food *and* good service. Whenever you are in a restaurant and the flow appears to be effortless, remember that a dedicated staff planned it that way.

Another source of satisfaction reported by many managers involves the people management side of the business. For example, teaching new employees the right way to do their jobs or motivating an employee to keep working even though a customer was rude or tipped poorly provides great satisfaction to most managers. Turning a discontented customer into a satisfied one is another aspect of the job which many find to be very rewarding.

Generically, sources of frustration can be described as breaks in the chain. A break can be defined as a purveyor who does not deliver goods when promised, equipment which breaks down, or employees who show up late or who don't show up at all. When these situations occur, the manager is left scrambling to fix the problem in order to ensure that the operation runs smoothly. Sometimes the manager cannot fix the problem—at times like these he or she may be unable to serve all items offered on the menu and/or provide exceptional service to the customer. Unlike many other jobs where a hang-up in one project is easily overcome by postponing it and accelerating work on another project, the restaurant project (i.e., the shift) cannot be postponed because management has made a commitment to the public to be open during specified hours, serving items listed on the menu. If any necessary system input it unavailable, management must be ready to fulfill the commitment to the public no matter what the circumstances.

What Is the Biggest Misconception About the Job?

Most restaurant workers say that the biggest misconception they had about the job was that it would be easy. Do not confuse the ease with which one can procure a restaurant job with the thinking that it is an easy job—physically or mentally. Regarding the physical aspect of the job, during their shift, restaurant managers probably spend most of their time either standing or walking around the restaurant. Some managers estimate that they log 3 to 5 miles in an 8-hour workday. Additionally, many managers end up doing a considerable amount of lifting: boxes, serving trays, pots and pans, etc. Unless managers are in good physical condition already, their first few weeks on the job will be very tiring. Eventually, however, most restaurant workers get used to the physical demands of the job and actually begin to enjoy the job.

The cerebral requirements of the job are no less demanding. Managers must become master organizers and coordinators to be considered top performers. Each restaurant worker—cook, manager, waiter, waitress, bartender—typically has four or five projects going at once. Waiters and waitresses may have three or four tables of customers in various stages of their meals. The cook may be preparing 20 to 25 meals at the same time. The manager organizes the process and jumps in to assist whenever necessary. Constant prioritization of tasks is the name of the game.

No less mentally demanding is the unavoidable, and unpredictable, human factor. Most managers can reasonably assume that they will have to deal with the moods, preferences, and personalities of their customers and the staff on a regular basis. Most restaurant workers say that this constant pressure to always be "on" is the most tiring aspect of their job.

What Is the One Thing You Would Have Wanted Someone to Tell You About This Career?

I would like to have known that the work is hard and that I would work the hardest when others are not working. The physical and mental demands which will be placed upon you if you choose a career in the restaurant business have already been described. The other aspect of a restaurant career which must be considered very carefully is that restaurant employees work while others are off work. A restaurant's busiest times are lunchtime, dinnertime, weekends, and holidays. If the restaurant employees' friends and family hold jobs with more traditional hours (i.e., 9 to 5, Monday through Friday), they may not see very much of them, particularly as new employees (i.e., the ones with the worst schedules). Many restaurant employees state that the offbeat hours are what they dislike most about the restaurant business. However, initially, most restaurant employees say that the flexible work schedules are very appealing to them. Flexibility can be a double-edged sword, however, particularly when one is working until 2:00 a.m. on a regular basis. It is imperative that the restaurant employees and their friends and family understand that they may not be able to see as much of each other as before. Everyone must be willing to bend to create quality time together.

What Three Pieces of Advice or Wisdom Would You Give Someone Thinking About This Career?

1. Never underestimate, or fail to appreciate, anyone—not the customers, not the employees, and not the purveyors. Everyone is important to the restaurant's success. Developing a good working relationship with each of these groups will increase the odds that the establishment will be a success. At the same time, managers enhance their own fortunes in the business as others begin to perceive them as people who can work with others to get the job done.

2. Managers must never compromise their standards. They must continually strive for excellence to succeed in this business. If they begin to cut corners by offering food of lesser quality or maintaining an inadequate waitstaff, their performance will be impaired. Make no mistake—the customers will notice the drop in quality and/or service immediately. Many will not tell the manager that they are dissatisfied; instead, they will vote with their feet and

begin frequenting a competitor's establishment. Once managers have compromised standards, and the customers have noticed, it is difficult to impossible to reestablish a good reputation.

3. Never forget the three most important words in the restaurant business: location, location, location. The establishment must be visible and accessible to the public or else no one will drop by to try the best steak in town. One restaurant in town failed simply because its parking lot was at such a steep grade that customers chose to go elsewhere. Restaurant owners and managers must also consider the right type of location for their establishment: Placing a fine dining restaurant in an area populated by fast food outlets is probably not a good idea.

19
Retail Sales

Robert Savage
Co-owner, The Toy School

One Month in the Career of a Retail Salesperson

It had really been a long day and my body was reminding me just how long it had been. But my brain kept telling me that there were at least 2 hours left before the store would close; and even that was no certainty. The store was still crowded with so many holiday shoppers—some of whom were looking pretty desperate and more than willing to refuse to leave us until they were finished.

As I began to walk over to the next shopper to ask how I could help him, I felt a touch on my elbow from the lady who had just walked in the front door. She came directly over to me, and in an insistent voice, said that she had to have another copy of "that little purple book you sold me this time last year." When I asked which book, she replied that she could not remember either the title or author.

I wondered to myself whether she had any concept of how many people I had waited on since "this time last year" or how many thousands of books were on the store's shelves or how many of those might be little and purple.

Customers are the one central focus for any successful retail salesperson. The old sales axiom that nothing really happens until there is a buying customer is an apt description of retail sales. As a result, good salespeople concentrate their efforts totally on each individual customer. Seldom is this moment chosen by the retail salesperson, and for this reason he or she must be ready at any time. This is one of the significant distinctions between retail and other types of selling. Further, the retail customer generally has many more choices and thus may give the retail salesperson fewer opportunities to make the sale.

For these reasons, the retail salesperson has to work smarter and make the best use of time spent with customers. They must recognize that many individuals simply do not know what they need or want or what actually brought them into the store in the first place. Others sometimes cannot describe the need even when they know it. Some may actually describe a secondary need or desire, leaving it up to the salesperson to figure out what they are really looking for.

Customers sometimes assume that the retail salesperson has greater abilities and/or resources than is actually the case. Customers often believe that the salesperson remembers past contacts in detail and are not understanding when the store runs out of a product. All these things require the retail salesperson to always be alert to what the customer is saying and to be very knowledgeable about other items which may be good substitutes for the product or service that the customer first had in mind.

From the moment she walked in, it was obvious that this lady had never been in the store. Just in the manner that her eyes scanned the shelves and displays I could tell that this potential new customer might be a little different.

I introduced myself in my best sales manner and asked how I might help. Her reply was a glare for which I was unprepared. Then, after what seemed like a very long time, she informed me that she only wanted to look around and that she was "quite capable of doing so" without any of my assistance.

I considered myself to be a competent salesperson who could handle any situation. So even as I left her on her own, I watched from a distance for clues and tried to reapproach her at least twice in the next half hour to see if there was anything I might do. Each time she told me that she was "personally capable." On the latter occasion I was further informed that she "could not find anything in the store worth buying."

It had been almost an hour when she finally walked to the checkout position with a large number of selections in hand. I was surprised when her bill amounted to much more than our average sale. Naturally I thanked her and invited her to come back in the future. Her answer was to reiterate sternly that nothing in the store was worth buying.

As she walked out, I was still trying to understand what had just happened.

An important aspect that virtually all successful retail salespeople understand and practice is that there is no single "correct" way to work with customers. Often approaches that work with some customers will not work with others. This also applies to other areas. For example, some customers want the salesperson to stay with them while they study the products and/or services. Others, however, do not want to be "bothered" in this way.

What is desirable is an outcome that is often referred to as a "win-win" situation. Customers win when products or services are purchased at prices that they believe are fair. The retail salesperson wins when a sale is completed or when the trust of the customer is built so that future sales prospects are enhanced.

Successful retail salespeople also know that they cannot rely solely on what a customer says. Thus, they must not only listen to the words, but they also must question customers and watch for nonverbal signs. Using all of these aids, a retail salesperson works to better understand what is needed or wanted by the customer.

One of the more important roles of salespeople is to get the customer to reach the point of a buying decision. However, they always must remember that the customer's pace cannot be rushed.

For some reason one of the store's best quality products—a children's stereo system—was just not selling. I knew that customers liked it very much but just could not seem to reach a decision to actually purchase it. I also knew that the buyer who had brought it in was concerned, as was the store's owner. As I thought about this, it occurred to me that maybe I could help. After all, poor sales did not do my commissions any good, and if all sales were this poor, even my job could be on the line.

Thinking back about those customers to whom I had tried to sell the system, I began to realize that it might be overpriced at $109.99. That was a lot to pay for a kid's stereo. Then as I thought about those customers' comments about their perception of its value to them, I began to feel that we should lower its price to the $95 to $98 range.

My thoughts about the system's market led me to conclude that it would sell best to young parents in the 28- to 37-years-of-age group who had children between the ages of 8 and 11. Thus, any targeted advertising should be done with this type of person in mind.

Then it dawned on me that the store's computer files had this data. That meant that we could identify addresses for customers in this group. I took my ideas—along with a sketch of a mailer pointing out the lower price and the product's best features—to the owner and the buyer, and they agreed to try my plan.

Three weeks later we had sold out of our initial supply and were anxiously awaiting our reorder. That was music to my ears.

While customers are—and should be—the central focus in the career of a retail salesperson, there are other areas which do not involve direct interaction with potential buyers. One of the most critical of these is pricing.

Pricing products and services requires finding that amount at which customers will receive at least as much benefit as they have paid, while at the same time the store will realize a positive margin over what it paid for the item sold. Pricing too high means the product simply will not sell. Pricing too low is also a problem because the store will not benefit from the margins necessary for the business to continue. Good retail salespeople can use their knowledge of their customers to help the store's owners or managers make the best pricing decisions possible. In many cases, the salesperson will actually be in charge of these important decisions.

Many other nonselling jobs also may be performed by retail salespeople. Examples include the design and layout of print advertising as well as physical displays within the store, efforts required to stage a store promotion (e.g., an author's visit to a bookstore to meet customers and autograph books), and research to help find new customers (e.g., adding to existing mailing lists) or to create entirely new markets (e.g., finding ways for an established store with many local customers to attract people visiting the city).

Additional jobs sometimes done by salespeople might include training recently hired employees or helping the store's buyers decide on possible new items. In a smaller store the good retail salesperson who has made him- or herself familiar enough with customers may even make buying decisions.

> *Despite what many people think, retail sales can be a "fun" line of work. This comes from having so much involvement with other people. Because customers are individuals, each presents unique challenges. Whether it is dealing with someone who is mild mannered or highly opinionated or the surprise that comes from working with someone who looks to be in a state of poverty but pays large amounts by using an unlimited gold credit card, few situations seem dull in retail sales.*
>
> *The fun feature of retail sales also comes because salespeople help others meet needs and desires in ways that improve their customers' lives. Being able to suggest a special, hard-to-find toy that will help a discouraged parent with a handicapped child or calling to tell a customer of an item bought at a trade show because the retail salesperson "knew they would want it," creates a feeling of genuine pleasure in a salesperson's work.*

Commonly Asked Questions About a Career in Retail Sales

What Tasks Do You Do Most Often?

The most important task and the one most often performed by a salesperson is selling to a customer. In this task the salesperson interacts with potential buyers to assist them in meeting needs. In fact meeting such needs (or desires), by finding ways to connect the store's products and services with a solution, is what selling is all about.

The actual amount of time involved is determined by the number of customers who come into the store and the amount of time each allows the seller to work with them. Some customers want the seller to work very closely with them. Others want him or her only to be available while they look. However, even this latter customer is still important in the sense that the good salesperson will watch and observe from a distance those items in which the potential buyer shows the most interest (e.g., by touching or returning for additional looks). This is a great opportunity for the seller to learn much about the customer's needs.

How Much Do You Work with People? Numbers? Computers?

The vast majority of a retail salesperson's work will almost always be with people. The successful salesperson must concentrate his or her energies on customers. Because salespeople work in a retail "store" environment, their schedules are mostly dictated by their customers, who choose when to come into the store, when to leave, and whether to return in the future.

Retail selling also requires that most of the salesperson's time be spent with people because personal interactions are the primary tool for learning what customers want. Often customers will not (or cannot) directly describe their real need(s). This makes it vital for the salesperson to gain as good an understanding as possible during the selling process.

While not the main focus, some work with numbers and computers improves the retail salesperson's knowledge about popular items and trends or about useful customer information in the store's computer databases. Today almost all sales are completed on a computer-based point-of-sale system. Thus, the ability to use these devices with ease is important.

How Much Time Do You Spend in Meetings? Writing? Other?

A typical retail salesperson should not expect to spend a great deal of time in meetings, writing reports, or other such activities. After all, the most important work is normally accomplished with customers. Meetings, reports, and other such activities would take time that could otherwise be spent making sales.

Recognizing this, there are some meetings such as a weekly or semi-monthly sales meeting that may be required. In fact, these can be very productive since they give salespeople excellent opportunities to exchange ideas, discuss new items (or price changes) in the store, and refresh one another on good sales practices. They also give retail salespeople a great chance to talk to their sales manager about ideas and experiences.

While not necessarily a formal meeting, there should be talks with the manufacturer's representatives. During these discussions, retail salespeople can get to know the store's products and services better and thus improve their ability to match specific items with customers' needs.

What Skills Do You Use Most Often?

The skills most often used by a retail salesperson are interpersonal ones. The skill of being able to solve problems or to find ways to help improve a situation for the customer is very important to the salesperson. Finding these solutions requires an easy command of the language, good conversational style, and intelligent questioning abilities.

Another area related to solving problems is that of observing and listening to the customer. First, in observing, the retail salesperson will learn to watch each customer for their body language (e.g., facial expressions shown in reaction to a suggestion) and other nonverbal means by which they communicate their likes and dislikes. Listening to what the customer says is also important, as are observations.

Another area includes acting and reacting to customers in an extremely tactful and diplomatic manner. While the majority of customers are easy to work with, there are those occasions when very difficult ones are encountered. Some very few will even be almost abusive (in a nonphysical way). Recognizing that the motivation for such a customer's comments and actions has nothing to do with the seller personally puts the difficult customer's actions in perspective.

What Training, Education, and/or Experience Are the Best Preparation for This Career?

One of the really good things about retail selling is that no one set of training, education, and/or experience is likely to be the best approach. What is important is that the retail salesperson be able to relate to other people on an interpersonal basis, to enjoy doing so, and to have a strong positive attitude. This positive attitude does not have to be loud and outgoing but should be one with which the retail salesperson is at ease.

Beyond being able to use these interpersonal skills, it is also important to have a good education. A college degree (or degrees) would be advantageous to anyone because of the additional knowledge and broader outlook they provide.

It is useful for salespersons to have experience and/or education related to the products and services with which they work. As an example, someone who has been a teacher or has an education degree would have a very strong edge in retail sales for a bookstore. Those who have worked in the assembly of electronics or as electrical engineers would clearly be able to greatly supplement their "people" skills in a retail outlet for stereo and television systems.

How Do Most People Get Their Jobs in This Career?

The majority of retail salespeople start out as clerks selling directly to customers in either smaller retail stores or in departments of a larger outlet (e.g., a department store). Many gain experience as part-time employees during high school and/or college years. A small percentage may begin as college trainees after graduation from college.

For those who begin on the floor of a retail store, the majority typically are hired by the owner or manager (in smaller shops), or they obtain the job through the employment office (in a large store).

Entering the retail sales field through a college training program would normally happen as a result of interviews set up by the campus graduate placement service. This would probably be part of an intern program leading to upper management.

What Do People in This Career Have in Common?

Good salespeople have a number of traits in common with their peers. They almost always genuinely enjoy interacting with other people. This is particularly true when their efforts are directed toward understanding and then assisting customers.

Being results oriented at a "macro" level is another trait that many good salespeople share. For example, they usually are very strongly motivated to always improve their own knowledge of their products and services. In addition, they are highly motivated to meet their over-all sales goals—even while being keenly aware that no single customer should be pressured to buy because of these revenue commitments.

How Much Are You Paid?

Retail salespeople who are just beginning in the field are typically paid by the hour. New workers are often paid at or near the prevailing minimum wage rate and also may experience situations where it is difficult to accumulate very many hours per pay period. Therefore, their total compensation in these early stages may well be less than they would like.

Good salespeople normally move up to higher hourly wage rates (e.g., $6.00 up to $9.00) or are changed to salaried workers (e.g., $1200 per month).

Most retail salespeople eventually move to an hourly wage plus commission or to a salary plus commission. Commissions are bonus amounts paid to reward salespeople for increasing the store's revenues and/or attracting more customers. A commission paid to help increase the store's revenues could be 10 percent of the individual's total sales for the month added to their earnings from regular hourly wages. Another type of commission would be 12 percent of that portion of the department's sales which exceed normal or expected levels. Such a bonus might be paid quarterly to that department's manager as extra compensation over and above his or her base salary.

What Is the Salary or Compensation Potential?

Retail selling is not a field generally thought of as a high-paying career. However, its potential in this area is often significantly better than its reputation. The reason for this reputation is that many beginners start at or near minimum hourly wages or may not be given enough hours to earn much on a weekly basis. However, good retail salespeople move upward on the hourly wage scale fairly quickly, and the number of hours they work also grows. Here they usually begin to achieve annual pay which ranges up to $30,000. Finally, with experience the best salespeople as well as assistants and managers of departments can add significantly to their wages or salary with various commissions. The bonus amounts grow with the level of sales achieved by their units. At this point, the potential is greatly increased for earning annual pay levels which are much higher. One's total compensation can reach $100,000 and more.

What Are the Short- and Long-Term Career Opportunities?

There are at least four career opportunities or paths for people in retail sales. The first is moving up in positions of increasing responsibility within a larger retail outlet such as a department store. In this case a good salesperson might become the assistant manager (and later the manager) of a department. Finally, one might even grow to become the store's manager.

A second path which is often followed is the move to a position as the store manager in a smaller retail outlet. In this situation, successful salespeople often become owners of their own store(s).

A third opportunity is to move to other areas of marketing either in a large store or in a consulting firm. Since sales is one of the major functions of marketing, other functions (e.g., advertising or distribution) often provide opportunity.

Moving from the retail environment to selling in the wholesale field is a fourth path. Here a retail salesperson can build on knowledge gained by dealing directly with customers who are the ultimate users of any product or service. He or she then uses that knowledge and experience to be a strong salesperson at the wholesale level.

What Is the Range of Jobs in This Career?

The range of jobs typically performed by retail salespeople is quite wide. Further, because there is such a long list of items available through retail sales, one is almost certain to be able to work with products and/or services that match the individual's personal interests.

The primary type of job that retail salespeople do is that of direct selling to a customer. The products and services being sold vary from soft goods (e.g., clothing) to hard goods (e.g., exercise equipment). They also include software (e.g., packaged personal computer programs) and services (e.g., travel reservations). Actually, retail sales in some form occurs for almost any item except the very biggest or most unique types of things (e.g., jumbo jet airplanes or an individually written computer program for a scientific research project).

What Provides the Greatest Satisfaction? Frustration?

The greatest source of satisfaction in retail sales is helping a customer. It adds to the salesperson's confidence, which in turn carries over to the next sale with that customer or another one. It even adds positively to other nonwork activities. The customer's goodwill is obvious to the salesperson as well as to his or her peers and boss(es).

The greatest frustration is a customer who is unhappy with a product or service that did not perform as expected. Closely related are those situations where customers cannot grasp how the product and/or service one is trying to sell would benefit them. These frustrations leave retail salespeople feeling that they are not capable of presenting the benefits to the customer in a clear enough fashion.

What Is the Biggest Misconception About the Job?

Several misconceptions are worth noting. Perhaps the first and most prevalent one is that salespeople are loud and/or fast-talking individuals who are only interested in convincing a customer to buy a product or service regardless of its usefulness. Actually, there *are* salespeople who are loud or fast-talkers (or both), but many excellent performers in this field are neither. Often some of the very best salespeople are soft-spoken and do not rush customers to close sales.

Another misconception is that retail salespersons are not good at numbers, "paperwork," or problem solving and they do not have any organizational skills. In reality, those who have the greatest success and last the longest in this career are usually good at solving problems for their customers. Further, these problem-solving skills are typically enhanced by being adept with numbers and/or quantitative analysis. In addition, many retail salespeople have strong organizational skills.

A third misconception is that retail salespeople generally care only about the pay they expect to receive. Most salespeople are concerned with their salaries and commissions—just as is anyone in any other field. However, the most successful ones are those who know that desirable earnings result from excellent work. Thus, they concentrate on those traits that make them an excellent salesperson first, realizing that the pay will follow.

What Is the One Thing You Would Have Wanted Someone to Tell You About This Career?

Because retail sales is sometimes perceived as a less than fulfilling career, the thing that would have been most helpful to have been told is just how vital sales activity is to the economies and societies in which people live.

In many ways retail selling can be viewed as an activity which completes a long process during which something of real value to people has been created. The retail salesperson is the one who takes a product or service to potential buyers. Viewed in this light, none of the process of creating something—whether inventions, manufacturing, or wholesale/distribution—has any benefit if that final retail sale is not made.

What Three Pieces of Advice or Wisdom Would You Give to Someone Thinking About This Career?

First is that one should always make sure that the store (i.e., their employer) has nothing but the highest regard for its customers. Stores that approach their business in this manner not only win more customers for the retail salesperson, but they also provide the extra support and backing during those occasions when the product or service fails or otherwise does not work as expected.

Second is to always make sure that the store's products and services are ones which provide real value when used by its customers. Further, they should be products and services which are at least good—and preferably outstanding—quality. Products or services which do not add real value (e.g., pet rocks) create downstream problems for the retail salesperson, and soon these difficulties and the reputation that they foster will seriously detract from one's ability and success.

Finally, retail salespeople should not spend any significant energies or time worrying about competitors. Good salespeople know about competitors, what they do, and how their products and services compare with those that they sell. This awareness is important in being able to find better solutions for customers. The product the salesperson sells is still most important.

20

Systems Analysis

Meril Thornton
Senior Vice President, NationsBank

One Month in the Career of a Systems Analyst

The ringing phone sounds like an explosion against the silence of the middle of the night. I struggle to answer it. "Sorry to bother you so late. We're having a problem with the system, and I don't know how to fix it." The caller is Greg, one of the programmers who reports to me. I am responsible for one of the bank's loan systems. The system keeps track of loans made to customers, the amount of interest charged, the amount still owed by the customer, and other pieces of information about the customer, and all the loan transactions.

Every night, our programs must update the loan files with new loans, payments, or other activity from that day and produce reports for our clients. The reports and the newly updated system must be available to our clients by 7:00 a.m. each morning. If there are problems during the night, a systems analyst gets a call and must fix the problem so the system will still be available when the bank opens in the morning.

I ask Greg what is different, since the system ran without problems last night. "I don't know. We didn't put in any changes today." After a lengthy discussion, we determine that the problem involves the interest charges for our Seniors' Bonus, a product for customers over 55 years old that gives discount pricing on a loan when combined with a savings account. The customer's loan is priced 2 percentage points over the interest rate we pay on the savings account and fluctuates as the savings interest rate changes, with a minimum, or floor, on the loan rate of 7 percent. This has been a popular product.

Greg has been able to locate the exact spot where the error is occurring. The program is producing the monthly combined loan and savings statements. It has read the savings information and determined the latest sav-

ings interest rate to calculate the loan interest rate. The current savings rate has dropped down to 4.5 percent. This would make the current loan rate less than 7 percent, which is lower than the minimum rate we charge.

When the program calculates the loan rate, it acknowledges that something is wrong and produces an error report and stops the system. When this product was developed and the program was written, it was probably assumed that any interest rate that low must be in error and needs to be corrected. But the low savings interest rate is correct. We must change this program to expect the low rate but calculate the loan interest as 7 percent, the minimum.

Because these changes must be thoroughly tested and approved, we decide to wait until the morning and delay the statements a few hours. This will give us a chance to design and test the changes, get the test approved by our client, rerun the system, and verify the statements before they are sent to the customer.

I reflect on what has happened as I try to fall back asleep. Why wasn't this caught during testing? I remember when this enhancement was installed. Not only did our team thoroughly test each program we added and each program we changed, but we produced all the reports and statements for our clients, and we verified everything. However, this particular event that caused tonight's problem, savings rates below 5 percent, was considered an exception that required human attention before proceeding. We had put this in as a safeguard so the system would not use a rate that may be in error, but here the rate was valid. The logic was designed to prevent an error from being made. I'll review the issues with our clients in the morning to review all the changes we need to make.

Systems analysts develop computer solutions to meet requirements and solve problems of businesses and government. They must bridge the gap between the nontechnical business user and the technical environment of computers and software. Systems analysts help make the translation from business requirements into the exact programming and computer commands to create or change the system. They become the primary line of contact for people who actually use the system every day. In the role of working as the liaison between the users of the system and the technical people who support the system, the systems analyst probably works more with people than with computers.

The work cycle for a computer systems change generally starts when the system users, or clients, have a requirement to build a new system or change an existing system. They may call the systems analyst with some initial information, like a description of a new product they want to sell. The systems analyst discusses it with them to make sure the request is feasible (i.e., perhaps the change really is not related to the system at all).

A good way to describe what a systems analyst does is to consider the analogy of the homeowner whose mother-in-law is moving in but has no additional bedrooms to accommodate the new resident. The homeowner could

*convert an existing room into a bedroom, which would require minimal
construction but could cause the homeowner to give up the use of the room
for other activities, such as having an office. Another approach would be to
finish the basement into a bedroom space. This would be a more costly
alternative but would fit well into the existing house structure since the
unfinished basement is relatively empty. The homeowner could elect to put
an addition on the home, causing modifications to the existing structure
and infrastructure improvements, like heating and plumbing.*

*The homeowner could elect to retain the integrity of the existing struc-
ture and purchase the home across the street for the mother-in-law. The
homeowner may also elect to sell the existing residence and purchase an
existing, larger residence that meets the majority of the homeowner's
needs or design and construct a new home that meets 100 percent of the
needs. Finally, the homeowner has the alternative of not doing any
enhancing to meet this new requirement and opt not to allow the mother-
in-law to join the residence after all.*

*When there are new needs for any system, an equally extensive list of pos-
sibilities can be generated. When we made the enhancement to the loan system, we could have taken the programs, screens, fields on the master file, and
reports from another product that wasn't very popular. We may not have
made as many changes to the system, but we would have had to take a product off the market. We could have used some available space on the master file
and created brand new screens and reports, if space were available. We could
have used the same system but created some new files just for this product.
We could have created a new set of programs and files just for the Seniors'
product and connected them to the old system for customer information (in
case the customer has other loans) and consolidated loan reporting.*

*We could have searched and found another loan software package that
had the Seniors' product, plus other new features we desired, and convert-
ed all of our loans to that system, perhaps giving up a few features we
have on our old system. Also, we could have designed a new loan system
from scratch that could accommodate all of our existing processing, the
Seniors' product, and some other loan products and features we would like
to offer. Finally, we could have decided not to offer the product at all
because the potential income benefits did not justify the expense required
in developing this product.*

Depending on the sophistication of the clients, they may only know
in broad high-level terms that they want a new product but not know
whether they could piggyback on an existing product or whether a
whole new system has to be written. Once the systems analyst has
made some high-level determinations, it is time to get details.

"Getting details" can take many forms. The systems analyst might
interview or meet with the requesters and anyone else who uses or
supports the system or who would use it to get all the details of the
request. The systems analyst then would write up a document that
would lay out the requirements of the system in terms the client can
understand. These requirements include any *inputs*, or information

coming into the system, either by people typing in transactions on screens or information coming in as "files" from other systems.

The requirement also includes *outputs,* which are things the system creates, such as reports, invoices, bills, information that can be displayed via screens, and files going to other systems. The systems analyst may also create samples of the new reports or screens so the client can get a sense of what they will look like. The systems analyst must also help the client determine who should have access to query or update the system and what functions or sets of information within the system need to be secured, or protected, from general access.

Next, once the systems analyst gets approval on this functional requirement, he or she goes about creating a document that mirrors the functional requirement but includes all the technical terms and instructions that programmers would understand. The systems analyst takes the functional requirements and determines programs that have to be written to create reports and screens or databases that have to be created or perhaps even recommends that new equipment be purchased.

The systems analyst may decide that a set of computer programs, or a software package, already exists which meets this need and can be purchased, thus saving the effort to develop the software within the company. When a software package is purchased, the analyst must determine the requirements to install the package on the computer and convert the existing information to the package.

I'm thinking back to when the Seniors' product was first conceived. Our clients came to us because they wanted to add this new feature for the loan product. The product had to work in conjunction with the savings product and produce a combined statement. We worked closely with the clients to determine exactly how the screens where the loan data is entered and displayed would change so the new Seniors' product could be identified, how the loan system would get information from the savings system, what additional calculations would be made, how the statements would be different, and how the new reports would look.

Once that was documented, we then analyzed what changes and additions the loan system needed, and we created the detailed design. This incorporated all the new and changed functions the client had requested. We also provided prototypes of the reports and screens so the client would know what they would get. The detailed design contained the specifications for all new programs, the "specs" for every program that would change, the new data files and fields required, and the new jobs that would run each night.

Greg then made all the program changes and wrote several new programs. We created a very comprehensive test plan, which would make sure each component in our system would be correct. We entered data for the new feature on the screens and made sure the calculations were correct, and the reports and statements were produced as specified. We found a lot of errors and had to fix our programs. When we were done testing, our clients did their own testing on the system. We had to correct each one of the problems they found. Finally, we put all the new and changed programs into the existing system, which we call the "production" system. Thus, the Seniors' product was ready to be introduced to the market.

There are many other decisions systems analysts must make when developing these technical requirements and designing systems. The type of hardware must be determined—PC, mainframe, or something in between. The analyst may need to decide the type of computer programming language to be used, although many systems departments have standards that direct the analysts to use certain languages. The systems analyst must decide how to provide the security needed to protect the data in the system and must determine how to "back up" the system and recover the data should something go wrong. The analyst determines how the data that the system uses and creates should be physically structured.

Now, it is finally time to start programming on the computer. The systems analyst can write very detailed specifications for each program, which describes in detail the inputs coming in the program, the processing flow, the calculations, the major decisions in the logic and the outcome of those decisions, and the outputs coming out of the program. For a new programmer, the systems analyst may write an English description of all the logic in the program. For a more experienced programmer, the systems analyst may write a high-level requirement and the programmer will design the program. The systems analyst may also do the programming and handle every phase of development of the system.

Greg has been "on-call" about 2 weeks. The loan system is very stable, so we generally don't have any problems at night. This is the first time he has gotten called. He was very nervous. I made a mental note to talk to him tomorrow about what to do when there are problems. My agenda was going to be pretty full tomorrow since I needed to coach Greg on handling such crises, review with the clients possible resolutions for tonight's problem, and get Greg started on the implementation, complete the running of the monthly statements, and attend a meeting to talk about adding another new feature to the system.

Handling situations like this where we have to meet a deadline and fix the system in the middle of the night is quite a challenge. But the thing is, what we do is vital to our business. If the system is not available tomorrow, our clients cannot balance and verify yesterday's work, enter new loans, or determine loan payoff amounts for customers who want to know. They need our system to run the business. Being able to provide this critical service really keeps me going. I was considering these benefits, yet trying to determine how I was going to get this all done as I finally started to fall back asleep.

Systems professionals and systems analysts are present in every industry that uses computers. Most industries are using computers to process financial data, and computers are used for a myriad of other applications, including manufacturing, marketing, scientific research, etc. The systems analyst is very familiar with the application of the system he or she is supporting.

Just about every company has some automation needs. The most basic needs stem from the company's need to bill its customers, receive payments from its customers, pay its employees, pay other vendors, produce periodic financial statements, and pay taxes. Small companies may use PCs and PC packages to automate these areas, but as the company grows, the company may have more specialized needs and more computing power and may require more complex computing equipment and a systems staff.

A manufacturing company may use automation to operate and maintain equipment, manage inventory and production of goods, and process and track customer orders. A marketing company may use computers to enter orders from remote terminals at the point of sale or track sales trends and monitor competitive research. A scientific company may use computers to do data analysis or build equipment.

Then there are companies that build computer software to support the functions of all the other industries. Financial services companies generally supply all their products via computers, such as securities trading and record keeping, lending, deposit taking, insurance policy tracking, etc. Government uses of automation include tax collection, property record keeping, law enforcement record keeping, and a host of other needs.

Commonly Asked Questions About a Career as a Systems Analyst

What Tasks Do You Do Most Often?

The tasks done most often by a systems analyst are to analyze requests, design and install systems, and solve problems. Most system users have numerous requests for changes and enhancements to the systems, requests for new systems, and problems with old systems. Some analysis of each of the requests is necessary to determine how long fulfilling the request would take and how much it would cost, whether the system can accommodate the change easily or the change would be extensive, and alternative approaches to accommodate the system that users need.

The systems analyst's role is to analyze the request; develop the exhausted list of alternatives with their costs, benefits, strengths, weaknesses, pros and cons; and work with the system user to select the best alternative given the prevailing circumstances, such as funding, opportunity costs, resources, etc. Once the alternative has been selected, the systems analyst has the task of designing the system.

The third task done frequently by the systems analyst is problem resolution. A system might have a problem that was not uncovered until it was tried with some unusual data, or there may have been a "bug" in the system which was caused by a human error. For example, the savings system could properly indicate that the latest savings rates are below 5 percent, but the modules in the combined loan/savings product were not attuned with the new trends in savings interests rates. The systems analyst would be called in to identify the problem, resolve it, and prevent it from reoccurring.

Systems analysts are constantly solving problems. There are sometimes urgent problems to solve, such as when the system blows up at night and they are called to fix it or help someone else fix it. That does not happen that often. More likely, a problem will be a report that does not show up in the client's mail box or a report that the client feels has some incorrect information on it. A programmer may test a new program and not be able to determine why it is not producing the results it should.

How Much Do You Work with People? Numbers? Computers?

The first 2 years, most systems professionals are programmers. They work more with computers, although they must interact with people constantly to understand how the system is structured, how jobs are run, how to test, etc. The design specifications are provided to programmers. From the design, the programmer writes, or *codes*, a computer program. Programmers prepare test data, test the program, and add it to the production system.

As programmers get more experienced, they start working directly with the system users to determine what needs to be automated, working on the design, and coding and testing the programs. When they grow into the systems analyst function, they usually organize the project, are responsible for the analysis and design, and produce the specifications for another person to do the programming. Systems analysts work almost all the time with people and get involved with the computer only for occasional problem solving.

The question on numbers is an interesting one. Any given programming assignment can require a lot of calculations and number crunching. On the other hand, many systems are only doing manipulation of data and not much number crunching at all. A newspaper company may have a system with a file of all of its delivery customers and may keep track of billing information, house location information, and records of problems with paper delivery, so not much number crunching may be required. However, that same system in the newspaper across town may be used to track sales information and revenue by geographical area, so it could be much more computational. The degree of numerical complexity depends on not just the application but the specific system. The bottom line is, although most systems analysts are not mathematicians, people who are out to avoid numbers may want to stay out of this profession.

How Much Time Do You Spend in Meetings? Writing? Other?

Whereas a programmer may spend 90 percent of the time coding and testing programs, the systems analyst probably spends 50 percent of each day in meetings, either with the programmers, the system users, the computer operators who run the jobs, or other analysts to learn about changes that will affect the system.

The systems analyst also has to do a lot of writing. There is writing involved in every task. When the systems analyst analyzes requests, the analyst may write up the alternatives and a proposal with the recommended alternative. During the design of the system, the analyst may write up the specification for the enhancement or new system. Once the system is complete, the analyst should write some documentation for future support.

What Skills Do You Use Most Often?

Systems analysts do a lot of negotiating. There are many demands on time, and there are many demands on the system. There are many requests for enhancements and new features. There are many small problems that need to be fixed and reports and screens the clients want rearranged. There are new product features wanted by the clients. There are improvements the operations area wants so they will not have to do as many manual tasks to operate the system each day. Each requester wants to be the top priority. There can only be a couple of top priorities, but each client is very important. If it were not for the clients, there would be no system and no role for a systems analyst, so the analyst does not want to constantly disappoint the clients. There is usually a process to help the clients collectively decide all they want and what the top priorities should be.

Another skill that systems analysts use a great deal is their analysis skill. When a client has a request or problem, the systems analyst has to analyze the request and the system and determine the most efficient way of handling the request. The analyst takes a lot of factors into account.

Another skill needed quite frequently is persistence and determination. When the system has a problem, an analyst cannot give up. The problem has to be found. If the systems analyst does not understand some new technology or new business function that is being automated, he or she has to stick with it, continue to ask questions, and continue to learn in small chunks about what is happening. Even if the systems analysts feel the questions are stupid and the clients are getting frustrated because the analyst does not understand their business, they need to keep asking and asking and asking until they understand. If the systems analysts give up trying to understand, they will not be successful.

The most critical need for a systems analyst is "people skills." Systems analysts need to be excellent communicators and make everyone feel comfortable with technology. They spend a lot of time writing, documenting, and making presentations.

What Training, Education, and/or Experience Are the Best Preparation for This Career?

Systems analysts need basic computer skills training, including knowledge of programming languages, operating systems, databases, and computer communications. Most have college degrees, but the type of degree varies from liberal arts to business to computer science. Regardless of the degree, there needs to be exposure to computers and programming languages.

Systems analysts also need to understand the application or business they are supporting, and this knowledge can come from on-the-job training. Many systems analysts started as programmers, but there are others who had the business knowledge or who knew how to manage projects and learned the technical side on the job.

How Do Most People Get Their Jobs in This Career?

Many people in systems began their careers in other parts of the same company and migrated into systems because they had exposure to computers and were intrigued. Many companies offer training to develop their staff into programmers. Other systems analysts began as programmers, either by receiving a college degree in a technical, business, or related field or by participating in a nondegree technical training program. The majority of systems analysts start off as programmers and work their way up to systems analysts by learning the technical environment of the company, the system they supported, and the application they supported.

The other entry into this field is to thoroughly understand the business. There are many systems analysts who used to be systems users or operations analysts or product analysts in an area that was heavily automated or needed to be. Business expertise is extremely valuable to the systems analyst, and many analysts moved over to the systems department from other areas and then got the technical skills needed to succeed through courses within the company or through external courses.

What Do People in This Career Have in Common?

Systems analysts like computers and are generally fascinated with the potential benefits that automation can bring to any situation. Systems analysts like to resolve problems and like working with people.

How Much Are You Paid?

A systems analyst's salary is usually in the low forties.

What Is the Salary or Compensation Potential?

Compensation for systems analysts varies drastically with type of industry, complexity of skills required to support the application, and region of the country. The salary can range from $30,000 to $60,000 a year. Progression with additional levels of responsibility in terms of system complexity or number of systems would lead to the upper end of the range.

What Are the Short- and Long-Term Career Opportunities?

Systems analysts have several different career options. They can continue to progress in technical computer knowledge and knowledge about the application and get subsequent "senior" labels in their title or perhaps even a title of "consultant." A seasoned, knowledgeable systems analyst is valuable to his or her firm and is rewarded and retained as such.

An experienced systems analyst with good technical, project, and communication skills is very marketable. There is an entire industry of contract programming, in which these analysts get contracts with different firms on a temporary basis, either through a contract programming firm or as an independent contractor.

Systems analysts can also go into management. They can start by managing small applications or systems or managing small projects to develop or enhance a system. As a project manager, you may not have direct management responsibility for the people on your project, but the people are assigned to the project based on skills needed, and the role of the project manager is to get the project objective done.

A systems manager can take on more responsibility and go on to more senior levels of systems and data processing management. A systems analyst can also move to the client area into a management or analyst role. Many systems analysts have become very familiar with the business and organization of the clients they support and can readily move into the client organization. Systems managers also go into other areas of data processing, such as computer operations, which is running the computer jobs and managing the computer hardware, or telecommunications or database support or other technical areas.

What Is the Range of Jobs in This Career?

Some definition is in order here. Job titles and their corresponding levels vary from firm to firm, industry to industry. You start your career as a systems professional, either straight from school or from a training program, as a programmer. In that job, you are given detailed specifications and write and test computer programs. To the degree that you also might interact with clients and design the programs, "analyst" may be added to your title. To the degree that you begin designing systems, you may be called a systems analyst. This may or may not imply that you do both programming and design.

There is no consistency with the titles. As you get more experienced, "senior" may be added to programmer analyst or systems analyst. Some firms have systems engineers or technical systems engineers. The engineer label may imply that your application is scientific as opposed to business, but it may not. The key is to understand the responsibilities of the entry-level and subsequent titles of progression at the firm you are interested in.

There also is a title, lead analyst, that denotes the most senior analyst working on a particular application. There may be some management responsibilities, but usually it means you just know the most about the system. Many systems analysts have management responsibilities. They may be managers of other programmers or programmer analysts on that system. Managers of a systems team are also called team leaders or systems managers or project managers.

There are also analysts in other systems areas that are needed anywhere computers are used in the company. Systems analysts support a variety of tasks for the business. Systems analysts are needed for every system, including the application systems or the more background type systems such as databases, telecommunications software, and systems software. Analysts who design how data files should be logically and physically organized are called database analysts.

Another area, sometimes called system programming or technical support or a related title, supports the more technical software that runs on the computer between the hardware and the application software. For example, running on a PC, you have DOS or DOS and Windows, you may have a program that manages your memory, and you may have a program of utilities that backs up or recovers your data. Then you have some software packages that help you do your job, such as spreadsheet software, software that does accounting, etc. These are considered applications. The operating system, the data storage management and memory management programs, and associated utilities are system software, as opposed to application software. System programmers maintain this in a mainframe or midrange environment. Analysts for problem resolution, request analysis, and system design are needed for this area as well.

What Provides the Greatest Satisfaction? Frustration?

Writing a computer program can be a tedious task. First you have to take your plans and translate them into the language you are using, such as COBOL, C, PASCAL, BASIC, etc. The program could be very short, like 100 lines, or extremely long, like 10,000 lines, or it could call in other programs called *subroutines,* to do parts of the logic. Then, you have to get rid of all the syntax errors, mistakes you made in using the grammar of the particular language. When people talk and they make grammar mistakes, we can still understand them. We know what they meant to say or should have said. Computers do not tend to be as flexible. When you write a language for the computer to interpret, you have to code the rules of the language exactly.

Once you have corrected all the syntax mistakes, you run the program. At first, you are likely to have logic mistakes. Logic mistakes are called *bugs.* Getting all those bugs out is called *debugging.* So you spend minutes or hours or days or months, depending on the size of your program, the degree of perfection of the plans you followed when you coded, and the degree of perfection in your coding. The output from your program finally starts to look a lot like what you were expecting. Then you have to continue to debug by thoroughly checking the contents and position, depending on what the program is doing, of each and every character in each and every position. This testing is very tedious. The whole process can be very tedious and frustrating. However, when the program runs and runs correctly, that moment is extremely exhilarating for programmers. It is analogous to a builder who has just finished a house. In the case of a systems analyst who has been working on a system with tens or hundreds or thousands of programs, it is like building a skyscraper.

Another great satisfaction for a systems professional is satisfying customers. Systems professionals are always working on something that will help them. The system or feature will either make their lives or business more manageable, automating a function that will now take less time or provide more accuracy or control or even doing a task that was completely impossible without a computer. This definitely has the potential for great customer service. Customers are also very appreciative for a job well done, either giving positive feedback for a system that fills an internal need or by purchasing the software if this is a packaged product.

Similar to building a computer program or set of programs from start to finish, it is also satisfying to work on a project from start to finish. Besides actually doing the coding and testing of the program, the project includes the steps of deciding what the scope of the effort should be and whether it is financially worth it, determining how all the roles will be filled, designing the project from the business perspective, designing the project from the technical perspective, and doing all the steps in bringing the project on-line.

Finally, going back to our beginning example, depending on the industry, there could be times when a crisis arrives, and you have a very short time to solve a critical problem. This is likely when it is critical for the business to have the system available. Solving a problem in a crisis takes a good understanding of the system and the trade-offs you can make to bring the system back up, a cool head, and a stomach for some level of stress.

What Is the Biggest Misconception About the Job?

One of the biggest misconceptions is that all systems professionals do is work on computers. There are many steps in the process of building systems and working on systems projects, and most of them require good people skills. Skills such as determining what the customer really needs or how the business works are just as crucial as technical skills.

Another misconception is that there are unlimited jobs for systems professionals. Job opportunities in this industry depend on the level of experience and expertise. Opportunity is very limited at the entry level and at the management level. The majority of jobs available seem to be for senior programmer analysts or systems analysts who do project management and analysis as well as programming, and they tend to be focused on particular languages and operating environments. Check any Sunday newspaper classifieds to identify which ones are in the most demand.

What Is the One Thing You Would Have Wanted Someone to Tell You About This Career?

The aspect that has been most surprising to me has been the degree of coordination required with so many entities to have a successful development process. A good systems analyst needs to consider every component that will make a system successful or make it fail. This can include knowledgeable clients with a good vision, a reliable computer hardware and telecommunications environment, a good operations staff, and standard design techniques and tools to produce maintainable and consistent coding. Any one of these may seem out of the control of the systems analyst. Problems with any one can also lead a development project quickly to failure. The systems analyst must manage all of these variables to guarantee the success of a development project.

What Three Pieces of Advice or Wisdom Would You Give Someone Thinking about This Career?

1. Get a solid technical foundation. Learn how to program. You do not have to be the best programmer on earth, but you should know how to look at programs to see what they are doing. You cannot be intimidated by what is in a computer program.

2. The range of systems you can support is very diverse. Do not just choose to want to be a systems analyst; also choose to support a certain range of industries or applications. It will help you focus your search, and once you start, it will allow you to learn more about the industry and be a better analyst.

3. You must want to constantly learn new skills in this career. Technology is changing rapidly, and systems analysts must keep up, not just to move up, but to stay employed.

PART 2
Career Tips

21
Ten Tips on
Choosing a Career

1. Evaluate your strengths and weaknesses.
2. Research various careers and future employment opportunities and trends.
3. Seek career advice from all sources.
4. Visit and intern with companies in careers you are considering.
5. Understand the job and the responsibilities thoroughly.
6. Choose a career you think you'll like and enjoy.
7. Consider how the career will affect other parts of your life.
8. Choose a career that will afford you the lifestyle you desire.
9. Think where you want to be 5, 10, and 20 years from now.
10. Don't be afraid to change careers.

1. *Evaluate your strengths and weaknesses.* When choosing a career, start by asking yourself questions like what are my strengths, what are my weaknesses, what do I like to do, what do I hate to do, where do I want to live, how much money do I need to make, and what kind of work environment would I like? List the answers to these questions *before* investigating career possibilities. Then begin the search. Most people look for careers without fully considering their complete lists of needs. As a result, a lot of people settle rather than optimize. To paraphrase a quote from *Alice in Wonderland,* if you don't care where you want to go, it doesn't matter which road you take. First decide where you want to go; then start to choose a career.

2. *Research various careers and future employment opportunities and trends.* You wouldn't go on a 3-day vacation without buying a guide book, reading various pamphlets, and talking to different people who have been to the place you're considering going. Neither should you choose a 30-year career without the same or greater due diligence. Most libraries are good places to find various career books, business publications, and trade journals. College and business school placement offices are especially good sources and keepers of career information. Look at which areas or careers are growing and which ones are likely to suffer from downsizing, cost cutting, technological advancement, and so on. The government issues a number of employment outlooks which can provide guidance into future growth opportunities.

3. *Seek career advice from all sources.* Friends, relatives, and professors, lend me your ears and wisdom. It's not like you're seeking advice on how to split the atom. If you are interested in sales, I'm sure that either you, your parents, or your friends know insurance agents, stock brokers, retail salespeople, and lots of others. Talk is cheap, so actively seek out people who work in careers you are thinking about. Talk to parents of friends of the family. They generally are established in a career and often are flattered to share their experiences. Talk with professors. You have just spent tens of thousands of dollars for the privilege of going to a college or university; you might as well use all the resources. When you think of all the people you can possibly talk to in a given career, your biggest limitation probably will be time. Network. Network. Network.

4. *Visit and intern with companies in careers you are considering.* If you are interested in banking, at the very least, call up a local bank and spend a day there observing and talking with some bank officers. Or, have the placement office at the school give you the name of an alumnus who works at a bank and then use him or her as your entry to learning about banking. Friends also can put you in touch with people they know at companies, who with a little prodding, might be willing to let you spend a career day with them. That of course is the minimum. A couple weeks to a year-long internship would provide you with even better insight into that career. Don't make money the major objective when doing an internship. Learning about a career in which you're going to spend your life will be worth far more than any amount of money you could ever make in a few months. Clearly, learning by doing is the best way to learn.

5. *Understand the job and the responsibilities thoroughly.* A lot of decisions are made with very limited knowledge. Some people pick colleges, buy houses, or choose cars after a day's consideration. While

you graduate in 4 years, live in a house an average of 5 years, and trade in a car after 4, careers usually last a lot longer. Once you spend time in a career, it becomes more and more difficult to switch since that's where your expertise is. Therefore, it is critical *before* deciding on a career to try to understand what skills are required, how is time spent working, how much math or computer knowledge is required, how much you work with people, what the compensation potential is, and so on. The more you know, the less surprised you'll be.

6. *Choose a career you think you'll like and enjoy.*   When all is said and done, you should like what you do. While that may seem intuitively obvious, many new job seekers initially look for high pay or high status coming out of college. They think that liking or loving the career will follow. Guess what? High pay and high status don't necessarily correlate with high job satisfaction. They may help, but all the money in the world can't make you like a job you hate. You should look forward to going to work. You should have high job satisfaction. While I am not saying that all jobs are fun or that every day will be a blast, if you like or love what you do, as the title of a recent career guide says, the money will follow.

7. *Consider how the career will affect others parts of your life.*   Even though you will spend most of your time at work, you still have to live. Remember, it's only a job. Decide how much time you want to spend at work, how much time you want to spend with friends and family, how much vacation time you want, and how much time you want to spend just reading and watching television. Then pick a career. Some careers, such as consulting and investment banking, require long, long hours at the beginning, middle, and end of that career. Other positions like marketing require long hours initially, then slack off somewhat. In some careers, such as real estate, you can decide how much or little you want to work. Different people have different needs; you must decide which career is best for you.

8. *Choose a career that will afford you the lifestyle you desire.*   Many people will tell you not to let money determine your career decision. These are people who usually are making big bucks, have two incomes, or inherited a fortune. While money should not be the only factor driving the career choice, money is clearly important. Some careers such as advertising and accounting are low paid initially while others such as investment banking and consulting usually command top dollar. While you earn the money you make in most careers, some careers clearly have greater earning potential than others. You must decide how much you can live on and then factor this into the career decision process. Once you have started a career, it is difficult to dramatically

change your compensation level. If you have champagne tastes, you need a career that will afford you the luxuries of life.

9. *Think where you want to be 5, 10, and 20 years from now.*   While it is sometimes difficult to picture where you will be 1 year or sometimes even 1 month from now, it is important to look into your personal crystal ball. In what position do you want to be in 5 or 10 years? How much money do you want to make? What kind of lifestyle do you want to lead? The answers should affect your career choice. While there are no guarantees for the future, advertising executives can have certain expectations about career progression and salary. Other more entrepreneurial positions fall much farther up the risk-return continuum. The future is yours; try to shape it by the decision you make now in your career choice.

10. *Don't be afraid to change careers.*   Nothing is forever. We all change. We all go for better opportunities. We all make mistakes. While changing careers is never easy, it also is not impossible. You really never can truly know your exact fit with a given career until you try it. If it appears the career is not working out to your satisfaction for whatever reason, make a change. Think about the worst thing that can happen, which is usually nothing, and then move on. Changing careers is like a visit to the dentist. It is not pleasant, but the anticipated pain is usually worse than the actual pain and usually you feel better afterward. Go for it. Unless you are James Bond, you only live once.

22

Ten Tips on Preparing a Résumé

1. Differentiate yourself.
2. Quantify and focus on specific accomplishments
3. Be positive.
4. Be honest.
5. Present a powerful résumé.
6. Target your résumé.
7. Use other résumés as a guide.
8. Proofread. Proofread. Proofread.
9. Put yourself in the reviewer's shoes.
10. Don't expect a résumé to get you a job—sell yourself in person or over the phone.

1. *Differentiate yourself.*   You're a hiring manager. You have a position open and a hundred résumés on your desk. How do you pick? Most of the candidates have very good credentials—good schools, good work experience, and good references. You look for ones that seem to fit exactly the profile of the position you are recruiting for and also for the ones that stand out. As a job applicant sitting on the other side of the table, it is unlikely that you will fit every profile perfectly. Therefore, you must differentiate yourself.

What experience have you had that is different? Did you travel to Asia for a school trip? Did you start a recycling business to support yourself through college? What did you do particularly well? Were you the youngest president of the marketing club? Did you win an award in your economics program? Why would someone pick your résumé over others? Is it an interesting résumé that invites the reader to want to speak to you? Does it shout achievement without being obnoxious? Make your résumé stand out from the pack.

2. *Quantify and focus on specific accomplishments.*   Résumés often list various activities such as "managed the computer training project" or "supervised three people" or "oversaw a budget of $100,000." While these activities are good, they don't tell the prospective employer what you have done to help the company make money or build its business. Focus on specific accomplishments and quantify results. For example, it is far stronger to list such things as "oversaw a computer project which generated over $100,000 in billings for the company in the first year" or "supervised a team of three professionals on a cost reduction project that resulted in a 15 percent savings in overall production costs." This tells the prospective company that you can help them too. If you accomplished something tangible for your last company, there is a good chance you can, and will, do the same for the new one.

3. *Be positive.*   There's a fine line between being positive and being overaggressive. If you don't believe in yourself, why should a company do so? If, on the other hand, only you believe in your worth or you over-promote your candidacy, this raises questions about why you are doing it. Put a positive spin on your résumé without straining credibility. For example, it is plausible that on your first job you saved your company $50,000 by reducing cycle time. You should promote this achievement. It is not believable that your suggestions resulted in multimillion dollars of savings the first year. Be proud of what you've done. Your résumé should reflect this pride in achievement and accomplishment.

4. *Be honest.*   While résumés don't blush, don't exaggerate or try to position yourself as something you're not. It is usually fairly obvious when someone is stretching the truth or trying to position themselves differently from who they really are. A résumé should put the most positive light on things you've done and your accomplishments. On the other hand, be sure the résumé also paints an accurate picture of yourself.

It is to both your benefit and the company's that the résumé be as accurate as possible so both sides can decide if there is a good fit. If your résumé is successful in helping you get a job and the résumé accurately represents you, chances are you will be happier in that job.

5. *Present a powerful résumé.*   Your résumé should not only be good, but it should look good. It should be typed or printed in bold, easy-to-read type. It should be printed on heavy paper. It should be

designed to look impressive. It should make bold statements using active verbs. It should be short and to the point, preferably one page long but never more than two. Your résumé should look as you want yourself to be presented because in some cases you may never get another chance. Go for the gold.

6. *Target your résumé.* One size doesn't fit all. If you are absolutely convinced that you want to be a management consultant and nothing else will be acceptable and that you only want to work for McKinsey or Bain, one résumé is probably okay. But if you're like most of us who send out multiple copies of our résumés to tens and even hundreds of companies, one universal résumé is not enough. You may want to target your résumé in terms of industry, job function, skills, expertise, and so on. You may want to emphasize one particular aspect of your experience to fit the needs of a particular job opening. While it is impossible to change your résumé for every job, two or three different versions are usually helpful.

7. *Use other résumés as guides.* Why reinvent the wheel? When you start to develop your résumé, go to your placement officer at your school and look at some examples. There also are books of résumés which can provide further direction. Ask your friends if you can look at copies of theirs or simply ask them to critique yours.

Some résumés clearly are better than others. In addition, there are parts of different résumés that you might want to incorporate into your own. In any case, it is easy to decide what you want your résumé to look like when you can point to another and say, "I want mine to look just like that one." When it comes to résumés, it is no crime to copy the format of the best.

8. *Proofread. Proofread. Proofread.* If someone makes a typo on a one-page résumé that was supposedly proofread 10 times or more, imagine what they would do on a 5-page report or a major project. It is unforgivable to have a mistake on your résumé. Your résumé represents you. A mistake communicates that you don't care about yourself or the work you do.

A résumé is short. Before you send it out, read it and proofread it. Then give it to at least two other people who have never seen it before and ask them to proof it. Only when you are sure it is perfect should you circulate it. The job you lose may be your own.

9. *Put yourself in the reviewer's shoes.* Most hiring managers have profiles of the positions they want to fill. These may or may not be written, but in any case there always are a few key skills, experience, and criteria that are essential to the open position. Put yourself in the reviewer's shoes and try to figure out what they are looking for.

While it may not always be possible to determine exactly what the profile, is, try to talk to the hiring manager or personnel recruiter to get insight into what type of individual they are seeking. Then adjust your résumé or write a cover letter that slants your application to fit their needs. It is critical that you break through the clutter of résumés by either differentiating yourself in some way or by positioning yourself as better meeting the prospective employer's needs.

10. *Don't expect a résumé to get you a job—sell yourself in person or over the phone.*   Many job hunters send out hundreds of résumés and only get a handful of responses. They then wonder why the mass résumé mailing didn't work. Simple. The résumé by itself usually will not get you a job.

Be proactive. In order to convince a company that they must hire you, you must sell yourself. Phone the company and ask to speak to the recruiter or hiring manager. Enquire about the status of your application and request an interview. What's the worst that can happen? They say no. In most cases, they will applaud or at least not look unfavorably on your candidacy. If you want a job, you must go for it.

23

Ten Tips on Interviewing Successfully

1. Project energy and enthusiasm.
2. Be yourself.
3. Demonstrate sincere interest.
4. Do your homework.
5. Dress for success.
6. Arrive early.
7. Lean forward and sit on the edge of your chair.
8. Consider the interview as a dialogue.
9. Never make your most important interview your first interview.
10. Write a thank-you note.

1. *Project energy and enthusiasm.* The interview is the first opportunity you have to sell yourself personally. If you are low key in the interview, that sends a signal that you probably will be low key on the job. While being mellow is okay for a Sunday afternoon, companies are looking for people who will take charge and give that extra regardless of what they are doing. Since a lot of applicants have great credentials, you have a wonderful opportunity to set yourself apart in the interview by projecting a high energy level.

This energy should carry over to everything you discuss in the interview. Show enthusiasm for past jobs and past activities. Don't down grade anything you've done or any company you've worked for. While clearly you probably will not have loved everything, it is important to show that you took on every challenge with vigor.

2. *Be yourself.*   While it is important that you understand what the interviewer is looking for, it is also crucial to be yourself. Don't try to portray yourself as a type A compulsively driven personality for a job with a consulting firm or stock brokerage if you are not. You probably wouldn't be happy in that environment anyway and would burn out in a short period.

Investigate careers to determine where you will best fit in terms of skills, interests, lifestyle, work environment, and so forth. Then, when you have chosen careers where there is a good fit, being yourself should be an advantage. In any case, you've got a better chance of getting a job and being happy in the long run if you get it by being yourself. And that, after all, is what work and life are all about.

3. *Demonstrate sincere interest.*   You've done it. Your résumé has managed to break through the clutter and has secured you an interview. You probably are one of only a handful of people they are going to talk to. What do you do? Start by showing sincere interest in the position and the company. You can always tell when someone is really interested in something or just going through the motions. Be careful not to ruin your chances by not actively pursuing the opportunity.

In this job market, companies have many choices. All other things being equal, are they going to pick someone who is dying for the job or someone who shows a casual interest? The answer is obvious. Either go for it or don't go at all.

4. *Do your homework.*   There is no greater turnoff than to interview someone who knows nothing about the company or the industry for which he or she is being considered. Before any interview, you should collect as much information as you can from company reports, newspaper and magazine articles, investment briefs, and so on. Any public library or college placement office should have files on companies, industries, and so forth. Go through them religiously.

First, being knowledgeable will enable you to answer questions intelligently. Second and equally important, it will help you ask great questions such as, "I see the company is embarking overseas. How will this affect your profitability" or "I have read that your new advertising campaign has been well received critically but hasn't affected sales. Are you going to change it?" This shows real interest and insight and will quadruple your chances of getting the job.

5. *Dress for success.*   Be sharp. Feel sharp. Look sharp. When you want to put your best foot forward, you should have on a nice pair of

shined shoes. Conservative business dress never goes out of style for either men or women. The more professional you look, the better your job chances. Men should always wear a tie, even if it is just an informal meeting. Women should be properly attired in business dress. If you take care of appearance, it tells the interviewer that you probably will show the same care and concern on the job. Clothes make the man or woman.

6. *Arrive early.* Do not be like the rabbit in *Alice in Wonderland.* Never let this happen to you: "I'm late. I'm late. For a very important date." Punctuality for a job interview is not only a virtue but a necessity. The interviewer has set aside valuable time in his or her busy schedule. Your ability to be there on time reflects not only on the interview but also on your interest in the job and your ability to complete projects on time. In other words, if you cared about the job, you would have made it your business to be there on time.

In order to be there when the interview is scheduled, plan to arrive early. While it is not good to show up to the interview too early, plan to be at the location a half hour before and then grab a Coke. Compose yourself and you're ready to go.

7. *Lean forward and sit on the edge of your chair.* Everything communicates, especially body language. When you go into the interview, your body language should signal interest and enthusiasm. Lean forward. Sit on the edge of your chair. Even though you might want the job badly, sitting back and relaxing indicates a lack of interest on your part, whether or not that's true. Be dynamic.

We've all seen boxing matches where there is little movement and everyone is bored and boos. The opposite is true in an exciting fight with lots of action. Your interview will generate a lot of sparks if it is successful. Be and act excited.

8. *Consider the interview as a dialogue.* All interviews are, or should be, two-way streets. You are interviewing the company just as much as they are interviewing you. In the same way that they want to find out whether you fit their needs, you must assess your own fit in terms of skills, experience, work style, personal chemistry, and so forth. Ask a lot of questions and hard ones, too. If you can't talk to them during the interview, you never will be able to do so during your employment.

You should want to find out, among other things, what you are expected to do, whom you will work for, what the career and promotional opportunities are, what the company's prospects are, and how they see you fitting into the company's future. Clearly, there are lots of other questions you might ask. Use the interview to determine whether you want to work there if a job is offered.

9. *Never make your most important interview your first interview.*
Practice. Before playing in a piano recital or a ball game, you would
practice. Before going on a job interview, go through several mock
interviews conducted by friends, family, or placement officers at your
school. Practice answering questions like these: What are your strengths
and weaknesses? What are your three best accomplishments? Why do
you want to work there? What value will you add? Take it seriously. If
possible, videotape one of these mock interview sessions.

When you are ready for real interviews, never make your most important one the first one. Interview with a few companies that you think you
might like but not the one you consider your favorite or the job you have
your heart set on getting. Interviews, like wine, get better with age. Your
third or fourth interview is guaranteed to be better.

10. *Write a thank-you note.*   Although this might sound like Miss
Manners, write a thank-you note. While this probably in and of itself
will not get you a job, if you are on the borderline, it could help
tremendously. It can reinforce favorable impressions and can confirm
that the interviewer made the right choice. Thank-you notes are sometimes circulated to other company employees who interviewed you. A
final reason for writing a thank-you is common courtesy. An interviewer has given his or her time, and this shows your appreciation for
it. Appreciation, interest, and courtesy will never hurt your job
chances.

24
Ten Tips on Getting a Great Job

1. Develop a plan and time schedule.
2. Want the job.
3. Be persistent.
4. Send out a lot of résumés and don't be discouraged.
5. Use your contacts.
6. Set realistic goals.
7. Make sure you feel good about the company's products and services.
8. Try to schedule an interview with the key decision maker.
9. Don't rule out quirky alternatives.
10. Take your time.

1. *Develop a plan and time schedule.* Getting a job is a full-time job. At the outset of your job search, establish some basic goals or objectives. Then make up a plan with a time schedule. For example, the first month you might plan to focus on banking. If after a month all your contacts or attempts to get interviews in banking are unsuccessful, you should expand to another field such as accounting or look for a slightly different position in the same field. The purpose of the time schedule is not so much to say that you will get a job in 2 months; rather it should indicate the level of activity you expect to do each week. For instance, every week you might plan to send out ten letters and call five companies. This may sound very artificial or structured, and it is. But it also will help keep you going in the face of rejection. Keep on plan.

2. *Want the job.* Desire is everything. The differences between successful athletes and minor leaguers are attitude and mental toughness. The pros want to win. The difference often between getting and not getting a job is desire. You must want the job and communicate this to the interviewer. Hiring managers look for desire in applicants because this attribute makes a successful employee.

Wanting the job means aggressively pursuing it. Without being obnoxious, call the company, follow up if you don't hear anything after a week, do your homework, and so on. If you want something enough, you generally have a better chance of getting it.

3. *Be persistent.* Persistence pays off. Many times employers go through an elaborate job search, select a candidate, and then notify the other prospective candidates that the job has been filled. Sometimes the successful candidate changes his or her mind. Then the search is reopened. In that case, the persistent but unsuccessful job seeker who had sent a thank-you note and followed up after being rejected will have a head start on the others. In addition, sometimes a candidate may not be right for a particular position but may be a good fit with the company. Therefore, just because you have been turned down for one position doesn't mean that there are no more opportunities with that firm. To paraphrase a popular baseball player, it's never over till it's over.

4. *Send out a lot of résumés and don't be discouraged.* Getting a job is like buying a house—you only need one. Some job hunters send out hundreds of résumés. In this market environment when companies are cutting costs and downsizing, job opportunities are limited. Therefore, it may require extra effort to get a job. You may need to send out lots of résumés. The more résumés you send out, the better the possibility of getting a job.

When you do send out a lot of résumés, you're going to get rejected a lot. But remember, rejection should not be taken personally. With heavy competition for few positions, rejection is part of the process. Almost everyone gets a job eventually. Stay with it and don't be discouraged.

5. *Use your contacts.* It's not only what you know, it's whom you know. While school officials and parents may frown at this, it's a fact of life that contacts can help greatly. First, they can break through the mass of résumés on an employer's desk. Second, a contact can vouch for you, which automatically lessens the risk for the prospective employer. Third and finally, contacts may suggest some companies and industries you might never even have thought about.

Some prospective job hunters are shy about using contacts. Don't be. Knowing influential people and using their help is readily acceptable in the business world and sometimes is even seen as a plus by employers who are looking for good people.

6. *Set realistic goals.* We all want great jobs in high-paying industries with great futures. The reality is that most jobs are not that way, especially when you start out. It is necessary for most new employees to pay their dues and work hard before they reap great rewards. Even investment bankers and management consultants are required to spend long hard hours the first couple of years in less than ideal conditions.

Decide what you want to do. Aim high but be realistic. Your first job in your chosen career may not be at a top company or may be at a lower level than you anticipated. But if that job has good long-term opportunity, the benefits will outweigh any short-term disadvantages.

7. *Make sure you feel good about the company's products and services.* Who would you rather work for, a company whose products you love or one whose products you consider second rate? While you don't necessarily have to personally use a product or service—for example a man could sell women's shampoo or a woman could market men's apparel—it is critical that you respect the company. You should feel good about the company's products, services, philosophy, the people who work there, and so forth because when you join the company you represent them and become part of the corporation.

You may not want to work in certain categories or industries such as cigarettes or alcohol, or you may not like the products or services of certain companies. Since you will be working a minimum of 40 hours a week for 46 weeks a year, you should like the company. Decide who you want to work for.

8. *Try to schedule an interview with the key decision maker.* When looking for a job, go directly to the source if possible. Try to find out who the hiring manager is and then call him or her and try to schedule an interview. The Personnel Department often is used to collect résumés and screen candidates. In other words, in many cases they decide whether or not a résumé goes forward, but they can't make the decision whether or not to hire. Therefore, while personnel managers are important in that they can block your candidacy, try to speak directly with the hiring manager.

Be careful not to offend personnel or make them feel you are going around them. On the other hand, if you can talk with the person who can say, "Yes you're hired," do it.

9. *Don't rule out quirky alternatives.* People sometimes rule out small companies they've never heard of or industries they're unfamiliar with when looking for a job. However, this may mean ignoring some great opportunities. Many of the most admired companies 10

years ago, such as IBM and Sears, have lost money and cut staff. Other companies which just started at that time and therefore were unknowns, such as Home Depot, have made millionaires of many of their employees.

There are many small unusual companies in the communications and computer/entertainment industries. Retailing is going through great changes, which means more nontraditional avenues may open. The implications of these and other changes for job seekers are that you should cast a wide net and not reject unknown companies or industries. Ten years from now these unknowns may dominate the industry.

10. *Take your time.* When looking for a job, each week may seem like an eternity, and it is. It is never easy to get a job. You go through a lot of interviews, receive a lot of positive signals, and then most often get rejected. It is easy to get discouraged, especially in a tight job market.

Concerned that you may not get a job for a long time, you may want to jump for the first thing that is offered. While you should not automatically turn down a job offer, decide whether the offer is right for you in terms of position, company, industry, etc. An extra couple of months in the job market may seem like forever, but in the overall scheme of working 30 to 40 years, it is worth it to wait.

25

Ten Tips on Succeeding on the Job

1. Carve out your own area of expertise.
2. Make sure what you are doing is really important to the company.
3. Put the company's customers first.
4. Be a team player.
5. Take the initiative.
6. Budget your time.
7. Meet deadlines.
8. Play office politics.
9. Create balance between your work activities and your personal life.
10. Never compromise your integrity and personal values.

1. *Carve out your own area of expertise.*   There's an ongoing debate about whether it's better to be a generalist or specialist in a particular industry. Regardless of which you choose, carve out your own area of expertise. When times get tough and companies have to cut back, they cut areas and individuals who are "nonessential." If you are an expert in some particular area or subject, the company is less likely to terminate you. Another advantage of developing expertise is that it will help you get promoted. If you can leverage your expertise to help the

company grow or make money, they are more likely to promote you. Make yourself as expert and as indispensable as possible.

2. *Make sure what you are doing is really important to the company.* If you are in a sales organization, you should be in sales. If you are in a research company, you should be doing research. Whatever is the heart of the company's business should be your primary area of focus. That's where you should work. That's where the most visibility is within the company. That's where they promote from. That's where they pay the most.

If you work in another area such as human resources, legal, or operations, make sure what you are doing is really important to the company. You should be supporting the primary function while at the same time helping the company improve the bottom line.

3. *Put the company's customers first.* The customer is king. All great companies believe this and preach superior customer service. The moment they forget this simple principle, the business suffers. As an employee, if you embrace serving the customer, you won't go far wrong. Increasing customer satisfaction greatly improves revenue. While it is necessary to balance the voice of the company or economic reality with the voice of a customer, customer service is a winning strategy. Therefore, if you put the customer first, you will do your job better, and the company should reward you for it.

4. *Be a team player.* No man or woman is an island. In order to succeed in business today, it is necessary to be a team player. All successful enterprises require the cooperation of different areas such as sales, marketing, operations, and others. In fact, today, the latest management theory is process innovation, which tries to break down functional barriers. In short, people must work together to succeed. You can try to be an individual superstar, which may work in the short run, but to be successful in the long term, you must work with others.

Practice team skills. Promote cooperation. Share the glory. It will be easier to get the job done and in the long run will lead to the greatest opportunity for you.

5. *Take the initiative.* The world belongs to those who take the initiative. Nothing gets done when people just do their jobs. In order to succeed in today's tough marketplace, you must seek competitive advantage. You must look for places where the company can outdo the competition or where the company can save money. Turn in assignments early. Make suggestions or suggest improvements for activities that are not assigned to you or are not a normal part of your job.

The people who get ahead in today's business combine skill and luck with initiative. Take chances. As long as you're right more than you're wrong, the company will reward you. Go for it.

6. *Budget your time.*   Time is your most precious commodity. In most jobs, there is always more to do than there is time available. Most managers could do nothing but attend meetings if they wanted to. But you also need to get your other work done. Therefore, budgeting your time is critical.

First, you need to figure out what you need to do. Then you need to prioritize your work load. Finally, set a time schedule with due dates. While it is obvious that we should do our most important tasks first, we often do the easiest ones or the ones which take the least time. Time management then becomes essential to get all the work done while completing the most important assignments first.

7. *Meet deadlines.*   Plain and simple, meet deadlines. Miss them and over time you will lose credibility. Obviously, critical to meeting deadlines is setting realistic ones in the first place. Always allow more time than you think you will need, especially if other people are involved. However, once you set a deadline, you are committed to it.

Keep track of your progress on it. If it appears that you wouldn't make your original estimate, revise it as early in the process as possible, explaining why this was necessary. However, if at all possible, keep to the original schedule. A former manager used to say the key to success is "quality work on time."

8. *Play office politics.*   Good, hard work always will triumph in the end. Maybe in books and movies this is true but not necessarily in real life. Doing good work is not enough if nobody knows about it. Your management has to know and appreciate what you are doing and what you have accomplished. Therefore, you have to promote your work without being seen as self-aggrandizing.

Always be responsive to your boss and other senior managers. When they make a request, respond immediately if not sooner. Always take the initiative and come up with good suggestions that make your boss look good. Finally, you can never win a nasty drag out argument with your boss. To succeed, work hard and play office politics hard.

9. *Create balance between your work activities and your personal life.* Keep telling yourself, it's only a job, it's only a job. While it is necessary to work hard and take the initiative, your personal life also is important. Make a clear separation between the two. Try to carve out personal time for yourself and free time to spend with family and

friends. It is very easy to get caught in the trap of working long hours during the week and then going in on the weekend to "catch-up."

However, we all need time to reenergize our batteries and to pay attention to non-work-related activities. If you give it your all while you're on the job, you need to create balance and devote time to your personal life. You'll do better at both.

10. *Never compromise your integrity and personal values.* Most important to you above everything else are your integrity and personal values. You always can lose a job and get another one. You always can lose money and then make more. But once you compromise your integrity and personal values, they can never be regained. Moreover, your long-term success is directly related to your integrity. While sometimes less than honorable characters get ahead in the short term, in the long term, honor and integrity always will win out. As Shakespeare once wrote, "This above all: to thine own self be true."